MENTOR SHAKESPEARE SERIES

MACBETH

BY WILLIAM SHAKESPEARE

NOTES BY HUGH HOLMES

Mentor Books Ltd.,
43 Furze Road
Sandyford Industrial Estate
Dublin 18
Republic of Ireland

Tel: +353 1 295 2112/2
Fax: +353 1 295 2114
e-mail: admin@mentorbooks.ie
www.mentorbooks.ie

A catalogue record for this book is available from the British Library

ISBN: 978–1–909417–83–0

Editor: Treasa O'Mahony
Cover, typesetting and design: Mary Byrne

MENTOR

Act 5

The Royal House of Scotland

Duncan:	King of Scotland
Malcolm:	Duncan's eldest son
Donalbain:	Duncan's youngest son

Macbeth's Household

Macbeth:	Thane (Lord) of Glamis and relative of Duncan
Lady Macbeth:	Macbeth's wife
Porter:	Gatekeeper of Macbeth's castle
Doctor:	A personal doctor for Macbeth's household
Seyton:	Macbeth's lieutenant and military advisor
Gentlewoman:	A personal servant to Lady Macbeth
Murderers:	Assassins hired by Macbeth

Banquo's Household

Banquo:	A thane (lord) and close friend of Macbeth
Fleance:	Banquo's son

Macduff's Household

Macduff:	Thane (Lord) of Fife
Lady Macduff:	Macduff's wife
Son:	Macduff's son

Supernatural Characters

Three Witches (The Weird Sisters)	
Hecate:	Goddess of witchcraft

Other Thanes (Scottish Noblemen)

Ross	**Caithness**
Lennox	**Mentieth**
Angus	

English Characters

Siward:	Earl of Northumberland, English general
Young Siward:	Siward's son
English Doctor:	

Setting

All of the scenes are set in 11th Century Scotland except for Act 4, Scene 3 which takes place at the court of King Edward, the English king.

Act 1 Scene 1

Scene Summary

- Against a background of thunder and lightning, three witches (the Weird Sisters) appear and discuss their plans to meet Macbeth as he returns from the battlefield.

A desert place.
Thunder and lightning. Enter three witches

FIRST WITCH
When shall we three meet again
In thunder, lightning, or in rain?

SECOND WITCH
When the hurlyburly's[1] done,
When the battle's lost and won.

THIRD WITCH
That will be ere[2] the set of sun.

FIRST WITCH
Where the place?

SECOND WITCH
Upon the heath.[3]

THIRD WITCH
There to meet with Macbeth.

FIRST WITCH
I come, Graymalkin![4]

SECOND WITCH
Paddock calls.[5]

THIRD WITCH
Anon.[6]

ALL
Fair is foul, and foul is fair:[7]
Hover through the fog and filthy air.

[*Exeunt*]

[1] **hurlyburly:** the noise and confusion of battle

[2] **ere:** before, i.e. the battle that Macbeth is fighting will be finished before dark

[3] **heath:** wasteland

[4] **Graymalkin:** a grey cat. Evil spirits supposedly appeared in the forms of animals and worked alongside witches.

[5] **Paddock:** an evil spirit in the form of a toad

[6] **Anon:** I'm coming now. The third witch has been called by her evil spirit.

[7] **Fair is foul, and foul is fair:** Good is bad and bad is good. This line illustrates the moral confusion at the heart of this play.

Key Quotations

THE WITCHES *When the battle's lost and won*
THE WITCHES *Fair is foul, and foul is fair*

Commentary

- This short scene sets the dark tone of *Macbeth.* The threatening figures of the witches combined with the violent weather create an air of menace. The witches' reference to the 'battle lost and won' establishes this as a time of war. It also illustrates how the witches often speak in riddles. Here, the witches suggest that Macbeth is about to win on the battlefield but his capacity for violence will also lead to his own downfall; Macbeth's initial triumph will eventually give way to disaster.

- The witches' paradoxical chant, 'Fair is foul, and foul is fair', neatly expresses how they encourage moral confusion by rejecting normal values. This is reflected in the 'fog and filthy air', the witches' natural element, which will obscure vision and confuse.

- The witches' ability to predict the future is displayed when they foresee that the battle will finish, 'ere the set of sun.' This is when they plan to meet Macbeth. Clearly his future is intertwined with these agents of evil.

- An audience in Shakespeare's time would have believed in the power of witchcraft. When *Macbeth* was first performed, King James I ruled England and Scotland. James I's book *Daemonologie* described and condemned the practice of witchcraft and he personally supervised witch trials. Shakespeare wrote *Macbeth* with the intention of flattering James I.

Questions

1. What evidence is there in this scene that the witches can predict the future?
2. What effect does the weather referred to in the scene have on the overall mood?
3. (a) The witches often speak in riddles. Find two examples of contradictory statements in this scene.
   (b) What do you think theses contradictory phrases mean?
4. If you were staging this scene, what props, set design and music/sound effects would you use, if any? Explain your ideas by referring to the scene.

Act 1 Scene 2

Scene Summary

- King Duncan meets soldiers and noblemen who tell him that the rebels and invaders who threatened his rule have been defeated.
- The former Thane of Cawdor is condemned to death for his treachery.
- Duncan instructs Ross to give Macbeth the title of Thane of Cawdor as a reward for his bravery in battle.

A camp near Forres.
Alarum[1] within. Enter DUNCAN, MALCOLM, DONALBAIN, LENNOX, with Attendants, meeting a bleeding SERGEANT

DUNCAN
What bloody man[2] is that? He can report,
As seemeth by his plight, of the revolt
The newest state[3].

MALCOLM
This is the sergeant
Who like a good and hardy soldier fought
'Gainst my captivity[4]. Hail, brave friend!
Say to the king the knowledge of the broil[5]
As thou didst leave it.

SERGEANT
Doubtful it stood;[6]
As two spent swimmers, that do cling together
And choke their art.[7] The merciless Macdonwald[8] –
Worthy to be a rebel, for to that
The multiplying villanies of nature
Do swarm upon him – from the Western Isles[9]
Of kerns and gallowglasses[10] is supplied;
And Fortune, on his damned quarrel smiling,[11]
Showed like a rebel's whore[12]: but all's too weak:[13]
For brave Macbeth – well he deserves that name –
Disdaining Fortune, with his brandished steel,
Which smoked with bloody execution,
Like Valour's minion[14] carved out his passage
Till he faced the slave;[15]
Which ne'er shook hands, nor bade farewell to him,
Till he unseamed him from the nave to the chops,
And fixed his head upon our battlements.[16]

DUNCAN
O valiant cousin![17] worthy gentleman!

1 **Alarum:** trumpets

2 **bloody man:** The visual spectacle of the wounded sergeant effectively establishes the backdrop of war. Images of blood occur throughout the play.

3 **newest state:** latest news (of the battle)

4 **'Gainst my captivity:** prevented my capture

5 **broil:** brawl (the battle)

6 **Doubtful it stood:** The outcome was uncertain.

7 **As two spent...choke their art:** Like two exhausted swimmers holding onto each other and drowning as a result

8 **Macdonwald:** a rebel leader

9 **Western Isles:** Ireland

10 **kerns and gallowglasses:** Kerns were Irish foot soldiers. Gallowglasses were soldiers on horseback.

11 **Fortune...smiling:** Fortune (fate/luck) at first favoured Macdonwald.

12 **rebel's whore:** Fortune prostituted herself to the rebels.

13 **all's too weak:** Even Fortune was too weak to defeat Macbeth.

14 **Valour's minion:** Bravery's favourite

15 **Disdaining...slave:** Treating fortune with contempt, Macbeth wielded his sword and fought his way through the rebels till he faced Macdonwald.

16 **Till he unseamed...battlements:** Until he cut him from the navel to his jaw and placed his decapitated head upon the parapet

17 **valiant cousin:** brave cousin, Macbeth is cousin to Duncan

SERGEANT
As whence the sun 'gins his reflection
Shipwrecking storms and direful thunders break,
So from that spring whence comfort seemed to come
Discomfort swells.[18] Mark, king of Scotland, mark:
No sooner justice had, with valour armed,
Compelled these skipping kerns to trust their heels,[19]
But the Norweyan lord surveying vantage,
With furbished arms and new supplies of men
Began a fresh assault.[20]

DUNCAN
Dismayed not this
Our captains, Macbeth and Banquo?

SERGEANT
Yes –
As sparrows eagles, or the hare the lion.[21]
If I say sooth, I must report they were
As cannons overcharged with double cracks,[22]
So they doubly redoubled strokes upon the foe.
Except they meant to bathe in reeking wounds,
Or memorise another Golgotha,[23]
I cannot tell –
But I am faint, my gashes cry for help.

DUNCAN
So well thy words become thee as thy wounds;
They smack of honour both. Go get him surgeons.
[*Exit SERGEANT, attended*]
Who comes here?
[*Enter ROSS*]

MALCOLM
The worthy Thane of Ross.

LENNOX
What a haste looks through his eyes! So should he look
That seems to speak things strange.

ROSS
God save the king!

DUNCAN
Whence camest thou, worthy thane?

ROSS
From Fife, great King;
Where the Norweyan banners flout[24] the sky

18 **As whence...Discomfort swells:** Just like storms can come from the same direction as the rising sun, new threats can appear on the horizon when safety seems certain.

19 **No sooner ... their heels:** No sooner had justice bravely forced the foot soldiers to retreat

20 **But the Norweyan...fresh assault:** than the Norwegian King saw the opportunity to launch a fresh attack

21 **As sparrows eagles, or the hare the lion:** As much as sparrows scare eagles or hares scare lions. The sergeant is being deliberately ironic here.

22 **As cannons...cracks:** like cannons charged with twice the normal amount of gunpowder

23 **Golgotha:** Calvary, the site of Christ's crucifixion

24 **flout:** flaunt/mock

And fan our people cold.
Norway himself, with terrible numbers,
Assisted by that most disloyal traitor
The Thane of Cawdor, began a dismal conflict;
Till that Bellona's bridegroom[25], lapped in proof,
Confronted him with self-comparisons,
Point against point,[26] rebellious arm 'gainst arm,
Curbing his lavish spirit:[27] and, to conclude,
The victory fell on us.

25 **Bellona's bridegroom:** Macbeth. Bellona was the Roman Goddess of War. Ross is suggesting that Macbeth's bravery on the battlefield makes him fit to be Bellona's husband.
26 **Point against point:** sword to sword
27 **Curbing his lavish spirit:** Restraining his (Cawdor's) wild behaviour

DUNCAN
Great happiness!

ROSS
That now
Sweno, the Norways' king, craves composition.[28]
Nor would we deign[29] him burial of his men
Till he disbursed[30] at Saint Colme's Inch[31]
Ten thousand dollars to our general use.

28 **craves composition:** begs to make peace
29 **deign:** grant
30 **disbursed:** paid
31 **Inch:** Island

DUNCAN
No more that Thane of Cawdor shall deceive
Our bosom interest: go pronounce his present death,
And with his former title greet Macbeth.[32]

32 **with his former title greet Macbeth:** Macbeth has been made Thane of Cawdor.

ROSS
I'll see it done.

DUNCAN
What he hath lost, noble Macbeth hath won.

[*Exeunt*]

Key Quotations

SERGEANT *For brave Macbeth – well he deserves that name –*
Disdaining Fortune, with his brandished steel,
Which smoked with bloody execution,
Like Valour's minion carved out his passage

SERGEANT *Till he unseamed him from the nave to the chops, / And fixed his head upon our battlements*

DUNCAN *What he hath lost, noble Macbeth hath won*

Commentary

- The atmosphere of treachery and violence from Scene 1 continues in Scene 2 with a detailed account of a bloody rebellion and battle. This is made visually apparent by the spectacle of the wounded and bleeding sergeant.

- Although the audience has yet to see Macbeth, much of his behaviour is reported in this scene. Shakespeare presents a character who is brave in battle and fights loyally for Scotland. He is referred to as 'brave Macbeth', 'Bellona's bridegroom', 'Valour's minion', 'noble Macbeth' and is rewarded for his actions with the title, Thane of Cawdor.

- However, Macbeth is also displayed as bloodthirsty: we learn that Macbeth 'unseamed' Macdonwald 'from the nave to the chops' and placed his head upon the parapet. Macbeth's sword 'smoked with bloody execution'; the image here of a violent soldier consumed by bloodlust is terrifying. It seems that Shakespeare wants to present a dual vision of Macbeth: a man capable of courageous acts of loyalty but also of violence and savagery.

Questions

1. Explain what happened in the battle against the rebels and the Norwegian invaders.
2. How was Macbeth rewarded for his part in the battle?
3. (a) Make a list of all the positive descriptions of Macbeth.
   (b) Make a list of quotations that display Macbeth as violent.
4. How is Banquo portrayed in this scene? Refer to the text in your answer.
5. Why do you think Shakespeare chose to have the battle reported by the characters rather than stage it for the audience?

Act 1 Scene 3

Scene Summary

- The witches appear before Macbeth and Banquo.
- They call Macbeth 'Thane of Cawdor' and tell him he will be King.
- They tell Banquo that his descendents will be kings.
- After this, Macbeth learns from Ross that he is to be made Thane of Cawdor.
- Macbeth begins to imagine that the witches' prophecy may come true and that he will become King.

A heath near Forres.
Thunder. Enter the Three Witches

FIRST WITCH
Where hast thou been, sister?

SECOND WITCH
Killing swine.

THIRD WITCH
Sister, where thou?

FIRST WITCH
A sailor's wife had chestnuts in her lap,
And munched, and munched, and munched:
'Give me,' quoth I:
'Aroint thee,[1] witch!' the rump-fed ronyon[2] cries.
Her husband's to Aleppo[3] gone, master o' the Tiger:[4]
But in a sieve I'll thither sail,[5]
And, like a rat without a tail,
I'll do, I'll do, and I'll do.[6]

SECOND WITCH
I'll give thee a wind.

FIRST WITCH
Thou art kind.

THIRD WITCH
And I another.

FIRST WITCH
I myself have all the other,[7]
And the very ports they blow,
All the quarters[8] that they know
I' the shipman's card.[9]
I will drain him dry as hay:[10]

1 **Aroint thee:** Go away
2 **rump-fed ronyon:** overfed hag
3 **Aleppo:** City in Syria
4 **master o' the Tiger:** captain of the Tiger (a ship)
5 **in a sieve I'll thither sail:** It was believed that witches could sail in sieves.
6 **I'll do:** I'll do him harm/I'll harm him

7 **the other:** power over all the other winds
8 **quarters:** sections of a compass
9 **shipman's card:** sailor's chart
10 **dry as hay:** The sailor will be thirsty because the winds will prevent him pulling into port and getting water.

Sleep shall neither night nor day
Hang upon his penthouse lid;[11]
He shall live a man forbid:[12]
Weary sev'nights, nine times nine[13]
Shall he dwindle, peak and pine:[14]
Though his bark cannot be lost,[15]
Yet it shall be tempest-tost.[16]
Look what I have.

SECOND WITCH
Show me, show me.

FIRST WITCH
Here I have a pilot's thumb,[17]
Wrecked as homeward he did come.
[*Drum within*]

THIRD WITCH
A drum! a drum!
Macbeth doth come.

ALL
The weird sisters, hand in hand,
Posters[18] of the sea and land,
Thus do go about, about:
Thrice to thine and thrice to mine
And thrice again, to make up nine.[19]
Peace! the charm's wound up.[20]

[*Enter MACBETH and BANQUO*]

MACBETH
So foul and fair a day[21] I have not seen.

BANQUO
How far is't called to Forres?[22] What are these
So withered and so wild in their attire,
That look not like the inhabitants o' the earth,
And yet are on't? Live you? Or are you aught
That man may question? You seem to understand me,
By each at once her choppy[23] finger laying
Upon her skinny lips:[24] you should be women,
And yet your beards forbid me to interpret
That you are so.

MACBETH
Speak, if you can: what are you?

[11] **penthouse lid:** eyelid
[12] **forbid:** cursed
[13] **sev'nights, nine times nine:** 81 weeks
[14] **dwindle, peak and pine:** grow thin, waste away.
[15] **Though his bark cannot be lost:** Though I don't have the power to sink his ship
[16] **tempest-tost:** tossed upon storms
[17] **pilot's thumb:** a sailor's thumb
[18] **Posters:** Speedy travellers
[19] **Thrice to thine...make up nine:** The witches circle each other nine times
[20] **the charm's wound up:** the spell is cast
[21] **foul and fair a day:** good and bad weather. This echoes the witches' chant in Scene 1.
[22] **How far is't called to Forres?:** How far is it supposed to be to Forres?
[23] **choppy:** chapped
[24] **By each ... skinny lips:** The witches seem to be telling Banquo to be quiet, presumably so they can address Macbeth.

FIRST WITCH
All hail, Macbeth! hail to thee, Thane of Glamis![25]

SECOND WITCH
All hail, Macbeth, hail to thee, Thane of Cawdor![26]

THIRD WITCH
All hail, Macbeth! that shalt be King hereafter!

BANQUO
Good sir, why do you start;[27] and seem to fear
Things that do sound so fair?[28] I' the name of truth,
Are ye fantastical, or that indeed
Which outwardly ye show?[29] My noble partner
You greet with present grace and great prediction
Of noble having and of royal hope,
That he seems rapt withal:[30] to me you speak not.
If you can look into the seeds of time,
And say which grain will grow and which will not,
Speak then to me, who neither beg nor fear
Your favours nor your hate.

FIRST WITCH
Hail!

SECOND WITCH
Hail!

THIRD WITCH
Hail!

FIRST WITCH
Lesser than Macbeth, and greater.

SECOND WITCH
Not so happy, yet much happier.

THIRD WITCH
Thou shalt get kings,[31] though thou be none:
So all hail, Macbeth and Banquo!

FIRST WITCH
Banquo and Macbeth, all hail!

MACBETH
Stay, you imperfect speakers,[32] tell me more:
By Sinel's[33] death I know I am Thane of Glamis;
But how of Cawdor? The Thane of Cawdor lives,
A prosperous gentleman; and to be King
Stands not within the prospect of belief,

[25] **Thane of Glamis:** Macbeth is already the Thane of Glamis.

[26] **Thane of Cawdor:** Macbeth does not yet know that Duncan has given him the title, Thane of Cawdor.

[27] **why do you start:** Macbeth seems shocked at the witches' prophecy.

[28] **fair:** good

[29] **Are ye fantastical...ye show?:** Are you imaginary or as real as you appear?

[30] **rapt withal:** stunned into silence

[31] **get kings:** beget/be the father of kings

[32] **imperfect speakers:** unclear speakers

[33] **Sinel:** Macbeth's father

No more than to be Cawdor. Say from whence
You owe this strange intelligence? Or why
Upon this blasted heath[34] you stop our way
With such prophetic greeting? Speak, I charge you.
[*Witches vanish*]

Banquo
The earth hath bubbles, as the water has,
And these are of them.[35] Whither are they vanished?

Macbeth
Into the air; and what seemed corporal[36] melted
As breath into the wind. Would they had stayed!

Banquo
Were such things here as we do speak about?
Or have we eaten on the insane root[37]
That takes the reason prisoner?

Macbeth
Your children shall be kings.

Banquo
You shall be King.

Macbeth
And Thane of Cawdor too: went it not so?

Banquo
To the selfsame[38] tune and words. Who's here?

[*Enter ROSS and ANGUS*]

Ross
The King hath happily received, Macbeth,
The news of thy success; and when he reads
Thy personal venture in the rebels' fight,
His wonders and his praises do contend
Which should be thine or his.[39] Silenced with that,
In viewing o'er the rest o' the selfsame day,
He finds thee in the stout Norweyan ranks,
Nothing afeard of what thyself didst make,
Strange images of death. As thick as hail
Came post with post,[40] and every one did bear
Thy praises in his kingdom's great defence,
And poured them down before him.

Angus
We are sent
To give thee from our royal master thanks;
Only to herald thee into his sight,[41]
Not pay thee.

[34] **blasted heath:** windswept wasteland

[35] **The earth hath...are of them:** The witches have disappeared into gaseous bubbles.

[36] **corporal:** having a body/physical

[37] **insane root:** a plant root (perhaps hemlock) which could cause madness/hallucinations

[38] **selfsame:** the very same

[39] **His wonders...should be thine or his:** The King's admiration competes with his desire to praise.

[40] **post with post:** message after message

[41] **herald thee into his sight:** escort you to the King

ORCHESTRAL CHART

SHOWING :—(1) The position of the players in the orchestra.
(2) The compass of the instruments as related to the Pianoforte Keyboard, and
(3) Illustrations of the instruments employed.

The above is a sketch of a symphonic orchestra of 40 players, comprising 12 Violins, 3 Violas, 3 Violoncellos, 2 Double Basses, 2 Flutes, 2 Oboes, 2 Clarinets, 2 Bassoons, 4 Horns, 2 Trumpets, 3 Trombones (2 Tenor and 1 Bass), Tuba and Tympani. The instruments of the orchestra, all directed by the Conductor (15), are divided into four main groups or families made up in the following manner :—

The Strings (1, 2, 3, 4, and 5) : Composed of First and Second Violins (1 and 2), Violas (3), Violoncellos (4), Double Basses (5), the tone being produced by drawing a bow across the strings. The Violins are divided into two groups—the First Violins (1) on the Conductor's left and the Second Violins (2) on his right.

The Wood-Wind :—Comprises Flutes (6), Oboes (7), Clarinets (8), and Bassoons (9), the various notes being obtained by the manipulation of the keys with the fingers. Additional instruments played in this group in large orchestras include Piccolo, Cor Anglais (English Horn), Bass Clarinet and Contra Bassoon.

The Brass—Comprises French Horns (10), Trumpets (11), Trombones (Tenor and Bass) (12), and Tuba (13), the required notes being produced by depressing the valves, except in the case of the Trombones, in which they are produced by means of a slide.

The Percussion :—A section of the orchestra of which the Tympani (14) is the most important. It includes all kinds of drums, cymbals, glockenspiel, etc., the sound being produced by striking the instruments.

Compiled and published in the furtherance of Music by

RUSHWORTH & DREAPER 11-17 ISLINGTON, LIVERPOOL

The Centre of Everything in Music.

[P.T.O.

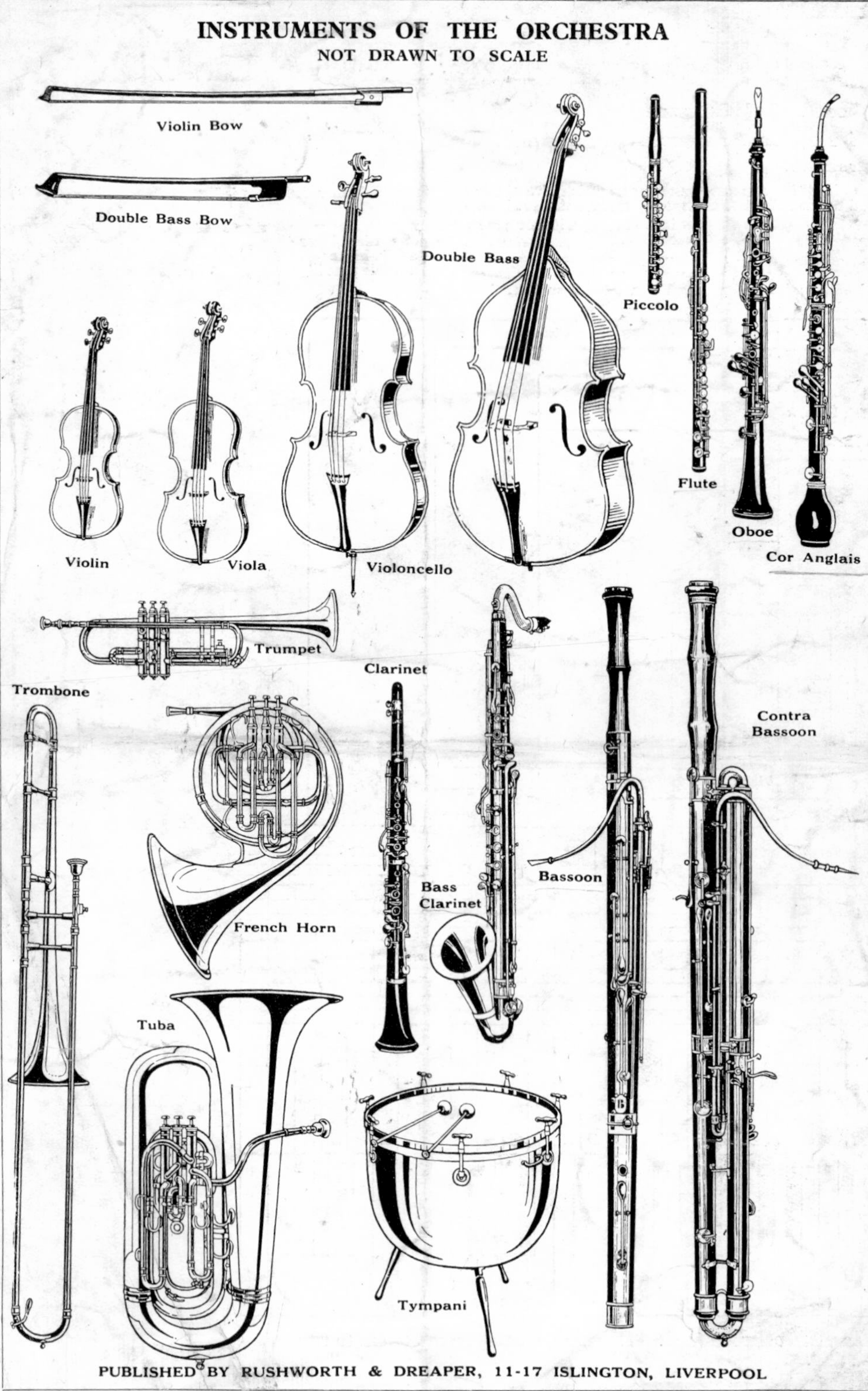
INSTRUMENTS OF THE ORCHESTRA
NOT DRAWN TO SCALE
Violin Bow
Double Bass Bow
Double Bass
Piccolo
Flute
Oboe
Cor Anglais
Violin
Viola
Violoncello
Trumpet
Clarinet
Trombone
Contra
Bassoon
Bassoon
Bass
Clarinet
French Horn
Tuba
Tympani
PUBLISHED BY RUSHWORTH & DREAPER, 11-17 ISLINGTON, LIVERPOOL

ORCHESTRAL CHART

SHOWING :—(1) The position of the players in the orchestra.

(2) The compass of the instruments as related to the Pianoforte Keyboard, and

(3) Illustrations of the instruments employed.

The above is a sketch of a symphonic orchestra of 40 players, comprising 12 Violins, 3 Violas, 3 Violoncellos, 2 Double Basses, 2 Flutes, 2 Oboes, 2 Clarinets, 2 Bassoons, 4 Horns, 2 Trumpets, 3 Trombones (2 Tenor and 1 Bass), Tuba and Tympani. The instruments of the orchestra, all directed by the Conductor (15), are divided into four main groups or families made up in the following manner :—

The Strings (1, 2, 3, 4, and 5) : Composed of First and Second Violins (1 and 2), Violas (3), Violoncellos (4), Double Basses (5), the tone being produced by drawing a bow across the strings. The Violins are divided into two groups—the First Violins (1) on the Conductor's left and the Second Violins (2) on his right.

The Wood-Wind :—Comprises Flutes (6), Oboes (7), Clarinets (8), and Bassoons (9), the various notes being obtained by the manipulation of the keys with the fingers. Additional instruments played in this group in large orchestras include Piccolo, Cor Anglais (English Horn), Bass Clarinet and Contra Bassoon.

The Brass—Comprises French Horns (10), Trumpets (11), Trombones (Tenor and Bass) (12), and Tuba (13), the required notes being produced by depressing the valves, except in the case of the Trombones, in which they are produced by means of a slide.

The Percussion :—A section of the orchestra of which the Tympani (14) is the most important. It includes all kinds of drums, cymbals, glockenspiel, etc., the sound being produced by striking the instruments.

Compiled and published in the furtherance of Music by

RUSHWORTH & DREAPER 11-17 ISLINGTON, LIVERPOOL

The Centre of Everything in Music.

[P.T.O.

THE RUSHWORT

COMPASS CHART OF O

Relative to the Pianofort

NOTE.—*The range of each instrument is not arbitrar*

★Transposi

The compass of each instrument is given in the *actual sounds* it produces. Those marked (★) are termed the music. The following table enables the student to understand the difference between the notes on the

Double Bass	The notes are printed	an octave higher	than sounding
Piccolo	,, ,, ,, ,,	an octave lower	,, ,,
Clarinet in B Flat ...	,, ,, ,, ,,	a whole tone higher	,, ,,
Cor Anglais (English Horn)	,, ,, ,, ,,	a fifth higher	,, ,,

Books on Orchestration by Corder, Forsyth, Jacob, Pr

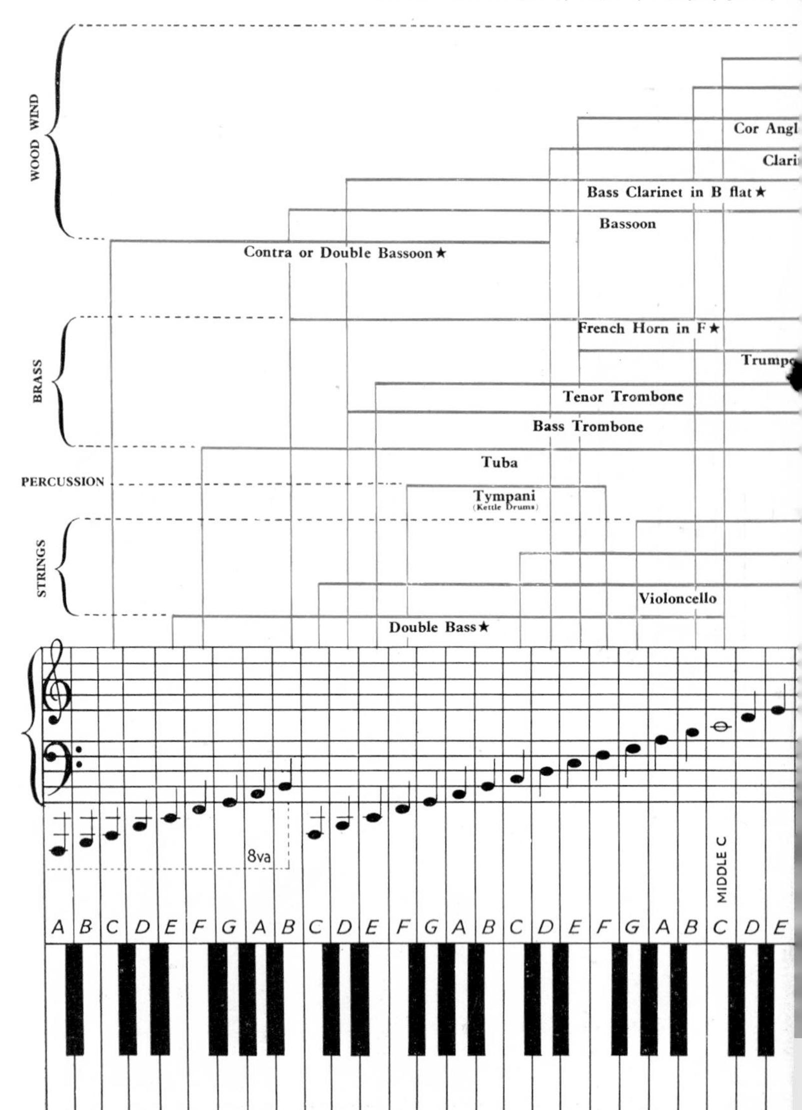

In this chart the order in which the instruments are arranged in orch the four groups or families are (1) Strings, (2) Percussion, (3) Brass, (4)

PUBLISHED BY RUSHWORTH & DRE

& DREAPER

CHESTRAL INSTRUMENTS

Keyboard of $7\frac{1}{2}$ Octaves.

but is the average compass used in Orchestral playing.

Instruments.

ransposing " instruments—instruments which give higher or lower sounds than the notes indicated on
re and the sounds these transposing instruments produce.

Bass Clarinet in B Flat		The notes are printed			a ninth higher	than sounding	
Double Bassoon	...	,,	,,	,, ,,	an octave higher	,,	,,
Horn in F ...	...	,,	,,	,, ,,	a fifth higher	,,	,,
Trumpet in B Flat	...	,,	,,	,, ,,	a whole tone higher	,,	,,

and Widor give fuller information on this subject.

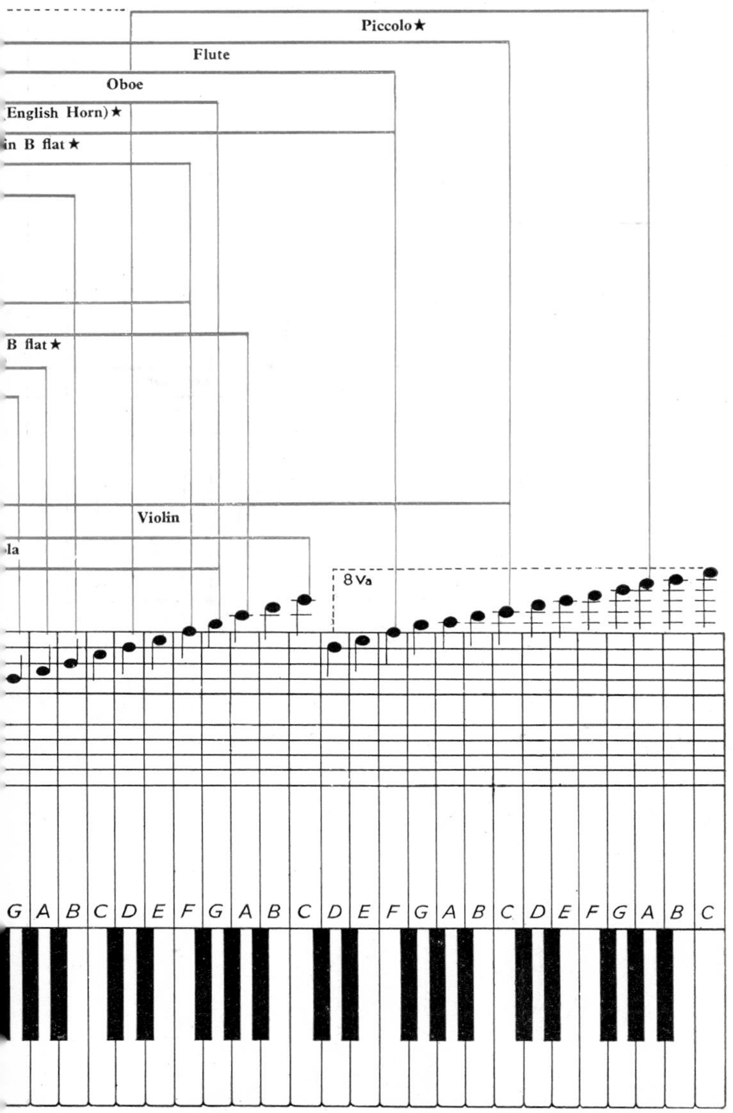

al score has been followed. Therefore, reading from bottom to top,
ood-Wind.

PER, 11-17 ISLINGTON, LIVERPOOL

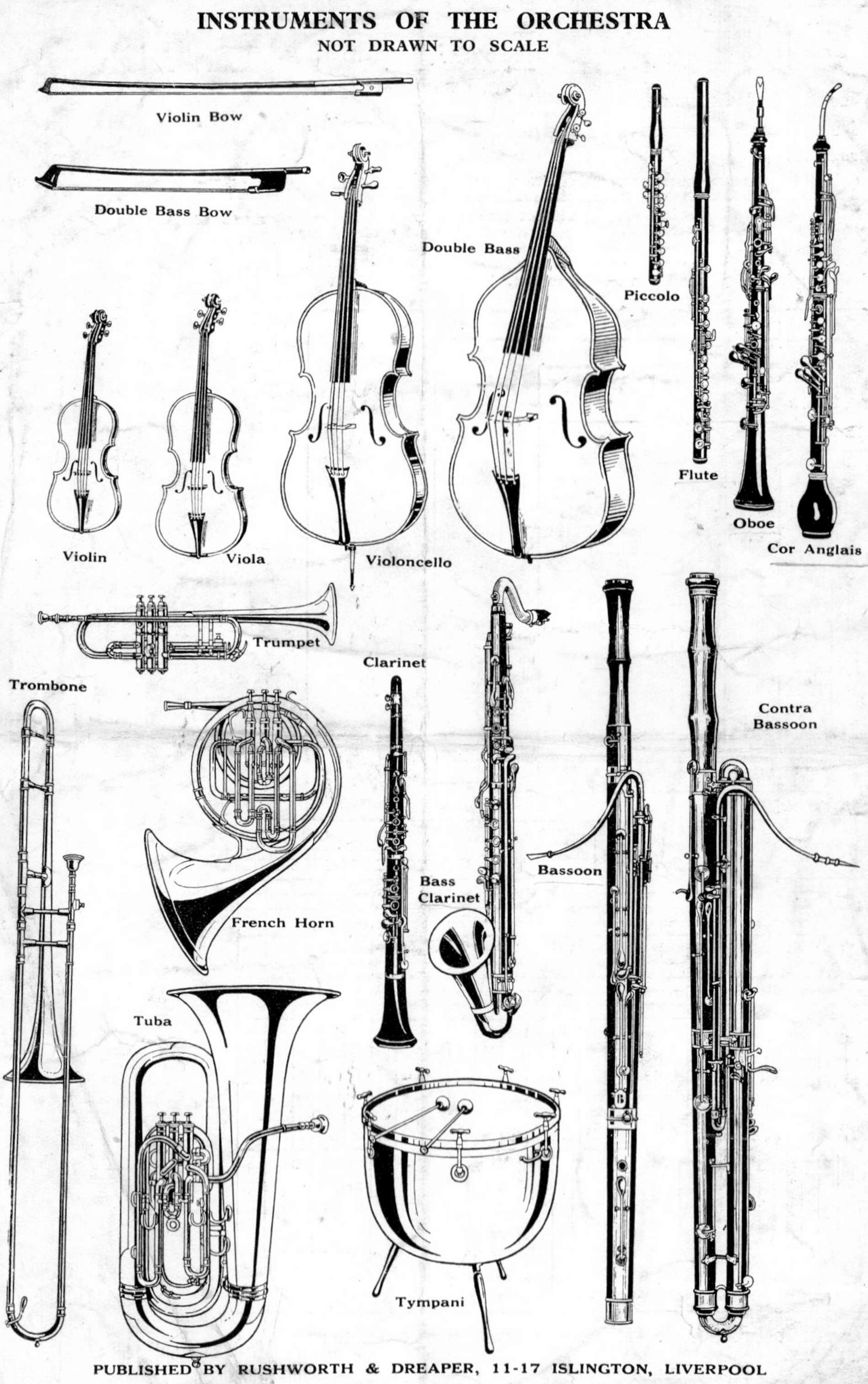
INSTRUMENTS OF THE ORCHESTRA
NOT DRAWN TO SCALE
Violin Bow
Double Bass Bow
Double Bass
Piccolo
Violin
Viola
Violoncello
Flute
Oboe
Cor Anglais
Trumpet
Clarinet
Trombone
Contra
Bassoon
Bassoon
Bass
Clarinet
French Horn
Tuba
Tympani
PUBLISHED BY RUSHWORTH & DREAPER, 11-17 ISLINGTON, LIVERPOOL

Ross

And, for an earnest of a greater honour,
He bade me, from him, call thee Thane of Cawdor:
In which addition, hail, most worthy thane!
For it is thine.

Banquo

What, can the devil speak true?

Macbeth

The Thane of Cawdor lives: why do you dress me
In borrowed robes?[42]

Angus

Who was the Thane lives yet;
But under heavy judgement[43] bears that life
Which he deserves to lose. Whether he was combined
With those of Norway, or did line the rebel
With hidden help and vantage, or that with both
He laboured in his country's wrack,[44] I know not;
But treasons capital,[45] confessed and proved,
Have overthrown him.

Macbeth

[*Aside*] Glamis, and Thane of Cawdor!
The greatest is behind.[46]
[*To ROSS and ANGUS*]
Thanks for your pains.
[*To BANQUO*]
Do you not hope your children shall be kings,
When those that gave the Thane of Cawdor to me
Promised no less to them?

Banquo

That, trusted home,[47]
Might yet enkindle[48] you unto the crown,
Besides the Thane of Cawdor. But 'tis strange:
And oftentimes, to win us to our harm,
The instruments of darkness tell us truths,
Win us with honest trifles, to betray's
In deepest consequence.[49]
Cousins, a word, I pray you.

Macbeth

[*Aside*] Two truths are told,
As happy prologues[50] to the swelling act
Of the imperial theme.[51] – [*Aloud*] I thank you, gentlemen.
[*Aside*] This supernatural soliciting
Cannot be ill, cannot be good. If ill,
Why hath it given me earnest of success,

42 **why do you dress me / In borrowed robes?:** why do you call me by a title that is not mine?

43 **heavy judgement:** death sentence

44 **laboured in his country's wrack:** worked to ruin/destroy Scotland

45 **treasons capital:** treason punishable by death

46 **The greatest is behind:** The greatest thing (i.e. Kingship) is yet to come

47 **trusted home:** trusted entirely

48 **enkindle:** encourage

49 **And oftentimes...deepest consequence:** Sometimes evil forces tell us half-truths to betray us, resulting in the worst consequences.

50 **happy prologues:** promising introductions

51 **the swelling act / Of the imperial theme:** the climax of Macbeth being crowned King

Commencing in a truth? I am Thane of Cawdor:
If good, why do I yield to that suggestion
Whose horrid image doth unfix my hair[52]
And make my seated[53] heart knock at my ribs,
Against the use of nature? Present fears
Are less than horrible imaginings:
My thought, whose murder yet is but fantastical,
Shakes so my single state of man[54] that function
Is smothered in surmise,[55] and nothing is
But what is not.[56]

BANQUO

Look, how our partner's rapt.[57]

MACBETH

[*Aside*] If chance will have me King, why, chance may crown me,
Without my stir.[58]

BANQUO

New honours come upon him,
Like our strange garments, cleave not to their mould
But with the aid of use.[59]

MACBETH

[*Aside*] Come what come may,
Time and the hour runs through the roughest day.[60]

BANQUO

Worthy Macbeth, we stay upon your leisure.

MACBETH

Give me your favour: my dull brain was wrought[61]
With things forgotten. Kind gentlemen, your pains
Are registered where every day I turn
The leaf to read them.[62] Let us toward the King.
[*Aside to BANQUO*]
Think upon what hath chanced, and, at more time,
The interim having weighed it, let us speak
Our free hearts each to other.[63]

BANQUO

[*Aside to MACBETH*] Very gladly.

MACBETH

[*Aside to BANQUO*] Till then, enough.
[*Aloud*] Come, friends.
[*Exeunt*]

52 **doth unfix my hair:** makes my hair stand up (in fright)

53 **seated:** firmly fixed

54 **Shakes so my single state of man:** disturbs my being/shakes me to the core

55 **function / Is smothered in surmise:** action is paralysed by speculation

56 **nothing is / But what is not:** nothing seems as it is

57 **rapt:** lost in thought

58 **Without my stir:** without me seeking it

59 **New honours...aid of use:** Just like one has to get used to new clothes, Macbeth will have to become accustomed to his new title.

60 **Time and the hour runs through the roughest day:** Every rough day will inevitably come to an end.

61 **wrought:** overcome/taken up

62 **your pains...to read them:** Every day I think of what you have done for me.

63 **Think upon...each to other:** Think about what has happened, and having weighed it up, let's speak honestly to each other.

Key Quotations

MACBETH *why do you dress me / In borrowed robes?*

BANQUO *That, trusted home, / Might yet enkindle you unto the crown*

BANQUO *... to win us to our harm,*
The instruments of darkness tell us truths,
Win us with honest trifles, to betray's
In deepest consequence

MACBETH *...why do I yield to that suggestion / Whose horrid image doth unfix my hair / And make my seated heart knock at my ribs*

MACBETH *If chance will have me King, why, chance may crown me, / Without my stir*

MACBETH *Come what come may, / Time and the hour runs through the roughest day*

Commentary

- The scene begins with one witch describing how she intends to do great mischief to a sea captain simply because the captain's wife refused to share chestnuts with her. This moment reveals how the witches perpetrate evil simply on a whim – evil is done for evil's sake.

- The image of the sailor 'tempest-tost' serves as a metaphor for the witches' powers to influence. However, they are unable to directly sink the ship ('Though his bark cannot be lost'), just as they are unable to directly harm Macbeth. The vision of an exhausted sea captain, unable to sleep, who will 'dwindle, peak and pine' and be drained 'dry as hay' foreshadows Macbeth's fate in Act 5. Macbeth's eventual spiritual draining, paranoia and sleeplessness are all anticipated here.

- This is the first time Macbeth and Banquo appear on stage. Both characters seem taken aback by the sudden appearance of the bearded witches. Banquo notes how Macbeth is stunned into silence by the witches' proclamation that he is Thane of Cawdor and will one day be King of Scotland: 'My noble partner...seems rapt withal'. In contrast, the witches' prediction that Banquo will father a line of kings doesn't seem to impress Banquo and he appears sceptical about their motives. Banquo argues that agents of evil may tell half-truths to encourage faith in them: 'to win us to our harm, /The instruments of darkness tell us truths, /Win us with honest trifles, to betray's /In deepest consequence'.

- Macbeth's belief in the witches' prophecy is bolstered by Ross's news that Duncan has given Macbeth the title of Thane of Cawdor. Macbeth is immediately troubled by dark thoughts: '...why do I yield to that suggestion / Whose horrid image doth unfix my hair / And make my seated heart knock at my ribs'. Although it is not explicitly stated, it can be assumed that Macbeth has been tempted by the witches' prophecy and is considering murdering Duncan to gain the crown for himself.

- In an aside Macbeth tries to console himself: 'If chance will have me King, why, chance may crown me, /Without my stir'. Here Macbeth seems willing to accept that Fate will crown him. However, this changes later in the Act as Macbeth actively looks to take the crown himself.

Questions

1. How does Shakespeare establish the witches as agents of evil at the start of the scene?
2. (a) What predictions do the witches make for Macbeth?
   (b) What prediction do they make for Banquo?
3. What evidence is there in the scene that suggests Macbeth is an ambitious individual?
4. Would you agree that Banquo is a more level-headed character than Macbeth? Explain your answer by referring to the scene.
5. What do you think are the 'horrible imaginings' that Macbeth mentions towards the end of the scene?
6. Clothing imagery is used twice in this scene. Write down both examples of this.

Act 1 Scene 4

Scene Summary

- Duncan warmly receives Macbeth and Banquo.
- Duncan names his son, Malcolm, as heir to the throne.
- Macbeth sees Malcolm as an obstacle to his ambition to be King.
- Duncan honours Macbeth by announcing a visit to Macbeth's castle at Inverness.
- Macbeth says he will ride ahead and tell his wife about Duncan's visit.

Forres. The Palace.
Flourish. Enter DUNCAN, MALCOLM, DONALBAIN, LENNOX, and Attendants

DUNCAN
Is execution done on Cawdor? Are not
Those in commission[1] yet returned?

MALCOLM
My liege,[2]
They are not yet come back. But I have spoke
With one that saw him die: who did report
That very frankly he confessed his treasons,
Implored your Highness' pardon and set forth
A deep repentance. Nothing in his life
Became him like the leaving it; he died
As one that had been studied in his death,[3]
To throw away the dearest thing he owed,
As 'twere a careless trifle.[4]

DUNCAN
There's no art
To find the mind's construction in the face:[5]
He was a gentleman on whom I built
An absolute trust.
[*Enter MACBETH, BANQUO, ROSS, and ANGUS*]
O worthiest cousin!
The sin of my ingratitude even now
Was heavy on me: thou art so far before
That swiftest wing of recompense is slow
To overtake thee.[6] Would thou hadst less deserved,
That the proportion both of thanks and payment
Might have been mine![7] Only I have left to say,
More is thy due than more than all can pay.

1 **Those in commission:** those sent to execute the former Thane of Cawdor

2 **liege:** lord

3 **he died / As one that had been studied in his death:** He died like somebody who had rehearsed the moment of his death.

4 **trifle:** something valueless

5 **There's no art / To find the mind's construction in the face:** Nobody can know another's mind simply by looking at the face.

6 **thou art so far...overtake thee:** Your achievements are so great that no reward can be given quickly enough.

7 **Would thou hadst...been mine:** I wish you deserved less so that I could reward you in proportion to your achievements.

MACBETH

The service and the loyalty I owe,
In doing it, pays itself. Your Highness' part
Is to receive our duties;[8] and our duties
Are to your throne and state, children and servants,
Which do but what they should, by doing everything
Safe toward your love and honour.[9]

DUNCAN

Welcome hither:
I have begun to plant thee,[10] and will labour
To make thee full of growing. Noble Banquo,
That hast no less deserved, nor must be known
No less to have done so – let me enfold[11] thee
And hold thee to my heart.

BANQUO

There if I grow,
The harvest is your own.[12]

DUNCAN

My plenteous joys,
Wanton in fulness, seek to hide themselves
In drops of sorrow.[13] Sons, kinsmen, thanes,
And you whose places are the nearest, know
We will establish our estate[14] upon
Our eldest, Malcolm, whom we name hereafter
The Prince of Cumberland; which honour must
Not unaccompanied invest him only,
But signs of nobleness, like stars, shall shine
On all deservers. From hence to Inverness,[15]
And bind us further to you.[16]

MACBETH

The rest is labour, which is not used for you:[17]
I'll be myself the harbinger[18] and make joyful
The hearing of my wife with your approach;
So humbly take my leave.

DUNCAN

My worthy Cawdor!

MACBETH

[*Aside*] The Prince of Cumberland! That is a step
On which I must fall down, or else o'er-leap,
For in my way it lies.[19] Stars, hide your fires!
Let not light see my black and deep desires:
The eye wink at the hand;[20] yet let that be,
Which the eye fears, when it is done, to see.
[*Exit*]

8 **duties:** obedience/service

9 **by doing everything / Safe toward your love and honour:** We do everything out of love and a sense of duty to you.

10 **plant thee:** give you honours/establish your power (i.e. by making Macbeth the new Thane of Cawdor)

11 **enfold:** embrace

12 **There if I grow…your own:** If I blossom, you will be rewarded with a faithful servant.

13 **Wanton in fulness…drops of sorrow:** unrestrained joy expressed in tears

14 **establish our estate upon / Our eldest, Malcolm:** Duncan names his eldest son Malcolm as his successor.

15 **Inverness:** Macbeth's castle is at Inverness.

16 **bind us further to you:** unite me (Duncan) with you (Macbeth)

17 **The rest is labour, / which is not used for you:** Leisure time seems like work if it is not spent in your company.

18 **harbinger:** herald; one who announces an arrival

19 **The Prince…it lies:** Macbeth sees Malcolm (Prince of Cumberland) as an obstacle to his ambition to be King.

20 **The eye wink at the hand:** Let my eyes ignore my actions. Macbeth is preparing to commit a crime but does not want to have to contemplate it.

DUNCAN
True, worthy Banquo; he is full so valiant,
And in his commendations I am fed;
It is a banquet to me. Let's after him,
Whose care is gone before to bid us welcome:
It is a peerless[21] kinsman.
[*Flourish. Exeunt*]

[21] **peerless kinsman:** unequalled/ unrivalled relative

Key Quotations

DUNCAN *There's no art / To find the mind's construction in the face*

MACBETH *The Prince of Cumberland! That is a step / On which I must fall down, or else o'er-leap*

MACBETH *Stars, hide your fires! / Let not light see my black and deep desires: / The eye wink at the hand*

Commentary

- Although short, this scene deepens the audience's understanding of Macbeth's ambitious nature. Despite the fact that Macbeth has considered murdering the King in the previous scene, he flatters Duncan and hypocritically swears his allegiance: 'The service and the loyalty I owe, / In doing it, pays itself'.

- There is a marked contrast between the dark tone of Macbeth's aside and Duncan's joyous proclamations. Macbeth's aside reveals the treachery of his thoughts: he says of Malcolm, 'That is a step / On which I must fall down, or else o'er-leap' and alludes to his overwhelming desire to be King and his dark fantasy of murdering Duncan: 'Stars, hide your fires! / Let not light see my black and deep desires'. Macbeth is torn between his ambition to be King and his desire to remain loyal.

- Duncan highlights how hard it is to see a person's true intentions: 'There's no art / To find the mind's construction in the face.' He explains how he once trusted the former Thane of Cawdor but was deceived by his appearance of loyalty. Ironically, as Duncan says this, Macbeth is hiding his own 'black and deep desires' for the crown.

- The audience now expects Macbeth to kill Duncan. This dark suspense creates tension as the audience watches how Macbeth has to wrestle with his own ambition.

Questions

1. What is your impression of Duncan from this scene?
2. Macbeth uses elaborate language to honour Duncan. Give two examples of this.
3. What is Macbeth's reaction to Duncan's announcement that Malcolm is heir to the throne?
4. Duncan states, 'There's no art / To find the mind's construction in the face'. Although Duncan doesn't have Macbeth in mind when he says this, do you think these lines are relevant to Macbeth? Explain your answer.
5. Basing your answer on the first four scenes of the play, would you agree that Macbeth is a conflicted character? Why / Why not?

Act 1 Scene 5

Scene Summary

- Lady Macbeth receives a letter from Macbeth telling her about the witches' prophecy.
- She worries that Macbeth does not have the necessary strength to kill Duncan. She decides to encourage Macbeth to carry out the murder.
- A messenger arrives informing her of the King's imminent arrival.
- Lady Macbeth calls on evil spirits to aid her part in killing Duncan.
- Macbeth and Lady Macbeth discuss the idea of murdering Duncan.
- The scene concludes ominously with Lady Macbeth saying, 'Leave all the rest to me.'

Inverness. Macbeth's castle.
Enter LADY MACBETH, reading a letter

LADY MACBETH

'They met me in the day of success:[1] and I have learned by the perfectest report,[2] they have more in them than mortal[3] knowledge. When I burned in desire to question them further, they made themselves air, into which they vanished. Whiles I stood rapt in the wonder of it, came missives[4] from the King, who all-hailed me 'Thane of Cawdor;' by which title, before, these weird sisters[5] saluted me, and referred me to the coming on of time, with 'Hail, king that shalt be!' This have I thought good to deliver thee, my dearest partner of greatness, that thou mightst not lose the dues of rejoicing, by being ignorant of what greatness is promised thee.[6] Lay it to thy heart, and farewell.'

Glamis thou art, and Cawdor; and shalt be
What thou art promised: yet do I fear thy nature;
It is too full o' the milk of human kindness
To catch the nearest way.[7] Thou wouldst be great;
Art not without ambition, but without
The illness should attend it:[8] what thou wouldst highly,
That wouldst thou holily;[9] wouldst not play false,
And yet wouldst wrongly win: thou'dst have, great Glamis,
That which cries 'Thus thou must do, if thou have it';
And that which rather thou dost fear to do
Than wishest should be undone. Hie thee hither,[10]
That I may pour my spirits in thine ear,[11]
And chastise with the valour of my tongue
All that impedes thee from the golden round,[12]
Which fate and metaphysical[13] aid doth seem

1 **day of success:** the day after the successful battle
2 **perfectest report:** most reliable source
3 **mortal:** human/earthly
4 **missives:** messengers
5 **weird sisters:** the witches
6 **greatness is promised thee:** i.e. queenship
7 **yet do I fear...nearest way:** I worry that you are too kind to take the type of wicked action that is needed in order to get what you want quickly.
8 **Thou wouldst be great...should attend it:** You could be great, you're not without ambition, but you don't have the ruthlessness needed to attain greatness.
9 **what thou wouldst...thou holily:** what you desire, you want to get by honest means
10 **Hie thee hither:** Come here quickly
11 **That I may pour my spirits in thine ear:** So I can whisper in your ear
12 **chastise...golden round:** attack with my persuasive words all that keeps you from the crown
13 **metaphysical:** supernatural

To have thee crowned withal.[14]
[*Enter a Messenger*]
What is your tidings?[15]

Messenger
The King comes here tonight.

Lady Macbeth
Thou'rt mad to say it!
Is not thy master with him? who, were't so,
Would have informed for preparation.

Messenger
So please you, it is true: our Thane is coming:
One of my fellows had the speed of him,[16]
Who, almost dead for breath, had scarcely more
Than would make up his message.

Lady Macbeth
Give him tending;[17]
He brings great news.
[*Exit Messenger*]
The raven[18] himself is hoarse
That croaks the fatal entrance of Duncan
Under my battlements. Come, you spirits
That tend on mortal thoughts, unsex me here,
And fill me from the crown to the toe top-full
Of direst cruelty![19] Make thick my blood;
Stop up the access and passage to remorse,
That no compunctious visitings of nature[20]
Shake my fell[21] purpose, nor keep peace between
The effect and it! Come to my woman's breasts,
And take my milk for gall,[22] you murdering ministers,
Wherever in your sightless substances
You wait on nature's mischief! Come, thick night,
And pall[23] thee in the dunnest[24] smoke of hell,
That my keen[25] knife see not the wound it makes,
Nor heaven peep through the blanket of the dark,
To cry 'Hold, hold!'

[*Enter MACBETH*]
Great Glamis! Worthy Cawdor!
Greater than both, by the all-hail hereafter!
Thy letters have transported me beyond
This ignorant present, and I feel now
The future in the instant.

Macbeth
My dearest love,
Duncan comes here tonight.

[14] **withal:** with
[15] **tidings:** news
[16] **had the speed of him:** was faster than him
[17] **Give him tending:** look after him
[18] **raven:** a bird associated with death; an ill-omen
[19] **Come, you spirits...direst cruelty!:** Come you evil spirits who listen to human thoughts, destroy my soft feminine nature and fill me from head to toe with vicious cruelty!
[20] **compunctious visitings of nature:** natural regretful thoughts
[21] **fell:** cruel/dire
[22] **gall:** bitterness
[23] **pall:** cover
[24] **dunnest:** darkest
[25] **keen:** sharp/eager

LADY MACBETH
And when goes hence?

MACBETH
Tomorrow, as he purposes.

LADY MACBETH
O, never
Shall sun that morrow see![26]
Your face, my Thane, is as a book where men
May read strange matters. To beguile the time,
Look like the time;[27] bear welcome in your eye,
Your hand, your tongue: look like the innocent flower,
But be the serpent under't.[28] He that's coming
Must be provided for:[29] and you shall put
This night's great business into my dispatch,[30]
Which shall to all our nights and days to come
Give solely sovereign sway and masterdom.[31]

MACBETH
We will speak further.

LADY MACBETH
Only look up clear;
To alter favour ever is to fear:
Leave all the rest to me.
[*Exeunt*]

26 **O, never / Shall sun that morrow see!:** O, he'll never see the sun tomorrow!
27 **To beguile...like the time:** To trick everybody, appear as they do.
28 **look like...serpent under't:** Look innocent on the outside, but be as vicious as a snake.
29 **provided for:** looked after/dealt with
30 **my dispatch:** in my hands
31 **solely sovereign sway and masterdom:** absolute power of being King

Key Quotations

LADY MACBETH *...I fear thy nature; / It is too full o' the milk of human kindness / To catch the nearest way*

LADY MACBETH *Hie thee hither,*
That I may pour my spirits in thine ear,
And chastise with the valour of my tongue
All that impedes thee from the golden round

LADY MACBETH *Come, you spirits*
That tend on mortal thoughts, unsex me here,
And fill me from the crown to the toe top-full
Of direst cruelty! Make thick my blood;
Stop up the access and passage to remorse

LADY MACBETH *look like the innocent flower, / But be the serpent under't*

Commentary

- Lady Macbeth is introduced to the audience as she reads a letter from Macbeth that recounts his meeting with the witches. This shows the trust Macbeth places in his wife. He doesn't mention anything about murder in his letter, but Lady Macbeth immediately assumes that this is the only way of gaining 'the golden round' (the crown).
- Lady Macbeth worries that her husband is 'too full o' the milk of human kindness' and that he may not have the murderous resolve to carry out an assassination. She sets herself up as a manipulator and clearly expresses her desire to persuade Macbeth with the phrase, 'Hie thee hither / That I may pour my spirits in thine ear'. Her intentions recall the methods employed by the witches.
- Lady Macbeth dramatically and shockingly calls on evil spirits to 'Stop up the access and passage to remorse'. This adds to the play's focus on supernatural evil. The fact that Lady Macbeth has to invoke evil spirits shows that she is not innately evil but is willing to give up her soul to acquire power.
- The appeal to evil spirits to 'unsex' her shows how Lady Macbeth equates manliness with violence. She seeks to suppress any 'feminine qualities' that may prevent her aiding in the murder of Duncan.
- Lady Macbeth's ambition outweighs her moral scruples and she celebrates the ability to act without guilt or regret: 'That my keen knife see not the wound it makes, / Nor heaven peep through the blanket of the dark, / To cry 'Hold, hold!'
- In this scene Lady Macbeth seems to take the lead and dominates her husband. She instructs Macbeth to 'put / This night's great business into my dispatch'. Later in the play we see how it is Lady Macbeth who plans the details of Duncan's murder.
- This scene also points to the relationship between power and false appearances. Lady Macbeth instructs her husband to 'look like the innocent flower, / But be the serpent under't.' This echoes Duncan's earlier comment about the former Thane of Cawdor: 'There's no art / To find the mind's construction in the face'.

Questions

1. What is your impression of Lady Macbeth from this scene?
2. (a) What is Lady Macbeth's view of her husband?
   (b) How is this view contradicted in Act 1, Scene 2?
3. In Act 1, Scene 4, Macbeth says, 'Stars, hide your fires! / Let not light see my black and deep desires: / The eye wink at the hand'. Write down a quotation from Lady Macbeth in this scene that expresses a similar idea.
4. Why do you think Lady Macbeth asks evil spirits to 'unsex' her?
5. What does Lady Macbeth mean when she tells Macbeth to 'look like the innocent flower, / But be the serpent under't'?
6. How would you describe the relationship between Macbeth and Lady Macbeth? Refer to this scene in your answer.
7. Imagine you are directing this scene. What advice would you give to the actor playing Lady Macbeth? Consider facial expressions, body language, tone of voice and the character's motivation. Refer to key lines in your response.

Act 1 Scene 6

Scene Summary

- Duncan and Banquo arrive at Macbeth's castle and are greeted by Lady Macbeth.

Inverness. Before Macbeth's castle.
Hautboys[1] and torches. Enter DUNCAN, MALCOLM, DONALBAIN, BANQUO, LENNOX, MACDUFF, ROSS, ANGUS and Attendants

DUNCAN
This castle hath a pleasant seat;[2] the air
Nimbly and sweetly recommends itself
Unto our gentle senses.

BANQUO
This guest of summer,
The temple-haunting martlet,[3] does approve,
By his loved mansionry,[4] that the heaven's breath[5]
Smells wooingly[6] here: no jutty, frieze,
Buttress, nor coign of vantage, but this bird
Hath made his pendent bed and procreant cradle.[7]
Where they most breed and haunt, I have observed,
The air is delicate.[8]
[*Enter LADY MACBETH*]

DUNCAN
See, see, our honoured hostess!
The love that follows us sometime is our trouble,
Which still we thank as love.[9] Herein I teach you,
How you shall bid God 'ield us for your pains,
And thank us for your trouble.[10]

LADY MACBETH
All our service
In every point twice done and then done double
Were poor and single business to contend
Against those honours deep and broad wherewith
Your Majesty loads our house: for those of old,
And the late dignities[11] heaped up to them,
We rest your hermits.[12]

DUNCAN
Where's the Thane of Cawdor?
We coursed him at the heels,[13] and had a purpose
To be his purveyor:[14] but he rides well,

1 **Hautboys:** oboe players

2 **seat:** location/position

3 **martlet:** house martin (a type of bird)

4 **loved mansionry:** favourite home

5 **heaven's breath:** air

6 **wooingly:** inviting/welcoming

7 **no jutty...procreant cradle:** The bird has nested in every protruding part of the building.

8 **Where they most breed... delicate:** Wherever these birds most commonly breed and hunt, the air is appealing.

9 **The love...thank as love:** Sometimes my subject's love is bothersome but I am grateful for it.

10 **Herein I teach you...for your trouble:** I say this to teach you to thank God for the inconvenience and me for the trouble, as it displays my love for you.

11 **late dignities:** recent honours, i.e. the title of Thane of Cawdor

12 **We rest your hermits:** We are in your debt. Hermits relied on charity to survive.

13 **coursed him at the heels:** rode close behind him

14 **purveyor:** an officer who rode ahead of a king to organise his accommodation

And his great love, sharp as his spur, hath holp[15] him
To his home before us. Fair and noble hostess,
We are your guest tonight.

LADY MACBETH

Your servants ever
Have theirs, themselves and what is theirs, in compt,[16]
To make their audit at your Highness' pleasure,
Still to return your own.[17]

DUNCAN

Give me your hand;
Conduct me to mine host: we love him highly,
And shall continue our graces towards him.
By your leave, hostess.

[*Exeunt*]

[15] **holp:** helped
[16] **in compt:** held in account
[17] **Your servants ... return to your own:** We are always your servants, as are our own servants, what they own, all that is held in account for you and can be returned to you.

Commentary

- The language used here starkly contrasts with that of the previous scene. Banquo's reference to the 'martlet' and the 'guest of summer' is in sharp relief to Lady Macbeth's image of the 'raven …That croaks the fatal entrance of Duncan' from Scene 5. Similarly, where Lady Macbeth called on the 'dunnest smoke of hell' and hoped that heaven would be unable to 'peep through the blanket of the dark', Banquo remarks how 'heaven's breath / Smells wooingly here'.
- This short scene is rich in dramatic irony*. The audience is acutely aware that Macbeth and Lady Macbeth are considering murdering King Duncan. However, Duncan, in his warm gratitude towards Macbeth and Lady Macbeth, is totally unaware of what awaits him. He believes that Macbeth's haste to reach the castle is the result of love rather than Macbeth's urgent need to discuss the assassination.
- Lady Macbeth's convincing performance as a welcoming hostess cements the idea of her as a cold-hearted murderer. Her ability to smile and flatter seems particularly chilling considering her conversation with Macbeth in the previous scene.

*__dramatic irony:__ when the audience knows something that the characters on stage are unaware of.

Act 1 Scene 7

Scene Summary

- Macbeth, in soliloquy, offers several reasons why he shouldn't kill Duncan.
- He decides not to go through with the murder.
- Upon hearing this Lady Macbeth uses her powers of persuasion to encourage Macbeth to change his mind.
- She formulates a plan whereby the chamberlains will be made drunk, drugged, smeared with blood and subsequently blamed for the killing.
- Macbeth agrees to carry out the murder.

Inverness. Macbeth's castle.
Hautboys and torches. Enter a Sewer[1], and divers Servants with dishes and service, and pass over the stage. Then enter MACBETH.

MACBETH
If it were done when 'tis done, then 'twere well
It were done quickly:[2] if the assassination
Could trammel up the consequence,[3] and catch
With his surcease[4] success; that but this blow
Might be the be-all and the end-all here – [5]
But here, upon this bank and shoal of time,
We'd jump the life to come.[6] – But in these cases
We still have judgement here;[7] that we but teach
Bloody instructions, which, being taught, return
To plague the inventor.[8] This even-handed justice
Commends[9] the ingredients of our poisoned chalice
To our own lips. – He's here in double trust:[10]
First, as I am his kinsman and his subject,
Strong both against the deed;[11] then, as his host,
Who should against his murderer shut the door,
Not bear the knife myself. – Besides, this Duncan
Hath borne his faculties so meek,[12] hath been
So clear in his great office,[13] that his virtues
Will plead like angels, trumpet-tongued,[14] against
The deep damnation of his taking-off;[15]
And pity, like a naked new-born babe,
Striding the blast, or heaven's cherubim, horsed
Upon the sightless couriers of the air,
Shall blow the horrid deed in every eye,
That tears shall drown the wind.[16] – I have no spur

1 **Sewer:** head servant
2 **If it were done…done quickly:** If the murder is to be done, it's best done sooner.
3 **trammel up the consequence:** prevent (or trap) any consequences
4 **surcease:** death
5 **the be-all and end-all here:** the end of the matter here on earth
6 **But here, upon…life to come:** But here upon the narrow stretch of human life we'd risk punishment in the afterlife.
7 **But in …judgement here:** But there is also the risk of being punished on earth (i.e. by the law).
8 **that we but teach…the inventor:** the violence we commit may be turned against us
9 **Commends:** presents
10 **double trust:** two reasons (that Duncan should trust Macbeth)
11 **First, as I am…the deed:** Firstly, I am his relative and his subject. These are both strong reasons not to kill him
12 **borne his faculties so meek:** used his power with restraint
13 **clear in his great office:** honest in his role as King
14 **trumpet-tongued:** proclaiming loudly like a trumpet
15 **taking off:** death
16 **And pity…drown the wind:** Pity, like a newborn child, will join the stormy outcry, or like angels riding on violent winds will blow Duncan's death into every eye until the sound of crying will drown out the wind.

To prick the sides of my intent, but only
Vaulting ambition, which o'erleaps itself
And falls on the other.[17]

[*Enter LADY MACBETH*]
How now! What news?

Lady Macbeth
He has almost supped: why have you left the chamber?

Macbeth
Hath he asked for me?

Lady Macbeth
Know you not he has?

Macbeth
We will proceed no further in this business:
He hath honoured me of late; and I have bought
Golden opinions from all sorts of people,
Which would be worn now in their newest gloss,
Not cast aside so soon.[18]

Lady Macbeth
Was the hope drunk
Wherein you dressed yourself?[19] Hath it slept since?
And wakes it now, to look so green and pale[20]
At what it did so freely? From this time
Such I account thy love. Art thou afeard
To be the same in thine own act and valour
As thou art in desire? Wouldst thou have that
Which thou esteem'st the ornament of life,[21]
And live a coward in thine own esteem,
Letting 'I dare not' wait upon 'I would,'
Like the poor cat i' the adage?[22]

Macbeth
Prithee,[23] peace:
I dare do all that may become a man;
Who dares do more is none.

Lady Macbeth
What beast was't, then,
That made you break this enterprise to me[24]?
When you durst[25] do it, then you were a man!
And, to be more than what you were, you would
Be so much more the man. Nor time nor place
Did then adhere, and yet you would make both.
They have made themselves, and that their fitness now

[17] **I have no spur...falls on the other:** I have nothing to drive me towards this murder but my own ambition which jumps too eagerly and falls on the other side.

[18] **I have bought...aside so soon:** I have earned new regard from people which should be enjoyed rather than cast aside like old clothes.

[19] **Was the hope...dressed yourself?:** Was your earlier ambition like a drunken promise?

[20] **green and pale:** hungover

[21] **ornament of life:** the crown

[22] **poor cat i' the adage:** an adage is a proverb. Here Lady Macbeth is referring to the proverb 'The cat would eat fish but not wet her feet', i.e. Macbeth is not willing to do something unpleasant to get what he wants.

[23] **Prithee:** I pray you

[24] **What beast... enterprise to me:** Then, what sort of beast were you when you first suggested this plot to me?

[25] **durst:** dared

Does unmake you[26]. I have given suck,[27] and know
How tender 'tis to love the babe that milks me:
I would, while it was smiling in my face,
Have plucked my nipple from his boneless gums,
And dashed the brains out, had I so sworn as you
Have done to this.

MACBETH

If we should fail?

LADY MACBETH

We fail!
But screw your courage to the sticking-place,[28]
And we'll not fail. When Duncan is asleep –
Whereto the rather shall his day's hard journey
Soundly invite him – his two chamberlains[29]
Will I with wine and wassail[30] so convince
That memory, the warder[31] of the brain,
Shall be a fume,[32] and the receipt of reason
A limbeck[33] only. When in swinish[34] sleep
Their drenched natures lie as in a death,
What cannot you and I perform upon
The unguarded Duncan? what not put upon[35]
His spongy[36] officers, who shall bear the guilt
Of our great quell?[37]

MACBETH

Bring forth[38] men-children only;
For thy undaunted mettle[39] should compose
Nothing but males. Will it not be received,
When we have marked with blood those sleepy two
Of his own chamber and used their very daggers,
That they have done't?

LADY MACBETH

Who dares receive it other,
As we shall make our griefs and clamour roar
Upon his death?

MACBETH

I am settled, and bend up
Each corporal agent[40] to this terrible feat.
Away, and mock the time[41] with fairest show:[42]
False face must hide what the false heart doth know.

[*Exeunt*]

26 **Nor time...unmake you:** Neither the time nor the place were right but you were willing to make them so. Now that the time and place are right you have lost your nerve.

27 **given suck:** breastfed

28 **screw your courage to the sticking place:** strengthen your resolve. The line suggests a tightening string on a musical instrument or crossbow.

29 **chamberlains:** attendants/ personal servants

30 **wassail:** strong alcoholic drink

31 **warder:** guardian

32 **fume:** foggy

33 **limbeck:** a distillation jug

34 **swinish:** pig-like

35 **put upon:** blame

36 **spongy:** soaked in drink

37 **quell:** murder

38 **Bring forth:** give birth to

39 **undaunted mettle:** fearless nature

40 **corporal agent:** body part

41 **mock the time:** trick everybody

42 **fairest show:** good performance

Key Quotations

MACBETH *I have no spur*
To prick the sides of my intent, but only
Vaulting ambition, which o'erleaps itself
And falls on the other.

LADY MACBETH *I have given suck, and know*
How tender 'tis to love the babe that milks me:
I would, while it was smiling in my face,
Have plucked my nipple from his boneless gums,
And dashed the brains out, had I so sworn as you
Have done to this.

MACBETH *Bring forth men-children only; / For thy undaunted mettle should compose / Nothing but males.*

MACBETH *False face must hide what the false heart doth know.*

Commentary

- This key moment reveals Macbeth's inner struggle between his desire for power and his moral scruples. In his soliloquy he offers several reasons not to go ahead with the murder.

  Macbeth:
  - fears punishment on earth and in the afterlife ('But here, upon this bank and shoal of time, / We'd jump the life to come. – But in these cases / We still have judgment here')
  - worries that the murder will come back to haunt him ('we but teach / Bloody instructions, which, being taught, return / To plague the inventor'.)
  - expresses his moral obligation to Duncan who is Macbeth's relative, King and guest ('He's here in double trust'; 'as his host, / Who should against his murderer shut the door, / Not bear the knife myself'.)
  - fears the public outcry that will follow Duncan's murder ('his virtues / Will plead like angels, trumpet-tongued, against / The deep damnation of his taking-off'.)
  - recognises that his only motivation for murder is his 'vaulting ambition' which will inevitably lead to disaster.

  At the end of his soliloquy Macbeth seems resolved to 'proceed no further in this business'.

- What is extraordinary about this scene is how Macbeth, despite his clear understanding of the immorality of the act and his fear of the consequences, changes his mind. Lady Macbeth uses a number of methods to try and convince Macbeth.

  She:
  - appeals to his sense of ambition ('Wouldst thou have that / Which thou esteem'st the ornament of life')
  - questions his love for her ('From this time / Such I account thy love')
  - taunts him ('Wouldst thou…live a coward in thine own esteem, / Letting 'I dare not' wait upon 'I would,' / Like the poor cat i' the adage?')
  - attacks his masculinity ('When you durst do it, then you were a man!')
  - employs the shocking image of murdering her child to illustrate her commitment to her husband:

'I have given suck, and know
How tender 'tis to love the babe that milks me:
I would, while it was smiling in my face,
Have plucked my nipple from his boneless gums,
And dashed the brains out, had I so sworn as you
Have done to this'

- At this point in the play, Lady Macbeth seems to be the driving force behind the conspiracy to murder Duncan. It is she who formulates the plan to blame the chamberlains for the murder and seems much stronger in her resolve to take the crown than Macbeth. However, it should be noted that despite Lady Macbeth's influence over her husband, Macbeth freely chooses to murder Duncan and is ultimately responsible for his own moral decisions.

- The scene also explores the idea of gender roles and particularly masculinity. Initially Macbeth equates manhood with acting in a proper and moral manner. He tells Lady Macbeth that to kill Duncan would not be the actions of a real man: 'I dare do all that may become a man; / Who dares do more is none'. However, Lady Macbeth equates manliness with the bravery and the capacity for violent action: 'When you durst do it, then you were a man!' She appeals to Macbeth's manly pride to encourage him to commit the murder. Macbeth later echoes his wife's vision of masculinity when he describes Lady Macbeth's steely determination as a masculine trait: 'Bring forth men-children only; / For thy undaunted mettle should compose / Nothing but males'. The question of what it means to be a man is recalled throughout the play.

Questions

1. List five reasons Macbeth offers in his soliloquy for not killing Duncan.
2. What impression of Duncan do you get from Macbeth's soliloquy?
3. How does Lady Macbeth try to convince Macbeth to kill Duncan?
4. What is Lady Macbeth's plan to avoid suspicion for the murder of Duncan?
5. What does Macbeth mean when he says, 'Bring forth men-children only; / For thy undaunted mettle should compose / Nothing but males'?
6. Explain why Macbeth says, 'False face must hide what the false heart doth know'.
7. (a) Macbeth uses a clothing image in this scene. Write it down.
   (b) Explain what Macbeth means in these lines.
8. From this scene alone, who do you think is more responsible for the decision to kill Duncan: Macbeth or Lady Macbeth? Explain your answer.

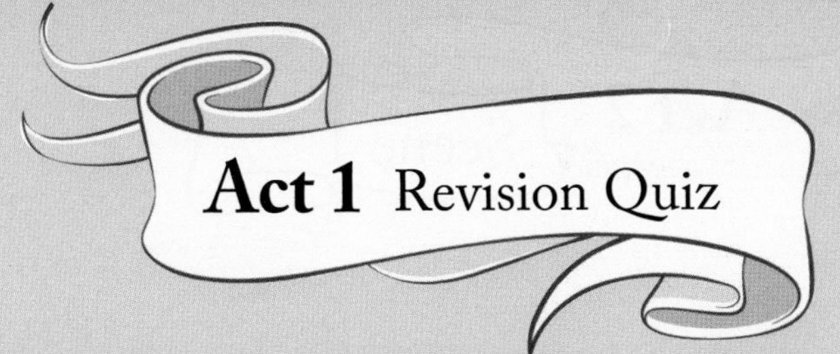

Act 1 Revision Quiz

1. What does Macbeth do to Macdonwald when he meets him on the battlefield?
- **(a)** Offers him a peace settlement
- **(b)** Takes him prisoner
- **(c)** Strips him of his crest and title
- **(d)** Cuts off his head and places it on the battlements

2. What prophecies do the witches make for Macbeth in Act 1, Scene 3?

3. What do the witches predict for Banquo?

4. What title did Macbeth have at the start of the play?

5. What new title does Duncan give him?

6. Who does Duncan name as his successor?

7. In his aside, how does Macbeth privately respond to the news of Duncan's announced successor?

8. Write down five reasons Macbeth gives for not killing Duncan.

9. Who says each of the following?:
- **(a)** '*Fair is foul, and foul is fair*'
- **(b)** '*to win us to our harm,*
  The instruments of darkness tell us truths,
  Win us with honest trifles, to betray's
  In deepest consequence.'
- **(c)** '*Yet do I fear thy nature;*
  It is too full o' the milk of human kindness
  To catch the nearest way.'
- **(d)** '*...look like the innocent flower, / But be the serpent under't.*'
- **(e)** '*I have no spur*
  To prick the sides of my intent, but only
  Vaulting ambition, which o'erleaps itself
  And falls on the other.'

10. Fill in the blanks:
- **(a)** '*Till he unseamed him from the* __nave__ *to the* __chops__, */ And fix'd his*
  __head__ *upon our* __battlements__.'
- **(b)** '*For* __brave__ *Macbeth – well he deserves that name –*
  Disdaining Fortune, with his brandish'd steel,
  Which __smoked__ *with bloody execution,*
  Like __Valour's__ *minion carved out his passage*'
- **(c)** '*...why do I yield to that suggestion*
  Whose __horrid__ *image doth* __unfix__ *my hair*
  And make my seated __heart__ *knock at my* __ribs__'

Scene Summary

- Banquo and his son Fleance meet Macbeth in the courtyard at night.
- There is an uneasy conversation between Macbeth and Banquo.
- Macbeth tells a servant to ring a bell at Lady Macbeth's bidding. This is to serve as the signal to kill Duncan.
- Macbeth sees a floating dagger pointing him towards Duncan's room.
- The hallucination disappears. The bell rings. Macbeth moves towards Duncan's bedchamber to commit the murder.

Inverness. Courtyard of Macbeth's castle.
Enter BANQUO, and FLEANCE bearing a torch before him

BANQUO
How goes the night, boy?

FLEANCE
The moon is down; I have not heard the clock.

BANQUO
And she goes down at twelve.

FLEANCE
I take't, 'tis later, sir.

BANQUO
Hold, take my sword.[1] There's husbandry[2] in heaven;
Their candles are all out[3]. Take thee that too.
A heavy summons lies like lead upon me,
And yet I would not sleep.[4] Merciful powers,
Restrain in me the cursed thoughts that nature
Gives way to in repose![5]
[Enter MACBETH, and a Servant with a torch]
Give me my sword.
Who's there?

MACBETH
A friend.

BANQUO
What, sir, not yet at rest? The king's a-bed:
He hath been in unusual pleasure, and
Sent forth great largess to your offices.[6]
This diamond he greets your wife withal,

1 **sword:** Banquo should feel relaxed i his friend's home but he is guardedly clutching his sword.
2 **husbandry:** good housekeeping
3 **candles are all out:** The night is starless.
4 **A heavy summons...not sleep:** I'm tired but can't sleep.
5 **cursed thoughts...in repose:** horrible ideas that enter my head when I rest

6 **great largess to your offices:** generous gifts to your servants' roon

By the name of most kind hostess; and shut up[7]
In measureless content.[8]

Macbeth
Being unprepared,
Our will became the servant to defect;
Which else should free have wrought.[9]

Banquo
All's well.
I dreamt last night of the three Weird Sisters:
To you they have showed some truth.

Macbeth
I think not of them:
Yet, when we can entreat an hour to serve,[10]
We would spend it in some words upon that business,
If you would grant the time.

Banquo
At your kind'st leisure.

Macbeth
If you shall cleave to my consent,[11] when 'tis,
It shall make honour for you.

Banquo
So I lose none
In seeking to augment it,[12] but still keep
My bosom franchised and allegiance clear,[13]
I shall be counselled.

Macbeth
Good repose the while!

Banquo
Thanks, sir: the like to you!
[Exeunt BANQUO and FLEANCE]

Macbeth
Go bid thy mistress, when my drink is ready,
She strike upon the bell. Get thee to bed.
[Exit Servant]
Is this a dagger which I see before me,
The handle toward my hand? Come, let me clutch thee.
I have thee not, and yet I see thee still.
Art thou not, fatal vision, sensible
To feeling as to sight?[14] or art thou but

7 **shut up:** in bed
8 **In measureless content:** with great satisfaction
9 **Being unprepared...have wrought:** As we were unprepared for the visit, our welcome was not as warm as we hoped.
10 **entreat an hour to serve:** find a convenient hour
11 **cleave to my consent:** follow my lead/ take my advice
12 **So I lose...augment it:** Just so long as I don't lose my honour by trying to get more.
13 **bosom franchised and allegiance clear:** heart loyal and conscience clear
14 **sensible/To feeling as to sight?:** able to be held as well as seen?

A dagger of the mind, a false creation,
Proceeding from the heat-oppressed brain?[15]
I see thee yet, in form as palpable[16]
As this which now I draw.
Thou marshall'st[17] me the way that I was going;
And such an instrument I was to use.
Mine eyes are made the fools o' the other senses,
Or else worth all the rest;[18] I see thee still,
And on thy blade and dudgeon[19] gouts of blood,[20]
Which was not so before. There's no such thing:
It is the bloody business which informs
Thus to mine eyes. Now o'er the one half-world
Nature seems dead, and wicked dreams abuse
The curtained sleep; witchcraft celebrates
Pale Hecate's[21] offerings, and withered murder,
Alarumed by his sentinel, the wolf,
Whose howl's his watch, [22] thus with his stealthy pace.
With Tarquin's[23] ravishing strides, towards his design
Moves like a ghost. Thou sure and firm-set earth,
Hear not my steps, which way they walk, for fear
Thy very stones prate[24] of my whereabout,
And take the present horror from the time,
Which now suits with it.[25] Whiles I threat, he lives:
Words to the heat of deeds too cold breath gives.[26]
[A bell rings]
I go, and it is done; the bell invites me.
Hear it not, Duncan, for it is a knell[27]
That summons thee to heaven, or to hell.
[Exit]

[15] **heat-oppressed brain:** feverish mir
[16] **palpable:** clearly present/tangible
[17] **Thou marshall'st:** You lead/direct
[18] **Mine eyes...all the rest:** Either my eyes are foolish compared to the other senses or are more perceptive than all the rest.
[19] **dudgeon:** handle
[20] **gouts of blood:** blood droplets
[21] **Hecate:** goddess of witchcraft
[22] **Alarumed...his watch:** Murder is awoken by his watchdog, the wolf
[23] **Tarquin:** a Roman prince who crept stealthily to rape a sleeping victim
[24] **prate:** tell
[25] **And take the present...suits with** And destroy the horrifying silence which suits my purposes tonight
[26] **Words to the heat of deeds too cold breath gives:** Words cool the heat of action.
[27] **knell:** the ringing of a funeral bell

Key Quotations

BANQUO *Merciful powers, / Restrain in me the cursed thoughts that nature / Gives way to in repose!*

MACBETH *Is this a dagger which I see before me, / The handle toward my hand?*

MACBETH *Thou marshall'st me the way that I was going*

Commentary

- At the start of the scene, Banquo is avoiding sleep as he is having nightmares. He protectively holds his sword and as Macbeth approaches he suspiciously calls out, 'Who's there?' This uneasy atmosphere is continued when Macbeth seems to warily test Banquo's loyalty to him: 'If you shall cleave to my consent, when 'tis, / It shall make honour for you.' Banquo is unsure what exactly Macbeth is proposing but he states clearly that he will only act in good conscience and seeks to keep his 'bosom franchised and allegiance clear'.

- When this play was written, King James I ruled England and Scotland. It was thought at the time that James I was Banquo's descendent. In this scene, Banquo is presented as a moral individual who prays for grace to resist temptation: 'Merciful powers, / Restrain in me the cursed thoughts that nature / Gives way to in repose!' This portrayal was meant to flatter James I. Through contrast, it also highlights Macbeth's immorality.

- Macbeth's dagger soliloquy dramatically illustrates his inner turmoil as he prepares for murder and is driven on by the irresistible allure of power. Some commentators see the dagger as a supernatural phenomenon much like the witches, others view it as a signal of Macbeth's loosening grip on reality. This soliloquy offers some interesting staging options: should the audience be able to see the dagger or is it more effective if Macbeth addresses the empty air?

- The soliloquy itself uses highly charged, poetic language that reveals Macbeth's overwrought mind. Macbeth imagines half the world is plunged in darkness and envisages 'withered murder' creeping like a ghost. The soliloquy draws out the tension as the audience waits in nervous expectation for the murder to be committed. Macbeth knows that agonising over his actions is only postponing the inevitable: 'Words to the heat of deeds too cold breath gives' and leaves to commit the murder.

Questions

1. What change has occurred in the relationship between Banquo and Macbeth? Refer to this scene and Act 1, Scene 3 in your answer.
2. Do you think the appearance of the dagger is a supernatural phenomenon like the witches or is it the product of Macbeth's imagination? Explain your viewpoint.
3. How does Shakespeare create tension in this scene?
4. Rewrite Macbeth's dagger soliloquy in modern English.

Scene Summary

- Having just killed King Duncan, Macbeth returns to his wife.
- He is shaken by the event and complains of hearing voices.
- Macbeth holds the daggers and has forgotten to plant them on the sleeping bodies of the chamberlains.
- Lady Macbeth brings the daggers to Duncan's chamber.
- Macbeth and Lady Macbeth wash the blood from their hands.
- Knocking is heard at the castle gate.

The same.
Enter LADY MACBETH

LADY MACBETH
That which hath made them drunk hath made me bold;
What hath quenched[1] them hath given me fire.[2] Hark! Peace!
It was the owl that shrieked, the fatal bellman,[3]
Which gives the stern'st[4] good-night. He is about it:
The doors are open; and the surfeited grooms[5]
Do mock their charge[6] with snores: I have drugged their possets,[7]
That death and nature do contend about them,
Whether they live or die.

MACBETH
[*Within*] Who's there? What, ho!

LADY MACBETH
Alack, I am afraid they have awaked,
And 'tis not done. The attempt and not the deed
Confounds[8] us. Hark! I laid their daggers ready;
He could not miss 'em. Had he not resembled
My father as he slept, I had done't.
[Enter MACBETH]
My husband!

MACBETH
I have done the deed. Didst thou not hear a noise?

LADY MACBETH
I heard the owl scream and the crickets cry.
Did not you speak?

MACBETH
When?

[1] **quenched:** put to sleep
[2] **fire:** energy
[3] **fatal bellman:** the bellringer at an execution or funeral
[4] **stern'st:** sternest/harshest
[5] **surfeited grooms:** drunken attendants
[6] **charge:** duties/the man they should protect, i.e. Duncan
[7] **possets:** late night alcoholic drink made with milk
[8] **Confounds:** ruins/undoes

→ Killing of King
– regicide

LADY MACBETH

Now.

MACBETH

As I descended?

LADY MACBETH

Ay.

MACBETH

Hark![9]
Who lies i' the second chamber?

LADY MACBETH

Donalbain.

MACBETH

[Looking at his hands] This is a sorry sight.

LADY MACBETH

A foolish thought, to say a sorry sight.

MACBETH

There's one did laugh in's sleep, and one cried 'Murder!'
That they did wake each other: I stood and heard them:
But they did say their prayers, and addressed them[10]
Again to sleep.

LADY MACBETH

There are two lodged together.

MACBETH

One cried 'God bless us!' and 'Amen' the other;
As[11] they had seen me with these hangman's hands.
Listening their fear, I could not say 'Amen,'
When they did say 'God bless us!'[12]

LADY MACBETH

Consider it not so deeply.

MACBETH

But wherefore could not I pronounce 'Amen'?
I had most need of blessing, and 'Amen'
Stuck in my throat.

LADY MACBETH

These deeds must not be thought
After these ways; so, it will make us mad.

[9] **Hark:** Listen!

[10] **addressed them:** they got ready

[11] **As:** As if

[12] **One cried... God bless us!:** Macbeth overhears the chamberlains praying and is unable to say 'Amen'. An Elizabethan audience would have seen an inability to pray as a sign of evil.

Macbeth
Methought I heard a voice cry 'Sleep no more!
Macbeth does murder sleep' – the innocent sleep,
Sleep that knits up the ravelled sleave[13] of care,
The death of each day's life, sore labour's bath,[14]
Balm[15] of hurt minds, great nature's second course,[16]
Chief nourisher in life's feast, –

Lady Macbeth
What do you mean?

Macbeth
Still it cried 'Sleep no more!' to all the house:
'Glamis hath murder'd sleep, and therefore Cawdor
Shall sleep no more – Macbeth shall sleep no more.'

Lady Macbeth
Who was it that thus cried? Why, worthy Thane,
You do unbend[17] your noble strength, to think
So brainsickly[18] of things. Go get some water,
And wash this filthy witness[19] from your hand.
Why did you bring these daggers from the place?
They must lie there: go carry them; and smear
The sleepy grooms with blood.

Macbeth
I'll go no more:
I am afraid to think what I have done;
Look on't again I dare not.

Lady Macbeth
Infirm[20] of purpose!
Give me the daggers: the sleeping and the dead
Are but as pictures: 'tis the eye of childhood
That fears a painted devil. If he do bleed,
I'll gild[21] the faces of the grooms withal;
For it must seem their guilt.
[*Exit. Knocking within*]

Macbeth
Whence is that knocking?
How is't with me, when every noise appals me?
What hands are here? Ha! they pluck out mine eyes.
Will all great Neptune's[22] ocean wash this blood
Clean from my hand? No, this my hand will rather
The multitudinous[23] seas incarnadine,[24]
Making the green one red.
[Re-enter LADY MACBETH]

[13] **ravelled sleave:** tangled thread
[14] **sore labour's bath:** soother of aches associated with work
[15] **Balm:** soothing ointment
[16] **second course:** main meal

[17] **unbend:** weaken
[18] **brainsickly:** hysterically/agitatedly
[19] **filthy witness:** i.e. the blood

[20] **Infirm:** unfit/weak

[21] **gild:** paint (with gold), a pun on 'guilt'

[22] **Neptune:** Roman god of the sea
[23] **multitudinous:** countless
[24] **incarnadine:** dye red

Lady Macbeth
My hands are of your colour; but I shame
To wear a heart so white *[Knocking within]*. I hear a knocking
At the south entry: retire we to our chamber;
A little water clears us of this deed:
How easy is it, then! Your constancy
Hath left you unattended[25] *[Knocking within]*. Hark! more knocking.
Get on your nightgown, lest occasion call us,
And show us to be watchers. Be not lost
So poorly in your thoughts.

Macbeth
To know my deed, 'twere best not know myself.[26]
[Knocking within]
Wake Duncan with thy knocking! I would thou couldst![27]
[Exeunt]

25 **Your constancy / Hath left you unattended:** Your determination has left you.

26 **To know my deed...myself:** I'd rather forget myself than see what I've done.

27 **I would thou couldst!:** I wish you could!

Key Quotations

Lady Macbeth *Had he not resembled / My father as he slept, I had done't.*

Lady Macbeth *These deeds must not be thought / After these ways; so, it will make us mad.*

Macbeth *Will all great Neptune's ocean wash this blood*
Clean from my hand? No, this my hand will rather
The multitudinous seas incarnadine,
Making the green one red.

Lady Macbeth *My hands are of your colour; but I shame / To wear a heart so white.*

Lady Macbeth *A little water clears us of this deed*

Macbeth *To know my deed, 'twere best not know myself.*

Macbeth *Wake Duncan with thy knocking! I would thou couldst!*

Commentary

- The murder of Duncan takes place offstage. This shifts the audience's attention away from the crime itself and onto Macbeth's sense of horror and guilt. The pitiful spectacle of Macbeth holding the bloody daggers keeps the audience focused on Macbeth's suffering.

- Shakespeare compounds the tension of the scene by making reference to the sounds of owls, crickets and knocking; this lends a spooky quality. The inclusion of nervous questions adds a further sense of uncertainty: 'Who's there?', 'Did not you speak?', 'As I descended?', 'Who lies i' the second chamber?'

- Lady Macbeth's calculating and composed behaviour lives up to the audience's expectations. She callously chides Macbeth for reflecting morbidly on the horrible crime: 'These deeds must not be thought / After these ways; so, it will make us mad' and it is she who returns the daggers to the room to 'gild the faces of the grooms' (i.e. smear the chamberlains' faces with blood). As Macbeth expresses his revulsion at what he has done, Lady Macbeth asserts her role in the crime but coldly states, 'My hands are of your colour; but I shame / To wear a heart so white'. She expresses no remorse and seems to think that there will be no consequences for what they have done: 'A little water clears us of this deed'.

- However, Lady Macbeth is trying to suppress her humanity in this scene. Despite her composed appearance, her reluctance to murder Duncan herself suggests that she is horrified by the crime: 'Had he not resembled / My father as he slept, I had done't' illustrates that she is horrified by the crime. Despite her brave exterior Lady Macbeth is just as shaken by the idea of murder as Macbeth.

- Macbeth seems traumatised by his crime and on the verge of hysteria. He reports hearing voices proclaiming that, 'Macbeth shall sleep no more' and is clearly on edge: 'How is't with me, when every noise appals me?'

- In Act 1 Macbeth took pride in his daring manliness. However, in this scene his courage seems to desert him. He tells Lady Macbeth that he will not look on the sight of Duncan's murdered body again: 'I'll go no more: / I am afraid to think what I have done; / Look on't again I dare not.'

- As Macbeth attempts to clean the 'filthy witness' from his hands, he realises the effect of his crime will spread rather than be washed away: 'Will all great Neptune's ocean wash this blood / Clean from my hand? No, this my hand will rather / The multitudinous seas incarnadine'. Macbeth's final statement is one of regret and clearly displays the depth of his guilt: 'Wake Duncan with thy knocking! I would thou couldst!'

Questions

1. (a) How does Macbeth feel after murdering Duncan? Refer to the text in your answer.

(b) How does Lady Macbeth feel after the murder? Refer to the text.

2. (a) What reason does Lady Macbeth give for not killing Duncan herself?

(b) Does this soften your view of her character? Why / why not?

3. Would you agree that in this scene, Lady Macbeth is the dominant character? Explain your viewpoint by referring to the text.

4. How does Shakespeare create tension in this scene?

5. Rewrite the following lines in your own words:

(a) *'These deeds must not be thought*
After these ways; so, it will make us mad'

(b) *'Methought I heard a voice cry 'Sleep no more!*
Macbeth does murder sleep' – the innocent sleep,
Sleep that knits up the ravelled sleave of care,
The death of each day's life, sore labour's bath,
Balm of hurt minds'

(c) *'The sleeping and the dead*
Are but as pictures: 'tis the eye of childhood
That fears a painted devil'

(d) *'Will all great Neptune's ocean wash this blood*
Clean from my hand? No, this my hand will rather
The multitudinous seas incarnadine,
Making the green one red'.

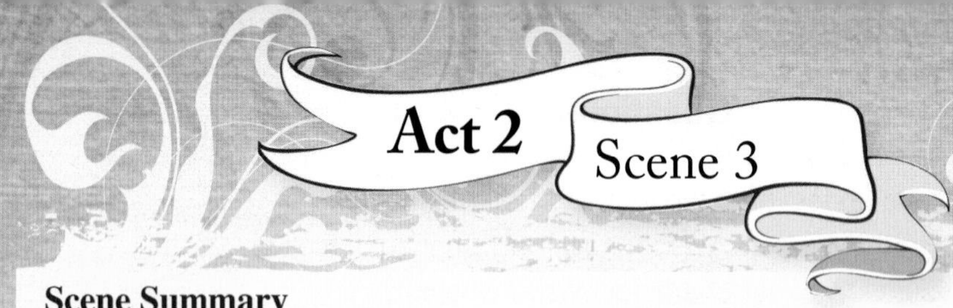

Act 2 Scene 3

Scene Summary

- The Porter grumbles as he opens the gate, providing a moment of comic relief for the audience.
- Macduff discovers Duncan has been murdered.
- Macbeth goes to the chamber and kills the chamberlains. He tells the other thanes that this was done in furious vengeance for the murder of Duncan.
- Lady Macbeth faints which shifts the attention away from Macbeth.
- Duncan's sons, Malcolm and Donalbain, decide to flee Scotland in fear for their lives.

The same.
Knocking within. Enter a Porter

PORTER
Here's a knocking indeed! If a man were porter of hell-gate, he should have old turning the key.[1] *[Knocking within.]* Knock, knock, knock! Who's there, i' the name of Beelzebub?[2] Here's a farmer, that hanged himself on the expectation of plenty:[3] come in time; have napkins enough[4] about you; here you'll sweat for't. *[Knocking within.]* Knock, knock! Who's there, in the other devil's name?[5] Faith, here's an equivocator,[6] that could swear in both the scales against either scale;[7] who committed treason[8] enough for God's sake, yet could not equivocate to heaven: O, come in, equivocator. *[Knocking within.]* Knock, knock, knock! Who's there? Faith, here's an English tailor come hither, for stealing out of a French hose:[9] come in, tailor; here you may roast your goose. *[Knocking within.]* Knock, knock; never at quiet! What are you? But this place is too cold for hell. I'll devil-porter it no further: I had thought to have let in some of all professions that go the primrose way[10] to the everlasting bonfire.[11] *[Knocking within.]* Anon,[12] anon! I pray you, remember[13] the porter. *[Opens the gate.]*

[Enter MACDUFF and LENNOX]

1 **have old turning the key:** plenty of practice turning the key
2 **Beezlebub:** Prince of the devils
3 **expectation of plenty:** expecting a good harvest that didn't arrive
4 **have napkins enough:** have plenty of handkerchiefs (because it's hot in hell)
5 **other devil:** possibly Satan
6 **equivocator:** One who speaks ambiguously in order to mislead or avoid the full truth.
7 **could swear...either scale:** whose answers are so ambiguous he could argue both sides of an argument
8 **treason:** betrayal of King or country
9 **stealing out of / a French hose:** not giving as much cloth as the customer paid for
10 **primrose way:** attractive path
11 **everlasting bonfire:** eternal hell
12 **Anon:** Right away/I'm coming now
13 **remember:** tip

MACDUFF
Was it so late, friend, ere you went to bed,
That you do lie so late?

PORTER
'Faith sir, we were carousing till the second cock:[14] and drink, sir, is a great provoker[15] of three things.

14 **carousing...second cock:** drinking till 3 a.m.
15 **provoker:** encourager

MACDUFF
What three things does drink especially provoke?

PORTER
Marry[16], sir, nose-painting,[17] sleep, and urine. Lechery,[18] sir, it provokes, and unprovokes; it provokes the desire, but it takes away the performance:[19] therefore, much drink may be said to be an equivocator with lechery: it makes him, and it mars[20] him; it sets him on, and it takes him off; it persuades him, and disheartens him; makes him stand to, and not stand to; in conclusion, equivocates him in a sleep, and, giving him the lie,[21] leaves him.

MACDUFF
I believe drink gave thee the lie last night.

PORTER
That it did, sir, i' the very throat o' me:[22] but I requited[23] him for his lie; and, I think, being too strong for him, though he took up my legs sometime, yet I made a shift to cast him.[24]

MACDUFF
Is thy master stirring?

[Enter MACBETH]

Our knocking has awaked him; here he comes.

LENNOX
Good morrow, noble sir.

MACBETH
Good morrow, both.

MACDUFF
Is the king stirring, worthy thane?

MACBETH
Not yet.

MACDUFF
He did command me to call timely[25] on him:
I have almost slipped the hour.

MACBETH
I'll bring you to him.

MACDUFF
I know this is a joyful trouble[26] to you;
But yet 'tis one.

16 **Marry:** by Mary
17 **nose-painting:** getting a red nose by drinking alcohol
18 **Lechery:** lust/sexual desire
19 **takes away the performance:** affects sexual performance
20 **mars:** damages/spoils
21 **giving him the lie:** pun: 1. deceives him 2. makes him lie down (asleep)
22 **the very throat o' me:** pun: 1. lied to my face 2. was poured down my throat
23 **requited him:** retaliated
24 **being too strong...cast him:** The Porter describes his drinking session as if it were a wrestling match in which the Porter fell down at times.
25 **timely:** early
26 **joyful trouble:** The King's visit is both a joy and extra work.

MACBETH
The labour we delight in physics pain.[27]
This is the door.

MACDUFF
I'll make so bold to call,
For 'tis my limited service.[28]
[Exit]

LENNOX
Goes the King hence today?

MACBETH
He does: he did appoint so.

LENNOX
The night has been unruly:[29] where we lay,
Our chimneys were blown down – and, as they say,
Lamentings[30] heard i' the air; strange screams of death,
And prophesying with accents terrible
Of dire combustion[31] and confused events,
New hatched to the woeful time:[32] the obscure bird[33]
Clamoured[34] the livelong night: some say, the earth
Was feverous and did shake.[35]

MACBETH
'Twas a rough night.

LENNOX
My young remembrance cannot parallel
A fellow to it.[36]
[Re-enter MACDUFF]

MACDUFF
O horror! Horror! Horror! Tongue nor heart
Cannot conceive[37] nor name thee!

MACBETH AND LENNOX
What's the matter?

MACDUFF
Confusion now hath made his masterpiece!
Most sacrilegious[38] murder hath broke ope[39]
The Lord's anointed temple, and stole thence
The life o' the building![40]

MACBETH
What is 't you say? the life?

[27] **The labour...pain:** Finding joy in our work is a cure for pain.

[28] **limited service:** the little I have been asked to do

[29] **unruly:** wild

[30] **Lamentings:** cries of sorrow

[31] **dire combustion:** terrible disruption

[32] **New hatched to the woeful time:** the product of this terrible age

[33] **obscure bird:** owl

[34] **Clamoured:** cried out

[35] **The night has been...did shake:** In Shakespeare's time, the King was seen as God's representative on earth. It wouldn't have surprised an audience to hear of strange weather events in the wake of regicide (murder of a king).

[36] **My young...fellow to it:** I can't remember a night like it in my young life.

[37] **conceive:** think of

[38] **sacrilegious:** against God. The King was seen as God's representative on earth.

[39] **ope:** open

[40] **broke ope...building:** The King's body is compared to a sacred temple.

Lennox
Mean you his majesty?

Macduff
Approach the chamber, and destroy your sight
With a new Gorgon[41] – Do not bid me speak;
See, and then speak yourselves.
[Exeunt MACBETH and LENNOX]

Awake, awake!
Ring the alarum-bell. Murder and treason!
Banquo and Donalbain! Malcolm! awake!
Shake off this downy[42] sleep, death's counterfeit,[43]
And look on death itself! Up, up, and see
The great doom's image![44] Malcolm! Banquo!
As from your graves rise up, and walk like sprites,[45]
To countenance[46] this horror! Ring the bell.
[Bell rings]
[Enter LADY MACBETH]

Lady Macbeth
What's the business,
That such a hideous trumpet calls to parley[47]
The sleepers of the house? Speak, speak!

Macduff
O gentle lady,
'Tis not for you to hear what I can speak:
The repetition, in a woman's ear,
Would murder as it fell.
[Enter BANQUO]
O Banquo, Banquo,
Our royal master's murdered!

Lady Macbeth
Woe, alas!
What? in our house?

Banquo
Too cruel anywhere.
Dear Duff, I prithee,[48] contradict thyself,
And say it is not so.
[Re-enter MACBETH and LENNOX, with ROSS]

Macbeth
Had I but died an hour before this chance,
I had lived a blessed time;[49] for, from this instant,
There's nothing serious in mortality:

[41] **Gorgon:** a Greek mythological creature that turned anyone who looked upon it to stone

[42] **downy:** soothing

[43] **death's counterfeit:** i.e. sleep is a false death

[44] **great doom's image!:** the picture of the end of the world

[45] **sprites:** spirits

[46] **countenance:** face

[47] **to parley:** to discuss (as in a battle conference)

[48] **prithee:** pray you

[49] **Had I…blessed time:** These words are said by Macbeth to suggest his innocence to the others. The irony is that his statement is actually true.

All is but toys: renown and grace is dead;
The wine of life is drawn, and the mere lees
Is left this vault to brag of.[50]
[Enter MALCOLM and DONALBAIN]

DONALBAIN
What is amiss?[51]

MACBETH
You are, and do not know't:
The spring, the head, the fountain of your blood
Is stopped;[52] the very source of it is stopped.

MACDUFF
Your royal father's murdered.

MALCOLM
O, by whom?

LENNOX
Those of his chamber, as it seemed, had done't:
Their hands and faces were all badged[53] with blood;
So were their daggers, which unwiped we found
Upon their pillows:
They stared, and were distracted. No man's life
Was to be trusted with them.

MACBETH
O, yet I do repent me of my fury,
That I did kill them.

MACDUFF
Wherefore did you so?

MACBETH
Who can be wise, amazed, temperate[54] and furious,
Loyal and neutral, in a moment? No man:
The expedition my violent love
Outrun the pauser, reason.[55] Here lay Duncan,
His silver skin laced with his golden blood;
And his gashed stabs looked like a breach[56] in nature
For ruin's wasteful entrance: there, the murderers,
Steeped[57] in the colours of their trade, their daggers
Unmannerly breeched with gore:[58] who could refrain,[59]
That had a heart to love, and in that heart
Courage to make's love known?

LADY MACBETH
Help me hence, ho!

50 **from this instant...brag of:** From now on, nothing in life is serious. Everything is trivialised; fame and good deeds are dead. The spirit of life is drained and only the dregs are left in the cellar to boast of.

51 **amiss:** wrong

52 **The spring...Is stopped:** The head of your family is dead.

53 **badged:** marked

54 **temperate:** calm

55 **The expedition...reason:** My passion overtook my ability to reason.

56 **breach:** large gap

57 **Steeped:** soaked

58 **Unmannerly breeched with gore:** indecently dressed in blood

59 **refrain:** restrain himself

MACDUFF
Look to the lady.

MALCOLM
[Aside to DONALBAIN] Why do we hold our tongues,
That most may claim this argument for ours?[60]

DONALBAIN
[Aside to MALCOLM] What should be spoken
Here, where our fate, hid in an auger-hole,[61]
May rush, and seize us? Let's away;
Our tears are not yet brewed.

MALCOLM
[Aside to DONALBAIN] Nor our strong sorrow
Upon the foot of motion.[62]

BANQUO
Look to the lady:
[LADY MACBETH is carried out]
And when we have our naked frailties[63] hid,
That suffer in exposure, let us meet,
And question this most bloody piece of work,
To know it further. Fears and scruples[64] shake us:
In the great hand of God I stand; and thence
Against the undivulged pretence I fight
Of treasonous malice.[65]

MACDUFF
And so do I.

ALL
So all.

MACBETH
Let's briefly put on manly readiness,[66]
And meet i' the hall together.

ALL
Well contented.
[Exeunt all but MALCOLM and DONALBAIN].

MALCOLM
What will you do? Let's not consort with them:[67]
To show an unfelt sorrow is an office[68]
Which the false man does easy. I'll to England.

[60] **Why do we...argument for ours?:** Why do we not speak when this matter is of greatest concern to us?

[61] **auger-hole:** drilled hole/spy hole

[62] **Nor our strong...of motion:** Our strong sorrow is not yet ready to be expressed.

[63] **naked frailties:** state of undress. Some of the characters are just out of bed and not fully dressed.
[64] **scruples:** doubts
[65] **Against the undivulged...malice:** I will fight against the unknown motives of treasonous enemies.

[66] **put on manly readiness:** 1. put on suitable clothes 2. adopt a 'manly', warlike attitude

[67] **consort with them:** stay in their company
[68] **office:** role

DONALBAIN

To Ireland, I; our separated fortune
Shall keep us both the safer. Where we are,
There's daggers in men's smiles: the near in blood,
The nearer bloody.[69]

MALCOLM

This murderous shaft that's shot
Hath not yet lighted,[70] and our safest way
Is to avoid the aim. Therefore, to horse;
And let us not be dainty[71] of leave-taking,
But shift[72] away: there's warrant in that theft
Which steals itself, when there's no mercy left.[73]

[Exeunt]

[69] **the near in blood, / The nearer bloody:** The more closely related somebody is the more likely they are to murder you.

[70] **This murderous shaft that's shot / Hath not yet lighted:** The murderous arrow that's been shot has not yet landed.

[71] **dainty:** courteous

[72] **shift:** sneak

[73] **there's warrant...no mercy left:** Leaving without saying goodbye is justifiable in a place where no mercy is left.

Key Quotations

MACDUFF *Most sacrilegious murder hath broke ope / The Lord's anointed temple, and stole thence / The life o' the building!*

MACBETH *Had I but died an hour before this chance,*
I had lived a blessed time; for, from this instant,
There's nothing serious in mortality:
All is but toys: renown and grace is dead;
The wine of life is drawn, and the mere lees
Is left this vault to brag of.

BANQUO *In the great hand of God I stand; and thence / Against the undivulged pretence I fight / Of treasonous malice*

DONALBAIN *There's daggers in men's smiles: the near in blood, / The nearer bloody*

Commentary

- After the horror of the previous scene, the drunken Porter provides much needed comic relief. His puns, cantankerous nature and innuendo help to amuse the audience.

- The character of the Porter also bring some of the play's themes into focus. His references to hell ('everlasting bonfire') and devils like 'Beelzebub' remind us that *Macbeth* is an exploration of good and evil. The Porter also provides a list of criminals entering the gates of hell; there can be no forgetting that this is a play that explores crime and its social and psychological impact.

- Notably the Porter mentions an 'equivocator… who committed treason'. This draws the audience's attention to how the three witches equivocate (mislead/tell half-truths) to Macbeth. The topic of equivocation was of importance when *Macbeth* was written. Fr. Garnet or 'Farmer'was tried for taking part in a failed assassination attempt on King James I (the Gunpowder Plot). Garnet famously equivocated (i.e. told half-truths) during the trial to avoid telling the whole truth. He was hanged. The witches' equivocation coupled with Macbeth's treason are brought to the fore here. Even in its lightest moment, *Macbeth* deals with weighty and serious ideas.

- Macduff describes Duncan's body using religious terminology. His murder is described as 'sacrilegious' and his corpse as 'The Lord's anointed temple'. This reflects the Elizabethan view that the King was God's chosen representative on earth and stresses the idea of Duncan as a good king.

- After the discovery of Duncan's body, Macbeth speaks eloquently: 'All is but toys: renown and grace is dead; / The wine of life is drawn, and the mere lees / Is left this vault to brag of'. This echoes the other thanes' grief for their murdered king. However, Macbeth's dark comments reveal his guilty conscience to the audience. This is most apparent in Macbeth's poetic lamentation – not for the loss of Duncan – but for the loss of his own innocence: 'Had I but died an hour before this chance, / I had lived a blessed time'.

- Macbeth attempts to hide his guilt from the other characters and live up to Lady Macbeth's demand that he 'look like the innocent flower, / But be the serpent under't.' He explains that his murder of the chamberlains was an act of passion: 'Who can be wise, amazed, temperate and furious, / Loyal and neutral, in a moment?' Macbeth's pretence is furthered when he assumes the leadership role and starts to give instructions to the other thanes: 'Let's briefly put on manly readiness, / And meet i' the hall together.'

- Lady Macbeth acts suitably shocked at the news of Duncan's death: 'Woe, alas! / What? in our house?' and reveals her ability to deceive others.

- Commentators often differ in their view of Lady Macbeth's fainting spell. It may occur because she is overwhelmed by Macbeth's description of the chamberlains: 'their daggers / Unmannerly breeched with gore'. Alternatively, she may faint as she realises Macbeth's capacity for evil without her influence. However, she 'conveniently' faints after Macduff starts to question Macbeth's motivation for killing the chamberlains. This suggests that Lady Macbeth's sudden swoon is simply a ploy to avoid suspicion of her husband.

Questions

1. How does Macduff react to the discovery of Duncan's body?
2. (a) What reason does Macbeth offer for killing the chamberlains?
   (b) What is his real motive?
3. Why do you think Lady Macbeth faints in this scene?
4. Looking at the reaction of all the characters to the news of Duncan's murder, do you think he was a good king? Refer to the scene in your answer.
5. Why do Malcolm and Donalbain 'shift away'?
6. In what way are the reports at the beginning of the scene of unnatural weather phenomena relevant?
7. Find a quotation from the scene for each of the following ideas:
   (a) The Porter provides some humour.
   (b) Strange weather has occurred in the night.
   (c) Macbeth says that life is drained of meaning now that Duncan is dead.
   (d) Donalbain is suspicious of his relatives.

Act 2 Scene 4

Scene Summary

- Ross and an old man speak about strange unnatural phenomena and the extraordinary behaviour of animals following Duncan's death.
- Macduff arrives and explains that Malcolm and Donalbain have left, and that some suspect that they ordered the murder of Duncan.
- Macbeth is to be crowned at Scone.
- Macduff says he is not going to the coronation; instead he is going home to Fife.

Inverness. Outside Macbeth's castle.
Enter ROSS and an OLD MAN

OLD MAN
Threescore and ten[1] I can remember well:
Within the volume[2] of which time I have seen
Hours dreadful and things strange; but this sore[3] night
Hath trifled former knowings.[4]

1 **Threescore and ten:** 70 years
2 **volume:** record
3 **sore:** awful
4 **Hath trifled former knowings:** Has trivialised things I have known before

ROSS
Ah, good father,[5]
Thou seest, the heavens, as troubled with man's act, [6]
Threaten his bloody stage: by the clock, 'tis day,
And yet dark night strangles the travelling lamp:[7]
Is't night's predominance, or the day's shame,
That darkness does the face of earth entomb,[8]
When living light should kiss it?

5 **father:** a term of respect; the old man is not Ross's father
6 **the heavens...man's act:** Heaven is upset by the actions of people.
7 **strangles the travelling lamp:** blocks out the sun
8 **entomb:** cover (as in a tomb)

OLD MAN
'Tis unnatural,
Even like the deed that's done. On Tuesday last,
A falcon, towering in her pride of place,
Was by a mousing owl hawked at and killed.[9]

9 **A falcon...and killed:** A falcon, soaring high, was attacked and killed by an owl.

ROSS
And Duncan's horses – a thing most strange and certain –
Beauteous and swift, the minions of their race,[10]
Turned wild in nature, broke their stalls, flung out,
Contending 'gainst obedience,[11] as they would make
War with mankind.

10 **minions of their race:** the best of their breed
11 **Contending 'gainst obedience:** rebelling against their training

OLD MAN
'Tis said they eat each other.

Ross
They did so, to the amazement of mine eyes
That look'd upon't. Here comes the good Macduff.
[Enter MACDUFF]
How goes the world, sir, now?

Macduff
Why, see you not?

Ross
Is't known who did this more than bloody deed?

Macduff
Those that Macbeth hath slain.

Ross
Alas, the day!
What good could they pretend?

Macduff
They were suborned:[12]
Malcolm and Donalbain, the King's two sons,
Are stolen away and fled; which puts upon them
Suspicion of the deed.

Ross
'Gainst nature still!
Thriftless ambition, that wilt ravin up
Thine own life's means![13] Then 'tis most like
The sovereignty will fall upon Macbeth.

Macduff
He is already named, and gone to Scone[14]
To be invested.[15]

Ross
Where is Duncan's body?

Macduff
Carried to Colmekill,[16]
The sacred storehouse of his predecessors,[17]
And guardian of their bones.

Ross
Will you to Scone?

Macduff
No, cousin, I'll to Fife.[18]

[12] **suborned:** bribed/induced

[13] **Thrifless ambition...life's means:** Purposeless ambition will devour the source of life (i.e. sons destroying their father).

[14] **Scone:** the place where Scottish kings were traditionally crowned

[15] **invested:** crowned

[16] **Colmekill:**The island of Iona: the place where Scottish kings were buried.

[17] **storehouse of his predecessors:** tomb of his ancestors

[18] **Fife:** Macduff's home

Ross

Well, I will thither.

Macduff

Well, may you see things well done there: adieu![19]
Lest our old robes sit easier than our new![20]

Ross

Farewell, father.

Old Man

God's benison[21] go with you; and with those
That would make good of bad, and friends of foes!

[Exeunt]

[19] **adieu:** goodbye

[20] **Lest our old robes...our new:** In case our old clothes (Duncan's reign) fit more comfortably than our new (Macbeth's reign).

[21] **bension:** blessing

Key Quotations

Ross *Thou seest, the heavens, as troubled with man's act*
Macduff *Lest our old robes sit easier than our new!*

Commentary

- Ross and an old man discuss the unnatural weather and the strange animal behaviour following Duncan's death: the night was exceptionally stormy, the sun failed to rise and an owl killed a falcon. Ross also says how Duncan's horses turned wild and ate each other. In Shakespeare's time, the King was seen as the natural ruler appointed by God. Shakespeare's superstitious audience would not have been surprised to see chaos in the natural world after the murder of a king. As Ross says: 'Thou seest, the heavens, as troubled with man's act'.

- Macduff seems worried about Macbeth ruling Scotland. Pointedly he says he will not go to the coronation at Scone. Although he states that Malcolm and Donalbain are under suspicion, he doesn't seem to believe that they are the killers. Macduff's final statement, 'Lest our old robes sit easier than our new!' clearly expresses this concern. In contrast, Ross takes events at face value and accepts the idea that Malcolm and Donalbain are to blame: 'Thriftless ambition, that wilt ravin up / Thine own life's means!' He has no difficulty in attending Macbeth's coronation.

- Macduff is established as a man of principle and innate goodness. His distrust of Macbeth and his refusal to go to Scone set him apart from the other thanes. However, this snub towards Macbeth is unwise as it eventually encourages Macbeth to feel threatened by Macduff.

Questions

1. Using quotations, make a list of all the strange animal behaviour and unnatural phenomena reported by Ross and the old man.
2. What evidence from the scene shows that Macduff is suspicious of Macbeth?
3. How do Macduff's and Ross's attitudes differ in this scene?

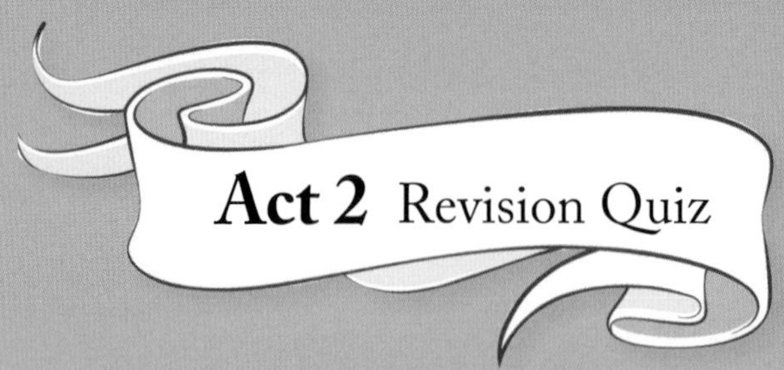

Act 2 Revision Quiz

1. **What instrument does Macbeth see floating in midair that points him towards Duncan's chamber?**
2. **Immediately after the murder of Duncan, Macbeth imagines he hears voices. Write down two things these voices say.**
3. **What offstage sounds are referred to in Scene 2 that heighten the tension of the scene?**
4. **What reason does Lady Macbeth offer for not killing Duncan herself?**
5. **Who plants the bloody daggers on the King's chamberlains?**
6. **In Scene 3, what does Lady Macbeth do that diverts attention away from Macbeth?**
7. **What do Malcolm and Donalbain decide to do after their father is murdered?**
8. **Name three strange phenomena that occur after Duncan is killed.**
9. **Who says each of the following?:**
   (a) '*Will all great Neptune's ocean wash this blood / Clean from my hand? No, this my hand will rather / The multitudinous seas incarnadine / Making the green one red*'.
   (b) '*These deeds must not be thought / After these ways; so, it will make us mad*'.
   (c) '*There's daggers in men's smiles: the near in blood, / The nearer bloody*'
   (d) '*Had I but died an hour before this chance, / I had lived a blessed time*'
10. **Fill in the blanks:**
   (a) '*My* hands *are of your colour; but I shame / To wear a heart so* white'
   (b) '*Wake* Duncan *with thy* knocking*! I would thou couldst!*'
   (c) '*A little* water *clears us of this* deed'

Act 3 Scene 1

Scene Summary

- Banquo suspects that Macbeth killed Duncan.
- Macbeth meets Banquo and enquires if he is going horse-riding in the afternoon. He also asks if Banquo's son Fleance is accompanying him.
- Macbeth meets with two murderers and instructs them to kill both Banquo and Fleance.

Forres. The Palace.
Enter BANQUO

Banquo
Thou hast it[1] now: King, Cawdor, Glamis, all,
As the weird women promised, and, I fear,
Thou play'dst most foully[2] for't: yet it was said
It should not stand in thy posterity,[3]
But that myself should be the root and father
Of many kings. If there come truth from them –
As upon thee, Macbeth, their speeches shine –
Why, by the verities[4] on thee made good,
May they not be my oracles[5] as well,
And set me up in hope? But hush! no more.
[*Sennet[6] sounded. Enter MACBETH, as king, LADY MACBETH, as queen, LENNOX, ROSS, Lords, Ladies, and Attendants*]

Macbeth
Here's our chief guest.

Lady Macbeth
If he had been forgotten,
It had been as a gap in our great feast,
And all-thing unbecoming.

Macbeth
Tonight we hold a solemn supper[7] sir,
And I'll request your presence.

Banquo
Let your Highness
Command upon me; to the which my duties
Are with a most indissoluble[8] tie
For ever knit.

Macbeth
Ride you this afternoon?[9]

1 **it:** i.e. the crown

2 **play'dst most foully:** committed foul deeds
3 **posterity:** descendents

4 **verities:** verified truth
5 **oracles:** prophets

6 **sennet:** trumpets/fanfare

7 **solemn supper:** formal dinner

8 **indissoluble tie:** unbreakable knot

9 **Ride you this afternoon?:** Notice how Macbeth asks specific questions about Banquo and Fleance's plans in a very casual manner.

BANQUO

Ay, my good lord.

MACBETH

We should have else desired your good advice,
Which still hath been both grave and prosperous,[10]
In this day's council; but we'll take tomorrow.
Is't far you ride?

BANQUO

As far, my lord, as will fill up the time
'Twixt[11] this and supper: go not my horse the better,
I must become a borrower of the night
For a dark hour or twain.[12]

MACBETH

Fail not our feast.[13]

BANQUO

My lord, I will not.

MACBETH

We hear, our bloody cousins are bestowed[14]
In England and in Ireland, not confessing
Their cruel parricide[15], filling their hearers
With strange invention[16]: but of that tomorrow,
When therewithal we shall have cause of state
Craving us jointly.[17] Hie you to horse: adieu,
Till you return at night. Goes Fleance with you?

BANQUO

Ay, my good lord: our time does call upon 's.

MACBETH

I wish your horses swift and sure of foot;
And so I do commend you to their backs.
Farewell.
[Exit BANQUO]
Let every man be master of his time[18]
Till seven at night: to make society
The sweeter welcome, we will keep ourself[19]
Till supper-time alone: while then, God be with you!
[Exeunt all but MACBETH, and an Attendant]
Sirrah,[20] a word with you: attend those men
Our pleasure?

ATTENDANT

They are, my lord, without[21] the palace gate.

[10] **grave and prosperous:** serious and profitable

[11] **'Twixt:** between

[12] **go not my horse...or twain:** If my horse doesn't ride faster than usual, I won't return until an hour or two after night falls.

[13] **Fail not our feast:** Don't fail to arrive at the feast.

[14] **bestowed:** lodged

[15] **parricide:** murder of a father

[16] **invention:** lies

[17] **cause of state / Craving us jointly:** State business will occupy both of us.

[18] **Let...his time:** Let everybody spend their time as they please.

[19] **ourself:** me. As Macbeth is now King he uses the royal 'we' to refer to himself.

[20] **Sirrah:** Sir

[21] **without:** outside

MACBETH

Bring them before us. [*Exit Attendant.*] To be thus is nothing;
But to be safely thus.[22] – Our fears in Banquo
Stick deep, and in his royalty of nature[23]
Reigns that which would be feared: 'tis much he dares;
And, to that dauntless[24] temper of his mind,
He hath a wisdom that doth guide his valour[25]
To act in safety. There is none but he
Whose being I do fear: and, under him,
My genius[26] is rebuked; as, it is said,
Mark Antony's[27] was by Caesar. He chid[28] the sisters
When first they put the name of King upon me,
And bade them speak to him: then prophet-like
They hailed him father to a line of kings:
Upon my head they placed a fruitless[29] crown,
And put a barren sceptre in my gripe,[30]
Thence to be wrenched with an unlineal[31] hand,
No son of mine succeeding. If 't be so,
For Banquo's issue[32] have I filed[33] my mind;
For them the gracious Duncan have I murdered;
Put rancours in the vessel of my peace
Only for them;[34] and mine eternal jewel
Given to the common enemy of man,[35]
To make them kings – the seed of Banquo kings!
Rather than so, come Fate into the list.
And champion me to the utterance![36] Who's there!
[Re-enter Attendant, with two Murderers]
Now go to the door, and stay there till we call.
[Exit Attendant]
Was it not yesterday we spoke together?

FIRST MURDERER

It was, so please your Highness.

MACBETH

Well then, now
Have you considered of my speeches? Know
That it was he[37] in the times past which held you
So under fortune, which you thought had been
Our innocent self: this I made good to you
In our last conference, passed in probation[38] with you,
How you were borne in hand,[39] how crossed, the instruments,
Who wrought with them,[40] and all things else that might
To half a soul and to a notion crazed
Say 'Thus did Banquo.'[41]

FIRST MURDERER

You made it known to us.

22 **To be thus...safely thus:** To be King is nothing unless the crown is secure.
23 **royalty of nature:** innate nobility
24 **dauntless:** fearless
25 **valour:** bravery
26 **genius:** guardian spirit
27 **Mark Antony:** a Roman general who resented Octavius Caesar becoming Emperor of Rome. Macbeth is comparing Banquo to Mark Antony and himself to Octavius Caesar.
28 **chid:** chided/reproached
29 **fruitless:** childless
30 **barren sceptre in my gripe:** a childless sceptre in my grip. A sceptre is a ceremonial staff held by a king.
31 **unlineal:** not of my line (unrelated)
32 **issue:** children
33 **filed:** defiled/made dirty
34 **Put rancours...for them:** ruined my peaceful mind with bitter thoughts, only for them (i.e. Banquo's children)
35 **mine eternal jewel...enemy of man:** my soul has been given to the Devil
36 **Rather than...utterance!:** Rather than let that happen, let Fate fight me to the death. Macbeth is challenging Fate here.
37 **he:** i.e. Banquo
38 **passed in probation:** proved to you
39 **borne in hand:** tricked
40 **wrought with them:** was involved with them
41 **all things else...'Thus did Banquo':** which even a halfwit or a lunatic could say it was Banquo

MACBETH

I did so, and went further, which is now
Our point of second meeting. Do you find
Your patience so predominant[42] in your nature
That you can let this go? Are you so gospelled[43]
To pray for this good man and for his issue,
Whose heavy hand hath bowed you to the grave
And beggared yours[44] for ever?

FIRST MURDERER

We are men, my liege.

MACBETH

Ay, in the catalogue[45] ye go for men;
As hounds and greyhounds, mongrels, spaniels, curs,
Shoughs, water-rugs and demi-wolves[46], are clept[47]
All by the name of dogs: the valued file[48]
Distinguishes the swift, the slow, the subtle,
The housekeeper, the hunter, every one
According to the gift which bounteous[49] nature
Hath in him closed; whereby he does receive
Particular addition, from the bill
That writes them all alike: and so of men.
Now, if you have a station[50] in the file,
Not i' the worst rank of manhood, say 't;
And I will put that business in your bosoms,[51]
Whose execution takes your enemy off,
Grapples you to the heart[52] and love of us,
Who wear our health but sickly in his life,
Which in his death were perfect.[53]

SECOND MURDERER

I am one, my liege,
Whom the vile blows and buffets of the world
Have so incensed that I am reckless what
I do to spite the world.[54]

FIRST MURDERER

And I another
So weary with disasters, tugged with[55] fortune,
That I would set my lie on any chance,
To mend it, or be rid on't.[56]

MACBETH

Both of you
Know Banquo was your enemy.

[42] **predominant:** dominant
[43] **gospelled:** religious/pious
[44] **beggared yours:** turned your children into beggars
[45] **catalogue:** general description
[46] **hounds...demi-wolves:** types of dog
[47] **clept:** called/named
[48] **valued file:** list of the qualities of each type of dog
[49] **bounteous:** generous
[50] **station:** position
[51] **put that business in your bosoms:** trust you with a secret plan
[52] **Grapples you to the heart:** holds you close to my heart
[53] **Who wear...were perfect:** I am unhealthy/insecure while Banquo is alive but I would be perfect if he was dead.
[54] **Whom the vile....spite the world:** I have been so enraged by the horrible blows from the world that I would do anything to get back at it.
[55] **tugged with:** knocked about by
[56] **I would set my lie...rid on't:** I am willing to gamble my life to improve my situation.

Both Murderers

True, my lord.

Macbeth

So is he mine; and in such bloody distance,[57]
That every minute of his being thrusts
Against my near'st of life: and though I could
With barefaced power sweep him from my sight[58]
And bid my will avouch[59] it, yet I must not,
For certain friends that are both his and mine,
Whose loves I may not drop, but wail his fall[60]
Whom I myself struck down; and thence it is,
That I to your assistance do make love,
Masking the business from the common eye
For sundry weighty reasons.[61]

Second Murderer

We shall, my lord,
Perform what you command us.

First Murderer

Though our lives –

Macbeth

Your spirits shine through you. Within this hour at most
I will advise you where to plant[62] yourselves;
Acquaint you with the perfect spy o' the time,[63]
The moment on't; for't must be done tonight,
And something from the palace;[64] always thought
That I require a clearness:[65] and with him –
To leave no rubs nor botches in the work –
Fleance his son, that keeps him company,
Whose absence is no less material to me
Than is his father's, must embrace the fate
Of that dark hour. Resolve yourselves apart;[66]
I'll come to you anon.

Second Murderer

We are resolved, my lord.

Macbeth

I'll call upon you straight:[67] abide within.[68]
[Exeunt Murderers]
It is concluded. Banquo, thy soul's flight,
If it find heaven, must find it out tonight.
[Exit]

57 **bloody distance:** close enough to draw blood (as with a fencer)

58 **barefaced...my sight:** kill him openly /kill him with my absolute power

59 **avouch:** justify

60 **wail his fall:** would cry if he died

61 **Masking the business...weighty reasons:** hide the affair from the public gaze for a variety of serious reasons

62 **plant:** place

63 **Acquaint you...o' the time:** Find yourself a perfect place to watch from i.e. for an ambush.

64 **something from the palace:** away from the palace

65 **always thought...clearness:** Bear in mind that I need to be free of any suspicion in this matter.

66 **Resolve yourselves apart:** Go away and decide for yourselves.

67 **straight:** straight away

68 **abide within:** wait inside

Key Quotations

MACBETH *To be thus is nothing; / But to be safely thus*

MACBETH *Our fears in Banquo*
Stick deep, and in his royalty of nature
Reigns that which would be feared: 'tis much he dares;
And, to that dauntless temper of his mind,
He hath a wisdom that doth guide his valour
To act in safety. There is none but he
Whose being I do fear: and, under him,
My genius is rebuked

MACBETH *Upon my head they placed a fruitless crown, / And put a barren sceptre in my gripe*

MACBETH *So is he mine; and in such bloody distance, / That every minute of his being thrusts / Against my near'st of life*

Commentary

- Banquo's suspicion of Macbeth is evident in his soliloquy at the start of this scene: 'I fear, / Thou play'dst most foully for't'. Banquo's mind is also drawn to the witches' prophecy for himself. He notes that the title was not predicted to stay within Macbeth's family and will instead pass through many generations of Banquo's line: 'myself should be the root and father / Of many kings'. No sooner does Banquo entertain the idea, then he silences the thought: 'But hush! no more'. Whether this is because of the arrival of Macbeth or because the allure of power is distasteful to him is not made clear.

- Macbeth is a changed figure from the preceding scenes. He seems less hysterical and is instead preoccupied by potential threats to his power. He tells the murderers that Banquo's existence is a source of anxiety to him: 'Who wear our health but sickly in his life, / Which in his death were perfect' and sees his power as useless if it cannot be held securely: 'To be thus is nothing; / But to be safely thus'.

- Macbeth sees Banquo as a threat, not solely because of the witches' prediction, but also because of Banquo's virtues and 'his royalty of nature'. He recognises that Banquo possesses a 'wisdom that doth guide his valour'. Macbeth feels both threatened and envious of Banquo, and is willing to challenge Fate to prevent Banquo's descendents from being crowned: 'the seed of Banquo kings! / Rather than so, come Fate into the list. / And champion me to the utterance!'

- Macbeth acts with sinister composure when he casually asks Banquo about his plans for the afternoon while all the time plotting to kill his former friend. However, Banquo appears reluctant to engage with him. Macbeth also arranges for the death of Fleance, Banquo's son, in order to 'To leave no rubs nor botches in the work'. Fleance's death would mean the end of Banquo's descendents and leave the witches' prophecy unfulfilled. Macbeth has become increasingly underhand, manipulative, treacherous and murderous. Furthermore, he seems to act independently of Lady Macbeth and no longer requires her to instruct or persuade him.

- In this scene there is an emphasis on manliness associated with courage. Macbeth's inflated pride in his own manly courage and his excessive ambition causes him to challenge Fate itself. Macbeth persuades the murderers to kill Banquo by appealing to their masculinity. He says that if they are to be considered real men ('if you have a station in the file, / Not i' the worst rank of manhood') they will carry out this 'courageous' act. This echoes Lady Macbeth's persuasive tactics in Act 1.

Questions

1. Summarise the main points of Banquo's soliloquy which he gives at the start of the scene.
2. Why does Macbeth arrange the murders of Banquo and Fleance? Use quotations in your response.
3. What reason does Macbeth give the murderers for not publicly ordering the death of Banquo?
4. Comparing this scene with the first two acts of the play, in what ways has Macbeth changed?

Act 3 Scene 2

Scene Summary

- Both Macbeth and Lady Macbeth mention fears about the security of their position.
- Macbeth hints at his plan to kill Banquo but doesn't involve Lady Macbeth directly in the plot.

Forres. The Palace
Enter LADY MACBETH and a Servant

Lady Macbeth
Is Banquo gone from court?

Servant
Ay, madam, but returns again tonight.

Lady Macbeth
Say to the king, I would attend his leisure
For a few words.

Servant
Madam, I will.
[Exit]

Lady Macbeth
Nought's had, all's spent,
Where our desire is got without content:[1]
'Tis safer to be that which we destroy
Than by destruction dwell in doubtful joy.[2]
[Enter MACBETH]
How now, my lord! Why do you keep alone,
Of sorriest fancies[3] your companions making,
Using those thoughts which should indeed have died
With them they think on? Things without all remedy
Should be without regard:[4] what's done is done.

Macbeth
We have scotched[5] the snake, not killed it:
She'll close[6] and be herself, whilst our poor malice[7]
Remains in danger of her former tooth.[8]
But let the frame of things disjoint,[9] both the worlds suffer,
Ere we will eat our meal in fear and sleep
In the affliction of these terrible dreams
That shake us nightly. Better be with the dead,
Whom we, to gain our peace, have sent to peace,
Than on the torture of the mind to lie

1 **Nought's had...without content:** We've earned nothing, but spent everything, when what we desired brings no contentment.
2 **'Tis safer ... doubtful joy:** It is better to be destroyed than to live with the constant fear of destruction.
3 **sorriest fancies:** dark, depressing thoughts
4 **Things without all...regard:** Problems that cannot be solved should not be reflected upon.
5 **scotched:** wounded/injured
6 **close:** heal
7 **poor malice:** inadequate violence
8 **former tooth:** original venom
9 **But let... disjoint:** but let the world collapse

In restless ecstasy.[10] Duncan is in his grave;
After life's fitful[11] fever he sleeps well;
Treason has done his worst: nor steel, nor poison,
Malice domestic, foreign levy, nothing,
Can touch him further.[12]

LADY MACBETH

Come on;
Gentle my lord, sleek o'er your rugged looks;[13]
Be bright and jovial[14] among your guests tonight.

MACBETH

So shall I, love; and so, I pray, be you:
Let your remembrance apply to Banquo;
Present him eminence,[15] both with eye and tongue:
Unsafe the while, that we
Must lave our honours[16] in these flattering streams,
And make our faces vizards[17] to our hearts,
Disguising what they are.

LADY MACBETH

You must leave this.

MACBETH

O, full of scorpions is my mind, dear wife!
Thou know'st that Banquo, and his Fleance, lives.

LADY MACBETH

But in them nature's copy's not eterne.[18]

MACBETH

There's comfort yet; they are assailable;[19]
Then be thou jocund:[20] ere the bat hath flown
His cloistered[21] flight, ere to black Hecate's[22] summons
The shard-borne beetle with his drowsy hums
Hath rung night's yawning peal,[23] there shall be done
A deed of dreadful note.

LADY MACBETH

What's to be done?

MACBETH

Be innocent of the knowledge, dearest chuck,[24]
Till thou applaud the deed. Come, seeling[25] night,
Scarf up the tender eye of pitiful day;[26]
And with thy bloody and invisible hand
Cancel and tear to pieces that great bond[27]
Which keeps me pale! Light thickens;[28] and the crow

[10] **to lie / in restless ecstasy:** to lie down in sleepless madness
[11] **fitful:** restless
[12] **nor steel...him further:** No sword, poison, trouble at home, foreign armies, nothing can hurt him (Duncan).
[13] **sleek o'er your rugged looks:** smooth over your haggard appearance
[14] **jovial:** in good spirits
[15] **Present him eminence:** Show him special respect.
[16] **lave our honours:** wash our achievements (titles)
[17] **vizards:** visors/masks
[18] **in them nature's copy's not eterne:** Nature has not given them eternal life.
[19] **assailable:** vulnerable to attack
[20] **jocund:** upbeat/in a good mood
[21] **cloistered:** hidden
[22] **Hecate:** goddess of witchcraft
[23] **The shard-borne...yawning peal:** The beetle flying on scaly wings has tolled night's bell.
[24] **chuck:** little chicken
[25] **seeling:** concealing
[26] **Scarf...pitiful day:** Blindfold the illuminating light of day.
[27] **great bond:** i.e. Macbeth's connection to Banquo
[28] **Light thickens:** Light dims

Makes wing to the rooky wood:
Good things of day begin to droop and drowse;
While night's black agents to their preys do rouse.[29]
Thou marvell'st at my words: but hold thee still;
Things bad begun make strong themselves by ill.
So, prithee, go with me.
[Exeunt]

[29] **rouse:** awaken

Key Quotations

LADY MACBETH *'Tis safer to be that which we destroy / Than by destruction dwell in doubtful joy.*

MACBETH *Better be with the dead,*
Whom we, to gain our peace, have sent to peace,
Than on the torture of the mind to lie
In restless ecstasy.

MACBETH *... make our faces vizards to our hearts, / Disguising what they are.*

MACBETH *Be innocent of the knowledge, dearest chuck, / Till thou applaud the deed.*

MACBETH *Come, seeling night,*
Scarf up the tender eye of pitiful day;
And with thy bloody and invisible hand
Cancel and tear to pieces that great bond
Which keeps me pale!

Commentary

- This scene highlights the psychological impact Duncan's murder has had on Macbeth and Lady Macbeth. In a short soliloquy, Lady Macbeth reveals how her new title has brought her anxiety rather than peace. She describes her elevated status as a 'doubtful joy' and explains how the crown has come at a high price and brought no contentment: 'Nought's had, all's spent, / Where our desire is got without content'.

- Lady Macbeth hides her anguish throughout the play. In this scene she conceals her doubts from Macbeth and instead criticises him for being aloof and consumed by dark thoughts. Adopting a pragmatic disposition, she scolds Macbeth and urges him to abandon his gloomy thoughts: 'Things without all remedy / Should be without regard: what's done is done'. Ironically, she could just as easily have directed these words at herself.

- Macbeth seems increasingly paranoid and worries about potential enemies: 'We have scotched the snake, not killed it: / She'll close and be herself, whilst our poor malice / Remains in danger of her former tooth'. Unconsciously, Macbeth echoes Lady Macbeth's envy of Duncan and the peace he has found in death: 'Duncan is in his grave; / After life's fitful fever he sleeps well'. Rather than finding happiness, Macbeth is beset by 'terrible dreams' and experiences a 'torture of the mind'.

- The relationship between Macbeth and Lady Macbeth has changed. Lady Macbeth hides her anxieties from her husband and Macbeth now asserts himself as the dominant partner. Although Macbeth hints at his plans for Banquo, he does not confide in Lady Macbeth. Instead he shields her from the horror of his plot: 'Be innocent of the knowledge, dearest chuck'. Macbeth also expects Lady Macbeth to 'applaud the deed'. His pride still causes him to crave approval.

- This scene clearly shows the fraying emotional state of both principal characters. Macbeth has clearly embarked on a path that will lead to more bloodshed and compound the guilt of his original crime.

Questions

1. Would you agree that Lady Macbeth is clearly troubled in this scene? Explain your answer.
2. Describe Macbeth's emotional and psychological state in this scene.
3. Describe the relationship between Macbeth and Lady Macbeth as revealed in this scene.
4. Why do you think Macbeth does not include Lady Macbeth in his plot to kill Banquo?
5. Find quotations from the scene that illustrate each of the following ideas:

   (a) Lady Macbeth is worried and has found no contentment.

   (b) Macbeth and/or Lady Macbeth must put on a brave face for those around them.

   (c) Macbeth is worried and restless.

   (d) Lady Macbeth envies the peace Duncan has found in death.

   (e) Macbeth envies the peace Duncan has found in death.

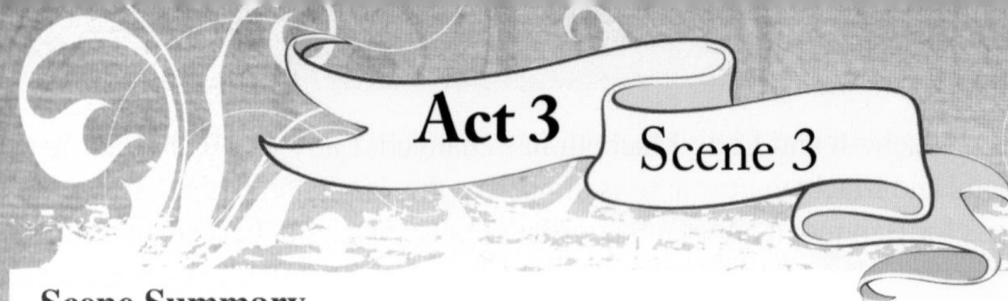

Scene Summary

- The two murderers wait to ambush Banquo and Fleance.
- They are joined by a third murderer sent by Macbeth.
- The murderers attack and kill Banquo.
- Fleance escapes.

A Park near the Palace.
Enter Three Murderers

FIRST MURDERER
But who did bid thee join with us?

THIRD MURDERER
Macbeth.

SECOND MURDERER
He needs not our mistrust, since he delivers
Our offices and what we have to do
To the direction just.[1]

FIRST MURDERER
Then stand with us.
The west yet glimmers with some streaks of day:
Now spurs the lated traveller apace[2]
To gain the timely inn[3], and near approaches
The subject of our watch.

THIRD MURDERER
Hark! I hear horses.

BANQUO
[Within] Give us a light there, ho!

SECOND MURDERER
Then 'tis he: the rest
That are within the note of expectation
Already are i' the court.[4]

FIRST MURDERER
His horses go about.[5]

1 **He needs...direction just:** We don't need to distrust him (i.e. 3rd Murderer OR Macbeth) as he (Macbeth) gives us our instructions.

2 **spurs the lated traveller apace:** The delayed traveller is spurred on (by the onset of evening).

3 **To gain the timely inn:** to reach the inn in good time

4 **the rest...i' the court:** The other guests are already in the court.

5 **go about:** are taking a roundabout route

Third Murderer
Almost a mile: but he does usually,
So all men do, from hence to the palace gate
Make it their walk.

Second Murderer
A light, a light!
[Enter BANQUO and FLEANCE with a torch]

Third Murderer
'Tis he.

First Murderer
Stand to't.[6]

Banquo
It will be rain[7] tonight.

First Murderer
Let it come down.
[They set upon BANQUO]

Banquo
O, treachery! Fly[8], good Fleance, fly, fly, fly!
Thou mayst revenge. O slave!
[Dies. FLEANCE escapes]

Third Murderer
Who did strike out the light?

First Murderer
Was't not the way?[9]

Third Murderer
There's but one down; the son is fled.

Second Murderer
We have lost
Best half of our affair.

First Murderer
Well, let's away, and say how much is done.
[Exeunt]

6 **Stand to't:** Get ready

7 **rain:** 1. weather 2. a rain of blows

8 **Fly:** Flee/Run

9 **Was't not the way?:** Wasn't that the plan?

Commentary

- Despite the fact that Macbeth personally hires the murderers and also convinces them that Banquo is their enemy, he still hires a third murderer to keep watch on the other two. This reveals Macbeth's deepening insecurity and mistrust of those around him.

- The witches foretold that Banquo 'shalt get kings' but will not be King himself. The murderers successfully kill Banquo, but Fleance's escape will only serve to deepen Macbeth's paranoia and add further anxieties to his already troubled mind.

- Macbeth tried to defy Fate by ordering the murders of Banquo and Fleance. Fleance escapes under cover of darkness as the torch is extinguished; it appears that he is fated to live and Macbeth is powerless to change this.

Scene Summary

- Macbeth meets with one of the murderers and learns of Banquo's death and Fleance's escape.
- Macbeth sees Banquo's ghost at his coronation banquet and is visibly shaken by the vision.
- Lady Macbeth tries to excuse Macbeth's behaviour as resulting from an illness.
- Macbeth decides to visit the witches.

Forres. A Hall in the Palace.
A banquet prepared. Enter MACBETH, LADY MACBETH, ROSS, LENNOX, Lords, and Attendants

MACBETH
You know your own degrees[1]; sit down: at first
And last[2], the hearty welcome.

LORDS
Thanks to your majesty.

MACBETH
Ourself will mingle with society,
And play the humble host.
Our hostess keeps her state[3], but in best time
We will require her welcome.

LADY MACBETH
Pronounce it for me, sir, to all our friends;
For my heart speaks they are welcome.

[First Murderer appears at the door]

MACBETH
See, they encounter thee with their hearts' thanks.
Both sides are even: here I'll sit i' the midst:[4]
Be large in mirth; anon we'll drink a measure
The table round.[5]
[Approaching the door]
There's blood upon thy face.

FIRST MURDERER
'Tis Banquo's then.

MACBETH
'Tis better thee without than he within.[6]
Is he dispatched?

1 **degrees:** rank
2 **at first/And last:** highest and lowest
3 **keeps her state:** will remain seated on her throne
4 **Both sides…midst:** Both sides of the table are even; I'll sit in the middle.
5 **Be large…table round:** Have fun; soon I'll drink a toast to the whole table.
6 **'Tis better…within:** It's better on you than inside him.

First Murderer

My lord, his throat is cut; that I did for him.

Macbeth

Thou art the best o' the cut-throats: yet he's good
That did the like for Fleance: If thou didst it,
Thou art the nonpareil.[7]

First Murderer

Most royal sir,
Fleance is 'scaped.

Macbeth

Then comes my fit[8] again: I had else been perfect,
Whole as the marble, founded as the rock,[9]
As broad and general as the casing air:[10]
But now I am cabined, cribbed,[11] confined, bound in
To saucy[12] doubts and fears. But Banquo's safe?

First Murderer

Ay, my good lord: safe in a ditch he bides,
With twenty trenched[13] gashes on his head;
The least a death to nature.[14]

Macbeth

Thanks for that:
There the grown serpent lies; the worm that's fled
Hath nature that in time will venom breed,
No teeth for the present.[15] Get thee gone: tomorrow
We'll hear, ourselves, again.
[Exit Murderer]

Lady Macbeth

My royal lord,
You do not give the cheer. The feast is sold
That is not often vouched, while 'tis a-making,
'Tis given with welcome:[16] to feed were best at home;[17]
From thence the sauce to meat is ceremony;[18]
Meeting were bare without it.

Macbeth

Sweet remembrancer![19]
Now, good digestion wait on appetite,
And health on both!

Lennox

May't please your highness sit?

7 **nonpareil:** unparalleled/unrivalled

8 **my fit:** my attack of anxiety

9 **Whole...the rock:** solid as marble, unshakeable as rock

10 **As broad ...casing air:** as free and unrestrained as the air around us

11 **cribbed:** trapped/shut in

12 **saucy:** nagging

13 **trenched:** as deep as a trench

14 **The least...nature:** the smallest being enough to kill him

15 **There the grown...for the present:** The old snake (Banquo) lies dead. The worm (Fleance) has fled and will develop venom later. He has no teeth at the moment.

16 **The feast is sold...welcome:** Unless the host welcomes the guests continually, they will feel like they paid for their meal.

17 **to feed were best at home:** They may as well eat at home.

18 **From thence...ceremony:** When eating out, it is the host that makes the meal special.

19 **Sweet remembrancer!:** Thanks for the reminder!

MACBETH
Here had we now our country's honour roofed,[20]
Were the graced person of our Banquo present;
[The GHOST OF BANQUO enters, and sits in MACBETH's place]
Who may I rather challenge for unkindness
Than pity for mischance![21]

[20] **country's honour roofed:** the most esteemed nobles under one roof

[21] **mischance:** accident

ROSS
His absence, sir,
Lays blame upon his promise. Please't your Highness
To grace us with your royal company?

MACBETH
The table's full.

LENNOX
Here is a place reserved, sir.

MACBETH
Where?

LENNOX
Here, my good lord. What is't that moves your Highness?

MACBETH
Which of you have done this?

LORDS
What, my good lord?

MACBETH
Thou canst not say I did it: never shake
Thy gory locks[22] at me.

[22] **gory locks:** bloody hair. Macbeth is addressing the ghost of Banquo whom none of the other characters can see.

ROSS
Gentlemen, rise: his Highness is not well.

LADY MACBETH
Sit, worthy friends: my lord is often thus,
And hath been from his youth: pray you, keep seat;
The fit[23] is momentary; upon a thought
He will again be well. If much you note him,
You shall offend him and extend his passion:
Feed, and regard him not. *[Aside to Macbeth.]* Are you a man?

[23] **fit:** spell of illness

MACBETH
Ay, and a bold[24] one, that dare look on that
Which might appal the devil.

[24] **bold:** brave

LADY MACBETH

O proper stuff![25]
This is the very painting of your fear:[26]
This is the air-drawn dagger which, you said,
Led you to Duncan. O, these flaws and starts,[27]
Impostors to true fear, would well become
A woman's story at a winter's fire,
Authorised by her grandam[28]. Shame itself!
Why do you make such faces? When all's done,
You look but on a stool.

MACBETH

Prithee, see there! Behold! Look! Lo! How say you?
Why, what care I? If thou canst nod, speak too.
If charnel-houses[29] and our graves must send
Those that we bury back, our monuments
Shall be the maws of kites.[30]
[GHOST vanishes]

LADY MACBETH

What, quite unmanned[31] in folly?

MACBETH

If I stand here, I saw him.

LADY MACBETH

Fie, for shame!

MACBETH

Blood hath been shed ere now, i' the olden time,
Ere human statute purged the gentle weal[32];
Ay, and since too, murders have been performed
Too terrible for the ear. The times have been,
That, when the brains were out, the man would die,
And there an end; but now they rise again,
With twenty mortal murders on their crowns,[33]
And push us from our stools. This is more strange
Than such a murder is.

LADY MACBETH

My worthy lord,
Your noble friends do lack you.

MACBETH

I do forget.
Do not muse[34] at me, my most worthy friends,
I have a strange infirmity,[35] which is nothing
To those that know me. Come, love and health to all;

[25] **O proper stuff!:** Absolute nonsense!
[26] **painting of your fear:** imagined out of fear
[27] **flaws and starts:** sudden outbursts and fits of emotion
[28] **Authorised by her grandam:** as true as an old grandmother's story
[29] **charnel-houses:** buildings for storing bones
[30] **our monuments...of kites:** Our graves should be the stomachs of carrion birds, i.e. to prevent the return of the dead.
[31] **unmanned:** stripped of manhood
[32] **Ere human...gentle weal:** before human laws made society civil
[33] **crowns:** heads
[34] **muse:** think about/reflect on
[35] **infirmity:** illness

Then I'll sit down. Give me some wine; fill full.
I drink to the general joy o' the whole table,
And to our dear friend Banquo, whom we miss;
Would he were here! To all, and him, we thirst,
And all to all.

LORDS

Our duties, and the pledge.[36]
[Re-enter GHOST]

[36] **pledge:** toast

MACBETH

Avaunt![37] and quit my sight! Let the earth hide thee!
Thy bones are marrowless, thy blood is cold;
Thou hast no speculation[38] in those eyes
Which thou dost glare with!

[37] **Avaunt!:** Get out!

[38] **speculation:** glimmer of life/ comprehension

LADY MACBETH

Think of this, good peers,
But as a thing of custom[39]: 'tis no other;
Only it spoils the pleasure of the time.

[39] **thing of custom:** a habit

MACBETH

What man dare, I dare:
Approach thou like the rugged Russian bear,
The armed rhinoceros, or the Hyrcan tiger;[40]
Take any shape but that, and my firm nerves
Shall never tremble: or be alive again,
And dare me to the desert with thy sword;[41]
If trembling I inhabit then, protest me
The baby of a girl.[42] Hence, horrible shadow!
Unreal mockery, hence!
[GHOST vanishes]
Why, so: being gone,
I am a man again. Pray you, sit still.

[40] **Hyrcan tiger:** a tiger from Hyrcania (a wild place, located mainly in present-day Iran)

[41] **dare me...sword:** Challenge me to a swordfight in the desert.

[42] **If trembling...a girl:** If I shake then you may call me a baby girl.

LADY MACBETH

You have displaced the mirth, broke the good meeting,
With most admired disorder.[43]

[43] **You have...admired disorder:** You have ruined the good time, broken up the party and earned attention with this disorderly behaviour.

MACBETH

Can such things be,
And overcome us like a summer's cloud,
Without our special wonder? You make me strange
Even to the disposition that I owe,
When now I think you can behold such sights,
And keep the natural ruby[44] of your cheeks,
When mine is blanched[45] with fear.

[44] **ruby:** red

[45] **blanched:** turned pale

Ross

What sights, my lord?

Lady Macbeth

I pray you, speak not; he grows worse and worse;
Question enrages him. At once, good night:
Stand not upon the order of your going,[46]
But go at once.

Lennox

Good night; and better health
Attend his majesty!

Lady Macbeth

A kind good night to all!
[Exeunt Lords and Attendants.]

Macbeth

It will have blood; they say, blood will have blood:
Stones have been known to move and trees to speak;
Augurs[47] and understood relations have
By maggot-pies[48] and choughs[49] and rooks brought forth
The secret'st man of blood.[50] What is the night?

Lady Macbeth

Almost at odds with morning, which is which.[51]

Macbeth

How say'st thou, that Macduff denies his person
At our great bidding?[52]

Lady Macbeth

Did you send to him, sir?

Macbeth

I hear it by the way; but I will send:
There's not a one of them but in his house
I keep a servant fee'd[53]. I will tomorrow,
And betimes[54] I will, to the Weird Sisters:
More shall they speak; for now I am bent[55] to know,
By the worst means, the worst. For mine own good,
All causes shall give way[56]: I am in blood
Stepped in so far that, should I wade no more,
Returning were as tedious as go o'er:[57]
Strange things I have in head, that will to hand;
Which must be acted ere they may be scanned.[58]

Lady Macbeth

You lack the season[59] of all natures, sleep.

46 **Stand not...going:** Don't wait to leave according to rank.

47 **Augurs:** prophecies

48 **maggot-pies:** magpies

49 **choughs:** a type of crow

50 **Augurs...of blood:** Prophecies and connections between events have been made by looking at magpies, crows and rooks, exposing the most secretive murderers.

51 **Almost...which:** Night and morning are arguing about which it is.

52 **How say'st...great bidding?:** Why did Macduff not come at my invitation?

53 **a servant fee'd:** a paid spy

54 **betimes:** very early

55 **bent:** determined

56 **All causes shall give way:** Everything else will be neglected.

57 **I am in blood...as go o'er:** I am so steeped in blood that I may as well continue on this path. The image is of Macbeth wading through a river of blood.

58 **Strange things...be scanned:** There are things in my mind that I need to act on before I have a chance to reflect upon them.

59 **season:** preserver (like salt)

MACBETH
Come, we'll to sleep. My strange and self-abuse
Is the initiate fear that wants hard use:
We are yet but young in deed.[60]
[Exeunt]

[60] **My strange...young in deed:** My odd, self-deception (imagining a ghost) is the result of my inexperience in crime. I need further practice. I am only new to crimes like this.

Key Quotations

MACBETH *But now I am cabined, cribbed, confined, bound in / To saucy doubts and fears.*

MACBETH *What man dare, I dare*

MACBETH *It will have blood; they say, blood will have blood*

MACBETH *I am in blood / Stepped in so far that, should I wade no more, / Returning were as tedious as go o'er*

MACBETH *My strange and self-abuse / Is the initiate fear that wants hard use: / We are yet but young in deed.*

Commentary

- Deception is an important element of *Macbeth*. We see this in Lady Macbeth's warm reception of the thanes to the banquet, while all the time hiding her personal doubts and fears. As Macbeth becomes hysterical at the sight of Banquo's ghost, Lady Macbeth attempts to smooth over the disturbance by pretending Macbeth suffers from strange fits.

- Macbeth reveals a claustrophobic sense of paranoia in this scene, as if he is snared by the anxiety of his own mind: 'I am cabined, cribbed, confined, bound in / To saucy doubts and fears'. We also learn that Macbeth employs spies in the other thanes' castles: 'There's not a one of them but in his house / I keep a servant fee'd'.

- Some commentators see the ghost as a product of Macbeth's imagination. The bloody spectacle of a man with 'twenty trenched gashes on his head' shaking his 'gory locks' effectively dramatises Macbeth's conscience for the audience. In a very physical way, we understand that Macbeth is haunted by his crimes. However, other commentators argue that in Shakespeare's time, it was thought that ghosts could appear to just one person. In this case, Banquo's ghost is literally haunting Macbeth.

- Macbeth continually protests his manliness and courage throughout this scene. As only Macbeth can see the ghost, Lady Macbeth dismisses it as the product of a fearful imagination: 'O proper stuff! / This is the very painting of your fear' and disparagingly compares it to a ghost story. Macbeth however says he is as brave as any man: 'What man dare, I dare' and would gladly take any test of bravery such as confronting wild animals or sword fighting in the desert. He wishes to act in a manly fashion but is also tormented by his conscience.

- Appearing world-weary at the end of the scene, Macbeth outlines his plans to commit more murders: 'I am in blood / Stepped in so far that, should I wade no more, / Returning were as tedious as go o'er'. The image of a man wading in blood is disturbing, but Macbeth's abandonment of moral responsibility is perhaps more upsetting. Macbeth blames his hysteria on inexperience and again expresses his intention to reign with a bloody hand: 'My strange and self-abuse / Is the initiate fear that wants hard use: / We are yet but young in deed'.

- Unlike the first Act where he was accosted by evil, Macbeth now seeks evil out for himself when he decides to consult the witches: 'I will, to the Weird Sisters: … for now I am bent to know, / By the worst means, the worst.' This indicates a deepening of evil intent.

- Macbeth's murder of Duncan subverted the natural order of Scotland. This is reflected by the disorderly conduct at the banquet. The thanes were seated according to their status, but as they are hurried out of the banquet hall, Lady Macbeth instructs them to ignore their rank as they leave: 'Stand not upon the order of your going'.

- At the start of the scene Lady Macbeth is the perfect hostess. However, by the end of the scene she appears fraught and exhausted. She expresses little interest in Macbeth's future plans. As his resolve and decisiveness grows, she becomes quieter. This is a turning point as we see Macbeth assume absolute power while Lady Macbeth becomes less of a force within the play.

Questions

1. What is Macbeth's reaction to the news that Fleance escaped the murderers?
2. (a) How does Lady Macbeth try to explain Macbeth's strange behaviour to the other thanes?

   (b) Where else in the play has she publicly intervened to protect Macbeth?
3. Lady Macbeth considers Macbeth's vision of Banquo's ghost as merely the 'painting' of Macbeth's fear, no more real than the 'air-drawn dagger' from Act 1. Do you agree with her? Why / why not?
4. Find two quotations that suggest that Macbeth intends to shed more blood.
5. How would you describe Macbeth's mental state at this point of the play? Use quotations to justify your ideas.
6. If you were directing *Macbeth*, how would you stage this scene? You may wish to discuss lighting, props, instructions to actors etc.
7. Imagine you are Lady Macbeth. Write a diary entry reflecting on the events of Macbeth's coronation banquet.

Act 3 Scene 5

Scene Summary

- Hecate, goddess of witchcraft, is angry that she hasn't been included in the dealings with Macbeth.
- She instructs the witches to further confuse Macbeth by showing him apparitions.

A Heath.
Thunder. Enter the Three Witches meeting HECATE

FIRST WITCH
Why, how now, Hecate! You look angerly[1].

HECATE
Have I not reason, beldams[2] as you are,
Saucy[3] and overbold? How did you dare
To trade and traffic[4] with Macbeth
In riddles and affairs of death;
And I, the mistress of your charms,
The close contriver[5] of all harms,
Was never called to bear my part,
Or show the glory of our art?
And, which is worse, all you have done
Hath been but for a wayward son[6],
Spiteful and wrathful, who, as others do,
Loves for his own ends[7], not for you.
But make amends now: get you gone,
And at the pit of Acheron[8]
Meet me i' the morning: thither[9] he
Will come to know his destiny.
Your vessels[10] and your spells provide,
Your charms and everything beside.
I am for the air; this night I'll spend
Unto a dismal and a fatal end:[11]
Great business must be wrought[12] ere noon:
Upon the corner of the moon
There hangs a vaporous drop[13] profound;
I'll catch it ere it come to ground:
And that distilled by magic sleights[14]
Shall raise such artificial sprites[15]
As by the strength of their illusion
Shall draw him on to his confusion:
He shall spurn[16] fate, scorn death, and bear
He hopes 'bove wisdom, grace and fear:
And you all know, security[17]
Is mortals' chiefest enemy.

1 **angerly:** angry
2 **beldams:** hags
3 **saucy:** cheeky/impertinent
4 **trade and traffic:** deal
5 **close contriver:** secret creator
6 **wayward son:** unreliable follower
7 **Loves for his own ends:** loves witchcraft to meet his own needs
8 **Acheron:** one of the rivers of the Underworld in Greek mythology
9 **thither:** there
10 **vessels:** cauldrons
11 **this night...fatal end:** I'll spend tonight plotting something deadly and ruinous.
12 **wrought:** worked/created
13 **vaporous drop:** It was thought that witches used drops from the moon for their spells.
14 **sleights:** tricks
15 **artificial sprites:** false apparitions
16 **spurn:** turn his back on
17 **security:** confidence

[Music and a song within: 'Come away, come away,' etc]
Hark! I am called; my little spirit, see,
Sits in a foggy cloud, and stays for me.
[Exit]

First Witch
Come, let's make haste; she'll soon be back again.
[Exeunt]

Commentary

- This scene provides a deeper vision of the witches' evil motivations and points to Macbeth's trust in their prophecies as an important element in his eventual downfall: 'And you all know, security / Is mortals' chiefest enemy'. From this point on Macbeth sees himself as invincible; as a result his actions become increasingly evil.

- Hecate is angry in this scene because she was left out of the dealings with Macbeth and also because she wants a deeper commitment to evil from Macbeth. She notes that Macbeth is drawn to the witches, not out of love of evil, but for his own needs: 'Loves for his own ends, not for you'.

- Hecate also hopes to further Macbeth's moral confusion by showing him 'artificial sprites' (apparitions). Again the witches' equivocation is shown as an influence on Macbeth.

Act 3 Scene 6

Scene Summary

- Lennox and another lord discuss Macbeth's guilt.
- Their conversation reveals that Macduff is in the court of King Edward (the King of England) and is planning to return with an army to overthrow Macbeth.

Forres. The Palace.
Enter LENNOX and another Lord

LENNOX
My former speeches have but hit your thoughts,
Which can interpret further:[1] only I say,
Things have been strangely borne.[2] The gracious Duncan
Was pitied of Macbeth: marry, he was dead:
And the right-valiant Banquo walked too late;
Whom, you may say, if't please you, Fleance killed,
For Fleance fled: men must not walk too late.
Who cannot want the thought how monstrous
It was for Malcolm and for Donalbain
To kill their gracious father? Damned fact!
How it did grieve Macbeth! Did he not straight
In pious rage the two delinquents tear,
That were the slaves of drink and thralls of sleep?
Was not that nobly done? Ay, and wisely too;
For 'twould have angered any heart alive
To hear the men deny't. So that, I say,
He has borne all things well:[3] and I do think
That had he Duncan's sons under his key[4] –
As, an't please heaven, he shall not – they should find
What 'twere to kill a father; so should Fleance.
But, peace! For from broad words and 'cause he failed
His presence at the tyrant's[5] feast, I hear
Macduff lives in disgrace. Sir, can you tell
Where he bestows himself?[6]

LORD
The son of Duncan,
From whom this tyrant holds the due of birth[7]
Lives in the English court, and is received
Of the most pious Edward[8] with such grace
That the malevolence of fortune nothing
Takes from his high respect.[9] Thither Macduff
Is gone to pray the holy king, upon his aid
To wake Northumberland and warlike Siward:[10]

1 **My former...interpret further:** What I've said to you before echoes your own thoughts; it's up to you to draw your own conclusions.
2 **Things have been strangely borne:** Unusual things have occurred.
3 **The gracious Duncan...things well:** Lennox with deliberate irony has listed all of the reasons why Macbeth could be considered innocent.
4 **under his key:** imprisoned
5 **tyrant:** a cruel ruler
6 **bestows himself:** is staying
7 **The son of...due of birth:** The son of Duncan (Malcolm) from whom Macbeth hold his birthright (the crown).
8 **Edward:** Edward the Confessor, the King of England
9 **That the malevolence...high respect:** that his misfortune does not lose him respect (in Edward's court)
10 **Northumberland and warlike Siward:** Siward was Earl of Northumbria and a powerful leader

That, by the help of these – with Him above
To ratify the work – we may again
Give to our tables meat, sleep to our nights,
Free from our feasts and banquets bloody knives,[11]
Do faithful homage and receive free honours:[12]
All which we pine[13] for now: and this report
Hath so exasperate[14] the King that he
Prepares for some attempt of war.

[11] **Free from...knives:** free ourselves from the threat of murder at our banquets
[12] **Do faithful...honours:** give the King honours and be rewarded honestly
[13] **pine:** crave/long for
[14] **exasperate:** annoyed

LENNOX

Sent he to Macduff?

LORD

He did: and with an absolute 'Sir, not I,'
The cloudy messenger turns me his back,
And hums, as who should say 'You'll rue the time
That clogs me with this answer.'[15]

[15] **The cloudy messenger...this answer:** The grumbling messenger turned his back as if to say 'You'll regret burdening me with this answer'. The messenger is not happy about having to give Macbeth such a rude reply from Macduff.

LENNOX

And that well might
Advise him to a caution, to hold what distance
His wisdom can provide.[16] Some holy angel
Fly to the court of England and unfold
His message ere he come, that a swift blessing
May soon return to this our suffering country
Under a hand accursed![17]

[16] **And that well...can provide:** And that alone should caution Macduff to keep his distance from Macbeth.

[17] **hand accursed:** evil ruler

LORD

I'll send my prayers with him.

[Exeunt]

Commentary

- The thanes have now come to suspect that Macbeth killed Duncan and Banquo. The audience learns that Macbeth's rule is considered tyrannical and that all want him overthrown. The scene also gives Shakespeare the opportunity to introduce the idea of a rebellion supported by English troops.

- The scene employs contrasting imagery that associates Macbeth with hell and his opposing forces with heaven. Scotland is said to suffer 'Under a hand accursed', i.e. Macbeth's. Whereas Edward is seen as a saintlike figure who has received Malcolm with 'grace'. Similarly, Macduff has gone to 'pray the holy king' (Edward). The lord appeals to 'Him above / to ratify the work' and Lennox hopes a 'holy angel' will bring a message to Edward sooner, to secure a 'swift blessing' for Scotland.

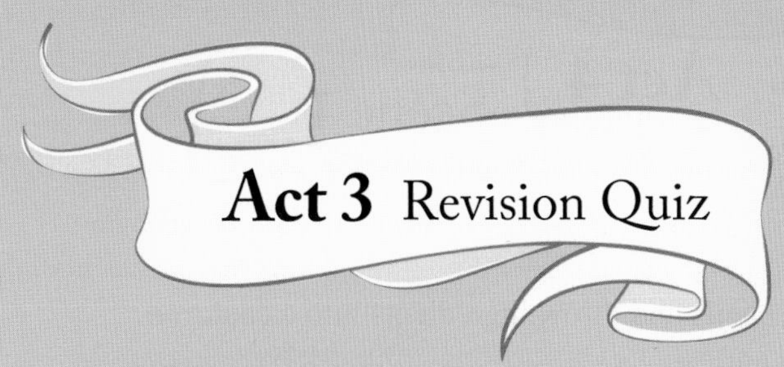

1. **Why does Macbeth say, 'Upon my head they placed a fruitless crown, / And put a barren sceptre in my gripe'?**

2. **Why does Macbeth ask Banquo where and when he is going riding?**

3. **Find a quotation from Scene 3 that shows Lady Macbeth has found no contentment in her position as Queen.**

4. **Why does Macbeth send a third murderer to meet the other two?**

5. **To whom does Macbeth say, 'never shake / Thy gory locks at me'?**

6. **How does Lady Macbeth explain Macbeth's unusual behaviour to the thanes during the Banquet Scene (Scene 4)?**

7. **Why is Hecate upset with the three witches?**

8. **Which of the thanes goes to England to seek military aid for a rebellion?**

9. **Who says each of the following?:**
   (a) *'To be thus is nothing;*
   But to be safely thus. – Our fears in Banquo
   Stick deep'
   (b) *'Tis safer to be that which we destroy / Than by destruction dwell in doubtful joy'*
   (c) *'Come, seeling night,*
   Scarf up the tender eye of pitiful day;
   And with thy bloody and invisible hand
   Cancel and tear to pieces that great bond
   Which keeps me pale!'
   (d) *But now I am cabined, cribbed, confined, bound in / To saucy doubts and fears'*

10. **Fill in the blanks:**
    (a) *'I am in* blood
    Stepped in so far that, should I wade *no more,*
    Returning were as tedious *as go o'er'*
    (b) *'It will have blood; they say,* blood *will have* blood *'*
    (c) *'And make our faces* vizords *to our hearts, /* disguising *what they are'*
    (d) *'My strange and self-abuse'*
    Is the initiate fear that wants hard use *:*
    We are yet but young *in deed'*

Act 4 Scene 1

Scene Summary

- The witches chant spells and throw ingredients into a cauldron.
- Macbeth visits the witches.
- He is shown three apparitions: an armed head, a bloody child and a crowned child.
- Each apparition gives Macbeth advice: to beware of Macduff, that Macbeth cannot be killed by a man born of a woman and that Macbeth is safe until Birnam Wood moves to Dunsinane Hill.
- Macbeth demands to know more and is shown a procession of eight kings. The last holds a mirror suggesting that the line continues further. The procession is followed by Banquo's ghost.
- Macbeth hears from Lennox that Macduff has gone to England.
- Macbeth decides to kill all in Macduff's castle.

A cavern. In the middle, a boiling cauldron[1].
Thunder. Enter the Three Witches

First Witch
Thrice the brinded[2] cat hath mewed.

Second Witch
Thrice and once the hedge-pig[3] whined.

Third Witch
Harpier[4] cries 'Tis time, 'tis time.

First Witch
Round about the cauldron go;
In the poisoned entrails[5] throw.
Toad, that under cold stone
Days and nights has thirty-one
Sweltered venom[6] sleeping got,[7]
Boil thou first i' the charmed pot.

All
Double, double toil[8] and trouble;
Fire burn, and cauldron bubble.

Second Witch
Fillet of a fenny snake,[9]
In the cauldron boil and bake;
Eye of newt[10] and toe of frog,
Wool of bat and tongue of dog,

1 **cauldron:** a large pot

2 **brinded:** brindled/striped/tabby

3 **hedge-pig:** hedgehog

4 **Harpier:** The third witch's creature/pet

5 **entrails:** intestines

6 **Sweltered venom:** sweated venom

7 **sleeping got:** taken while he was sleeping

8 **toil:** work/struggle

9 **fenny snake:** marsh snake

10 **newt:** a type of salamander

Adder's fork and blind-worm's sting,[11]
Lizard's leg and howlet's[12] wing –
For a charm of powerful trouble,
Like a hell-broth boil and bubble.

All
Double, double toil and trouble;
Fire burn and cauldron bubble.

Third Witch
Scale of dragon, tooth of wolf,
Witches' mummy,[13] maw and gulf
Of the ravined salt-sea shark,[14]
Root of hemlock[15] digged i' the dark,
Liver of blaspheming Jew,
Gall of goat, and slips of yew[16]
Slivered in the moon's eclipse,
Nose of Turk and Tartar's[17] lips,
Finger of birth-strangled babe
Ditch-delivered by a drab,[18]
Make the gruel thick and slab:[19]
Add thereto a tiger's chaudron,[20]
For the ingredients of our cauldron.

All
Double, double toil and trouble;
Fire burn and cauldron bubble.

Second Witch
Cool it with a baboon's blood,
Then the charm is firm and good.
[Enter HECATE]

Hecate
O well done! I commend your pains;[21]
And every one shall share i' the gains.
And now about the cauldron sing,
Live elves and fairies in a ring,
Enchanting all that you put in.
[Music and a song: 'Black spirits,' etc]
[HECATE retires]

Second Witch
By the pricking of my thumbs,[22]
Something wicked this way comes.
Open, locks,
Whoever knocks!

[Enter MACBETH]

[11] **blind-worm's sting:** also known as a slow-worm's sting. A slow-worm is a limbless lizard.
[12] **howlet:** young owl
[13] **Witches' mummy:** powder made from ground Egyptian mummies
[14] **maw and gulf...shark:** the stomach and throat of a well-fed shark
[15] **hemlock:** poisonous root
[16] **yew:** a type of tree
[17] **Turk and Tartar:** these were non-Christian people and therefore attractive to the witches
[18] **Ditch-delivered by a drab:** born in a ditch to a prostitute
[19] **slab:** sticky
[20] **chaudron:** internal organs
[21] **commend your pains:** congratulate your hard work
[22] **pricking of my thumbs:** tingling sensation in my thumbs. This was supposed to signal approaching evil.

MACBETH
How now, you secret, black, and midnight hags!
What is't you do?

ALL
A deed without a name.

MACBETH
I conjure you, by that which you profess,[23]
Howe'er you come to know it – answer me:
Though you untie the winds and let them fight
Against the churches; though the yesty[24] waves
Confound and swallow navigation up;[25]
Though bladed corn be lodged[26] and trees blown down;
Though castles topple on their warders' heads;
Though palaces and pyramids do slope[27]
Their heads to their foundations; though the treasure
Of Nature's germens[28] tumble all together,
Even till destruction sicken – answer me
To what I ask you.

FIRST WITCH
Speak.

SECOND WITCH
Demand.

THIRD WITCH
We'll answer.

FIRST WITCH
Say, if thou'dst rather hear it from our mouths,
Or from our masters?

MACBETH
Call 'em; let me see 'em.

FIRST WITCH
Pour in sow's blood, that hath eaten
Her nine farrow;[29] grease that's sweaten[30]
From the murderer's gibbet[31] throw
Into the flame.

ALL
Come, high or low;
Thyself and office deftly show!
[Thunder. FIRST APPARITION: an Armed Head[32]]

[23] **I conjure...profess:** I call upon you in the name of your dark profession.

[24] **yesty:** frothy

[25] **Confound...navigation up:** confuse and drown ships

[26] **bladed corn be lodged:** unripe corn is blown down

[27] **slope:** bend

[28] **Nature's germens:** seeds of nature

[29] **farrow:** piglets

[30] **sweaten:** sweated

[31] **gibbet:** gallows

[32] **armed head:** This foreshadows Macbeth's armoured head which will be severed by Macduff

Macbeth
Tell me, thou unknown power, –

First Witch
He knows thy thought:
Hear his speech, but say thou nought.

First Apparition
Macbeth! Macbeth! Macbeth! Beware Macduff;
Beware the Thane of Fife. Dismiss me. Enough.
[Descends]

Macbeth
Whate'er thou art, for thy good caution, thanks;
Thou hast harped[33] my fear aright: but one word more, –

First Witch
He will not be commanded: here's another,
More potent[34] than the first.
[Thunder. Second Apparition: A Bloody Child[35]]

Second Apparition
Macbeth! Macbeth! Macbeth! –

Macbeth
Had I three ears, I'd hear thee.

Second Apparition
Be bloody, bold, and resolute; laugh to scorn
The power of man, for none of woman born
Shall harm Macbeth.
[Descends]

Macbeth
Then live, Macduff: what need I fear of thee?
But yet I'll make assurance double sure,[36]
And take a bond of fate:[37] thou shalt not live;
That I may tell pale-hearted fear it lies,
And sleep in spite of thunder.[38]
[Thunder. Third Apparition: A child crowned[39], with a tree in his hand]
What is this
That rises like the issue of a king,
And wears upon his baby brow the round
And top of sovereignty?

All
Listen, but speak not to't.

33 **harped:** guessed

34 **more potent:** more powerful

35 **bloody child:** represents Macduff born by caesarean section

36 **assurance double sure:** make doubly sure

37 **take a bond of fate:** make Fate keep its word

38 **That I may tell...thunder:** That I might call fear a liar and sleep soundly even through the sound of thunder.

39 **child crowned:** represents Malcolm. The tree he holds represents Birnam Wood.

THIRD APPARITION

Be lion-mettled,[40] proud, and take no care
Who chafes, who frets,[41] or where conspirers are:
Macbeth shall never vanquished[42] be until
Great Birnam wood[43] to high Dunsinane hill[44]
Shall come against him.
[Descends]

MACBETH

That will never be
Who can impress[45] the forest, bid the tree
Unfix his earth-bound root? Sweet bodements![46] good!
Rebellion's head, rise never till the wood
Of Birnam rise, and our high-placed Macbeth
Shall live the lease of nature,[47] pay his breath
To time and mortal custom.[48] Yet my heart
Throbs to know one thing: tell me (if your art
Can tell so much), shall Banquo's issue ever
Reign in this kingdom?

ALL

Seek to know no more.

MACBETH

I will be satisfied: deny me this,
And an eternal curse fall on you! Let me know.
[Hautboys]
Why sinks that cauldron? and what noise is this?

FIRST WITCH

Show!

SECOND WITCH

Show!

THIRD WITCH

Show!

ALL

Show his eyes, and grieve his heart;
Come like shadows, so depart!
[A show of eight kings, the last with a glass in his hand;[49] GHOST OF BANQUO following]

MACBETH

Thou art too like the spirit of Banquo: down!
Thy crown does sear[50] mine eye-balls. And thy hair,
Thou other gold-bound brow, is like the first.
A third is like the former. Filthy hags!

40 **lion-mettled:** brave as a lion
41 **Who chafes, who frets:** who is angry, who worries
42 **vanquished:** beaten
43 **Birnam wood:** A forest close to Macbeth's castle
44 **Dunsinane hill:** The hill upon which Macbeth's castle sits

45 **impress:** conscript/force into doing
46 **bodements:** predictions

47 **live the lease of nature:** live a full lifespan
48 **pay his...custom:** breathe until old age and natural death come for him

49 **glass in his hand:** holding a mirror. The mirror reflects a further stretch of kings. Banquo's line will reign indefinitely.

50 **sear:** scorch

Why do you show me this? A fourth! Start, eyes!
What, will the line stretch out to the crack of doom?[51]
Another yet! A seventh! I'll see no more:
And yet the eighth appears, who bears a glass[52]
Which shows me many more; and some I see
That two-fold balls and treble sceptres[53] carry:
Horrible sight! Now, I see, 'tis true;
For the blood-boltered[54] Banquo smiles upon me,
And points at them for his.
[Apparitions vanish]
What, is this so?

First Witch
Ay, sir, all this is so: but why
Stands Macbeth thus amazedly?
Come, sisters, cheer we up his sprites,
And show the best of our delights:
I'll charm the air to give a sound,
While you perform your antic round:[55]
That this great king may kindly say,
Our duties did his welcome pay.
[Music. The witches dance and then vanish]

Macbeth
Where are they? Gone? Let this pernicious[56] hour
Stand aye accursed in the calendar!
Come in, without there!
[Enter LENNOX]

Lennox
What's your Grace's will?

Macbeth
Saw you the Weird Sisters?

Lennox
No, my lord.

Macbeth
Came they not by you?

Lennox
No, indeed, my lord.

Macbeth
Infected be the air whereon they ride;
And damned all those that trust them! I did hear
The galloping of horse: who was't came by?

[51] **crack of doom:** doomsday

[52] **eighth...a glass:** The eighth king is James I who was thought to be descended from Banquo. He carries a mirror ('glass') which suggest his line extends further.

[53] **two-fold balls and treble sceptres:** represents the coronation of James I (England & Scotland)

[54] **blood-boltered:** hair thick with blood

[55] **antic round:** grotesque dance

[56] **pernicious:** evil

LENNOX
'Tis two or three, my lord, that bring you word
Macduff is fled to England.

MACBETH
Fled to England!

LENNOX
Ay, my good lord.

MACBETH
[Aside.] Time, thou anticipat'st my dread exploits:[57]
The flighty purpose never is o'ertook
Unless the deed go with it.[58] From this moment
The very firstlings of my heart shall be
The firstlings of my hand.[59] And even now,
To crown my thoughts[60] with acts, be it thought and done:
The castle of Macduff I will surprise;
Seize upon Fife; give to the edge o' the sword
His wife, his babes, and all unfortunate souls
That trace him in his line.[61] No boasting like a fool;
This deed I'll do before this purpose cool.
But no more sights! *[Aloud.]* Where are these gentlemen?
Come, bring me where they are.
[Exeunt]

57 **Time...dread exploits:** Time, you have anticipated my terrible planned deeds.
58 **The flighty...go with it:** Our plans are never overtaken if we act immediately.
59 **The very...my hand:** As soon as I think, I will act.
60 **crown my thoughts:** finish my thoughts

61 **his line:** descendants

Key Quotations

THE WITCHES *Double, double toil and trouble; / Fire burn and cauldron bubble.*

SECOND APPARITION *Be bloody, bold, and resolute; laugh to scorn / The power of man, for none of woman born / Shall harm Macbeth.*

THIRD APPARITION*Macbeth shall never vanquished be until / Great Birnam wood to high Dunsinane hill / Shall come against him.*

MACBETH *The very firstlings of my heart shall be / The firstlings of my hand.*

Commentary

- The fact that Macbeth has sought the witches' advice shows how desperate and alone he is. It also cements his commitment to evil as he attempts to suppress his conscience. Macbeth is desperate to know his fate regardless of the havoc the witches bring.

- The witches personify pure evil in *Macbeth*. Their gruesome broth of grotesque animals, poison and human body parts dramatically shows their depravity. The simple rhythm (trochaic tetrameter) of their incantation: 'Double, double toil and trouble; / Fire burn and cauldron bubble' sounds like a corrupted children's rhyme and contrasts with the iambic pentameter used by the human characters. However, despite the horrendous spells and awful chanting, the real evil lies in the heart of Macbeth – the witches have merely encouraged it.

- Macbeth is presented with three apparitions. The first warns Macbeth, 'Beware Macduff!' thus confirming Macbeth's suspicions of Macduff. The second apparition gives Macbeth confidence by instructing him to 'Be bloody, bold, and resolute; laugh to scorn/ The power of man' as 'none of woman born / Shall harm Macbeth'. Just as Hecate predicted in Act 3, Macbeth becomes overconfident thinking no man may harm him. The third apparition buoys Macbeth's confidence further. He learns that 'Macbeth shall never vanquished be until / Great Birnam wood to high Dunsinane hill / Shall come against him'. As such a thing seems impossible, Macbeth assumes that he will live a full lifespan. Despite the last two seemingly positive predictions, Macbeth decides to murder Macduff to 'make assurance double sure'.

- Macbeth doesn't reflect on the possible meanings of the apparitions. Instead he takes them as positive signs: 'Sweet bodements! good!'

- Macbeth is shown a procession of kings, all descendants of Banquo. The eighth king is James I, King of England and Scotland when *Macbeth* was first performed. Shakespeare intended to flatter James I in this play.

- Macbeth's moral decline continues in this scene. He decides to murder Macduff's family in an unnecessary act of vindictive evil: 'give to the edge o' the sword / His wife, his babes, and all unfortunate souls / That trace him in his line'. Macbeth promises he will now act without reflection, satisfying every murderous whim: 'The very firstlings of my heart shall be / The firstlings of my hand'. Macbeth's transformation from the noble warrior of Act 1 to a cruel tyrant is now complete.

Questions

1. Compare Macbeth's encounter with the witches in Act 1 Scene 3 with his meeting in this scene.

2. (a) Describe each of the apparitions that Macbeth sees.
(b) State what advice each of them gives.
(c) What effect does this advice have on Macbeth?

3. In Act 3, Scene 5 Hecate predicts that Macbeth,

'shall spurn fate, scorn death, and bear
His hopes 'bove wisdom, grace and fear:
And you all know, security
Is mortals' chiefest enemy'

Is she correct? Explain your answer by referring to the text.

4. There seems to be no logical reason for Macbeth to murder Macduff's family. Why do you think he does it?

5. Why does Macbeth say, 'The very firstlings of my heart shall be / The firstlings of my hand'?

Scene Summary

- Ross tells Lady Macduff that her husband has gone to England.
- After Ross leaves, a messenger warns her of immediate danger.
- Before she has time to flee, Lady Macduff and her children are murdered upon the orders of Macbeth.

Fife. Macduff's castle.
Enter LADY MACDUFF, her SON, and ROSS

LADY MACDUFF
What had he done, to make him fly[1] the land?

ROSS
You must have patience, madam.

LADY MACDUFF
He had none:
His flight was madness: when our actions do not,
Our fears do make us traitors.[2]

ROSS
You know not
Whether it was his wisdom or his fear.

LADY MACDUFF
Wisdom! to leave his wife, to leave his babes,
His mansion and his titles in a place
From whence himself does fly? He loves us not;
He wants the natural touch:[3] for the poor wren,
The most diminutive[4] of birds, will fight,
Her young ones in her nest, against the owl.
All is the fear and nothing is the love;[5]
As little is the wisdom, where the flight
So runs against all reason.[6]

ROSS
My dearest coz,[7]
I pray you, school yourself:[8] but for your husband,
He is noble, wise, judicious, and best knows
The fits o' the season.[9] I dare not speak much further;
But cruel are the times, when we are traitors
And do not know ourselves, when we hold rumour

[1] **fly:** flee

[2] **when our actions...us traitors:** Even if he doesn't appear like a traitor, fleeing in fear makes him look like one.

[3] **He wants the natural touch:** He doesn't have the normal feelings of a father and husband.

[4] **diminutive:** smallest

[5] **All is the fear...love:** Fear motivates him, not love.

[6] **As little is the wisdom...all reason:** He is as lacking in wisdom as his flight is lacking in common sense.

[7] **coz:** cousin

[8] **school yourself:** learn/control yourself

[9] **The fits o' the season:** the unpredictability of our times

From what we fear, yet know not what we fear,
But float upon a wild and violent sea
Each way and move.[10] I take my leave of you:
Shall not be long but I'll be here again:
Things at the worst will cease, or else climb upward
To what they were before.[11] My pretty cousin,
Blessing upon you!

LADY MACDUFF
Fathered he is, and yet he's fatherless.

ROSS
I am so much a fool, should I stay longer,
It would be my disgrace and your discomfort:
I take my leave at once.[12]
[Exit]

LADY MACDUFF
Sirrah, your father's dead;
And what will you do now? How will you live?

SON
As birds do, mother.

LADY MACDUFF
What, with worms and flies?

SON
With what I get, I mean; and so do they.

LADY MACDUFF
Poor bird! thou'dst never fear the net nor lime,
The pitfall nor the gin.[13]

SON
Why should I, mother? Poor birds they are not set for.
My father is not dead, for all your saying.

LADY MACDUFF
Yes, he is dead; how wilt thou do for a father?

SON
Nay, how will you do for a husband?

LADY MACDUFF
Why, I can buy me twenty at any market.

SON
Then you'll buy 'em to sell again.

[10] **But float upon a wild and violent sea / Each way and move:** Are tossed about by these violent times and are swept this way and that.

[11] **Things at the worst...were before:** When things are at their worst, they must either end or improve.

[12] **I am so much...leave at once:** Ross is afraid that he will cry if he stays and leaves quickly to avoid embarrassment.

[13] **thou'dst never fear...nor the gin:** You never fear bird-nets, birdlime (a sticky substance used to trap birds), traps nor snares, i.e. you are never afraid of the many dangers in the world.

LADY MACDUFF
Thou speak'st with all thy wit: and yet, i' faith,
With wit enough for thee.

SON
Was my father a traitor, mother?

LADY MACDUFF
Ay, that he was.

SON
What is a traitor?

LADY MACDUFF
Why, one that swears and lies.

SON
And be all traitors that do so?

LADY MACDUFF
Every one that does so is a traitor, and must be hanged.

SON
And must they all be hanged that swear and lie?

LADY MACDUFF
Every one.

SON
Who must hang them?

LADY MACDUFF
Why, the honest men.

SON
Then the liars and swearers are fools, for there are liars and swearers enow[14] to beat the honest men and hang up them.

LADY MACDUFF
Now, God help thee, poor monkey!
But how wilt thou do for a father?

SON
If he were dead, you'd weep for him: if you would not, it were a good sign that I should quickly have a new father.

LADY MACDUFF
Poor prattler,[15] how thou talk'st!
[Enter a Messenger]

[14] **enow:** enough

[15] **prattler:** chatterbox

MESSENGER
Bless you, fair dame! I am not to you known,
Though in your state of honour I am perfect.[16]
I doubt[17] some danger does approach you nearly:
If you will take a homely[18] man's advice,
Be not found here; hence, with your little ones.
To fright you thus, methinks, I am too savage;
To do worse to you were fell[19] cruelty,
Which is too nigh[20] your person. Heaven preserve you!
I dare abide[21] no longer.
[Exit]

LADY MACDUFF
Whither[22] should I fly?
I have done no harm. But I remember now
I am in this earthly world; where to do harm
Is often laudable,[23] to do good sometime
Accounted dangerous folly.[24] Why then, alas,
Do I put up that womanly defence,
To say I have done no harm?
[Enter Murderers]
What are these faces?

FIRST MURDERER
Where is your husband?

LADY MACDUFF
I hope, in no place so unsanctified[25]
Where such as thou mayst find him.

FIRST MURDERER
He's a traitor.

SON
Thou liest, thou shag-haired[26] villain!

FIRST MURDERER
What, you egg!
[Stabbing him]
Young fry[27] of treachery!

SON
He has killed me, mother:
Run away, I pray you!
[Dies]
[Exit LADY MACDUFF, crying 'Murder!' Exeunt Murderers, following her]

[16] **Though in your...perfect:** I know perfectly well how noble you are.
[17] **I doubt:** I am worried/I suspect
[18] **homely:** ordinary/humble
[19] **fell:** awful
[20] **nigh:** near to
[21] **abide:** stay
[22] **Whither:** Where
[23] **laudable:** commendable
[24] **folly:** foolishness
[25] **unsanctified:** unholy
[26] **shag-haired:** unkempt. Some editors think the intended phrase was 'shag-eared'.
[27] **fry:** spawn

Commentary

- This scene momentarily shifts the focus away from Macbeth himself and onto the victims of his crimes. Instead of merely mentioning the murder of Lady Macduff and her son, Shakespeare devotes an entire scene to the characters so that their deaths create pathos*.

- The clever banter between Lady Macduff and her son give the audience an intimate view of Macduff's family; this intensifies the horror of their deaths. The messenger's urgent warning, coupled with our foreknowledge of Macbeth's plan, creates suspense as we wait for the inevitable murders.

- Shakespeare is keen to highlight the innocence of these victims. Lady Macduff herself protests this, 'I have done no harm'. It is particularly distressing to see the young boy defend the honour of his father by pathetically calling the murderer a 'shag-haired villain'. Just moments later the boy is stabbed to death.

- Although the murders of Duncan and Banquo were horrendous deeds, there was at least a criminal logic to them. However, the senseless slaughter of a mother and her children illustrates Macbeth's descent into evil.

- This episode gives Macduff further motivation to act against Macbeth. However, it also begs the question why Macduff left his family so vulnerable to attack. Lady Macduff criticises her husband's wisdom in this regard: 'Wisdom! to leave his wife, to leave his babes, / His mansion and his titles in a place / From whence himself does fly?' Some commentators see this as a flaw in Macduff; others argue that Macduff places his loyalty to Scotland above all else.

***pathos:** *the quality of arousing pity in the audience*

Questions

1. Lady Macduff heavily criticises Macduff for going to England. Do you agree with her criticism?
2. Considering they play little part in the overall plot, why do you think Shakespeare devotes an entire scene to Lady Macduff and her son?
3. Some scholars see the character of Macduff's son as distracting from the seriousness of the scene. Do you agree with them? Explain your answer.
4. Both Ross and Lady Macduff make reference to society in general. What is their view of how Scotland is being run?
5. Why do you think Shakespeare introduced a messenger into the scene?

Act 4 Scene 3

Scene Summary

- Macduff meets with Malcolm and seeks to enlist his help against Macbeth.
- Malcolm is distrustful of Macduff and tests his loyalty.
- Once Malcolm is satisfied by Macduff, he agrees to help in the fight against Macbeth. He tells Macduff that Edward, the English King, is sending troops to Scotland.
- Ross arrives and tells Macduff that his family are well.
- Ross is told about the plan to fight Macbeth; he then reveals the truth about Macduff's family.
- Macduff is devastated and determined more than ever to kill Macbeth.

England. Before King Edward's palace.
Enter MALCOLM and MACDUFF

MALCOLM
Let us seek out some desolate shade, and there
Weep our sad bosoms empty.[1]

MACDUFF
Let us rather
Hold fast the mortal sword,[2] and like good men
Bestride our down-fall'n birthdom.[3] Each new morn
New widows howl, new orphans cry, new sorrows
Strike heaven on the face, that it resounds[4]
As if it felt with Scotland and yelled out
Like syllable of dolour.[5]

MALCOLM
What I believe I'll wail,
What know, believe; and what I can redress,[6]
As I shall find the time to friend, I will.
What you have spoke, it may be so perchance.[7]
This tyrant, whose sole name[8] blisters our tongues,
Was once thought honest: you have loved him well.
He hath not touched you yet. I am young; but something
You may deserve of him through me,[9] and wisdom
To offer up a weak, poor, innocent lamb
To appease an angry god.[10]

MACDUFF
I am not treacherous.

1 **Weep our...empty:** cry our hearts out

2 **Hold fast the mortal sword:** grip the deadly sword tightly

3 **Bestride...birthdom:** defend the country of our birth

4 **resounds:** echoes

5 **syllable of dolour:** sound of grief

6 **redress:** put right

7 **perchance:** perhaps

8 **whose sole name:** whose name alone

9 **but something...through me:** You might use me to earn a reward from him.

10 **and wisdom...angry god:** You may think it wise to offer me up as a sacrificial lamb to calm an angry god (i.e. Macbeth).

MALCOLM

But Macbeth is.
A good and virtuous nature may recoil
In an imperial charge.[11] But I shall crave your pardon;
That which you are my thoughts cannot transpose:[12]
Angels are bright still, though the brightest fell;[13]
Though all things foul would wear the brows of grace,
Yet grace must still look so.[14]

MACDUFF

I have lost my hopes.

MALCOLM

Perchance even there where I did find my doubts.
Why in that rawness[15] left you wife and child –
Those precious motives,[16] those strong knots of love –
Without leave-taking? I pray you,
Let not my jealousies be your dishonours,
But mine own safeties.[17] You may be rightly just,[18]
Whatever I shall think.

MACDUFF

Bleed, bleed, poor country!
Great tyranny! lay thou thy basis sure,[19]
For goodness dare not check thee:[20] wear thou thy wrongs;
The title is affeered![21] Fare thee well, lord:
I would not be the villain that thou think'st
For the whole space[22] that's in the tyrant's grasp,
And the rich East to boot.[23]

MALCOLM

Be not offended:
I speak not as in absolute fear of you.
I think our country sinks beneath the yoke;[24]
It weeps, it bleeds; and each new day a gash
Is added to her wounds: I think withal[25]
There would be hands uplifted in my right;[26]
And here from gracious England have I offer
Of goodly thousands. But, for all this,
When I shall tread upon the tyrant's head,
Or wear it on my sword, yet my poor country
Shall have more vices[27] than it had before,
More suffer and more sundry[28] ways than ever,
By him that shall succeed.

MACDUFF

What should he be?

[11] **A good...imperial charge:** A good and moral man might behave immorally if asked to by a king.
[12] **transpose:** change
[13] **Angels...brightest fell:** i.e. Satan
[14] **Though all...look so:** Although evil men can appear good, a virtuous appearance is not necessarily false.
[15] **rawness:** vulnerability
[16] **motives:** those who inspire love
[17] **Let not...safeties:** Don't look at my suspicions as a sign of your dishonour but rather as ensuring my safety.
[18] **rightly just:** genuinely honest
[19] **lay thou thy basis sure:** lay firm foundations
[20] **check thee:** stop you
[21] **afeered:** legally certain
[22] **space:** country
[23] **to boot:** as well
[24] **yoke:** harness, i.e. harness of Macbeth's cruel rule
[25] **withal:** also/ besides/as well
[26] **There would...my right:** There are people willing to fight by my side.
[27] **vices:** sins/evils
[28] **sundry:** various

MALCOLM

It is myself I mean: in whom I know
All the particulars of vice so grafted[29]
That, when they shall be opened, black Macbeth
Will seem as pure as snow, and the poor state
Esteem him as a lamb, being compared
With my confineless harms.[30]

MACDUFF

Not in the legions[31]
Of horrid hell can come a devil more damned
In evils to top Macbeth.

MALCOLM

I grant him bloody,
Luxurious,[32] avaricious,[33] false, deceitful,
Sudden,[34] malicious, smacking of every sin
That has a name: but there's no bottom, none,
In my voluptuousness.[35] Your wives, your daughters,
Your matrons and your maids, could not fill up
The cistern of my lust,[36] and my desire
All continent impediments would o'erbear
That did oppose my will: better Macbeth
Than such an one to reign.

MACDUFF

Boundless intemperance[37]
In nature is a tyranny; it hath been
Th'untimely emptying of the happy throne
And fall of many kings. But fear not yet
To take upon you what is yours: you may
Convey your pleasures in a spacious plenty,[38]
And yet seem cold, the time you may so hoodwink[39].
We have willing dames enough. There cannot be
That vulture in you, to devour so many
As will to greatness dedicate themselves,
Finding it so inclined.

MALCOLM

With this there grows
In my most ill-composed affection such
A stanchless avarice[40] that, were I King,
I should cut off the nobles for their lands,
Desire his jewels and this other's house;
And my more-having would be as a sauce
To make me hunger more, that I should forge
Quarrels[41] unjust against the good and loyal,
Destroying them for wealth.

[29] **grafted:** strongly rooted

[30] **Esteem him...confineless harms:** You'll think of him (Macbeth) as a lamb next to my unrestrained evil.

[31] **legions:** armies

[32] **Luxurious:** lustful

[33] **avaricious:** greedy

[34] **Sudden:** quick to commit violence

[35] **voluptuousness:** lust

[36] **could not...of my lust:** could satisfy my lust

[37] **Boundless intemperance:** unrestrained lack of control

[38] **Convey...spacious plenty:** secretly enjoy your pleasures

[39] **hoodwink:** trick

[40] **stanchless avarice:** unstoppable greed

[41] **forge / Quarrels:** create arguments

MACDUFF
This avarice
Sticks deeper, grows with more pernicious[42] root
Than summer-seeming lust, and it hath been
The sword of our slain kings: yet do not fear;
Scotland hath foisons[43] to fill up your will.
Of your mere own: all these are portable,[44]
With other graces weighed.

MALCOLM
But I have none: the king-becoming graces,
As justice, verity,[45] temperance,[46] stableness,
Bounty,[47] perseverance, mercy, lowliness,
Devotion, patience, courage, fortitude,[48]
I have no relish[49] of them, but abound
In the division of each several crime,
Acting it many ways. Nay, had I power, I should
Pour the sweet milk of concord[50] into hell,
Uproar the universal peace, confound
All unity on earth.

MACDUFF
O Scotland, Scotland!

MALCOLM
If such a one be fit to govern, speak:
I am as I have spoken.

MACDUFF
Fit to govern!
No, not to live. O nation miserable,
With an untitled tyrant bloody-sceptred,
When shalt thou see thy wholesome days again,
Since that the truest issue[51] of thy throne
By his own interdiction stands accused,
And does blaspheme his breed? Thy royal father
Was a most sainted king; the queen that bore thee,
Oftener upon her knees than on her feet,[52]
Died every day she lived. Fare thee well!
These evils thou repeat'st upon thyself
Have banished me from Scotland. O my breast,
Thy hope ends here!

MALCOLM
Macduff, this noble passion,
Child of integrity,[53] hath from my soul
Wiped the black scruples,[54] reconciled my thoughts
To thy good truth and honour. Devilish Macbeth

[42] **pernicious:** wicked
[43] **foisons:** plentiful supply of wealth
[44] **portable:** bearable
[45] **verity:** truthfulness
[46] **temperance:** self-restraint
[47] **Bounty:** generosity
[48] **fortitude:** strength in the face of adversity
[49] **relish:** trace
[50] **concord:** peace
[51] **truest issue:** rightful heir
[52] **Oftener…her feet:** i.e. on her knees praying
[53] **Child of integrity:** born out of your good character
[54] **scruples:** reservations

By many of these trains[55] hath sought to win me
Into his power, and modest wisdom plucks me
From over-credulous haste:[56] but God above
Deal between thee and me! for even now
I put myself to thy direction, and
Unspeak mine own detraction, here abjure[57]
The taints and blames I laid upon myself,
For strangers to my nature. I am yet
Unknown to woman,[58] never was forsworn[59],
Scarcely have coveted[60] what was mine own,
At no time broke my faith, would not betray
The devil to his fellow and delight
No less in truth than life: my first false speaking
Was this upon myself. What I am truly
Is thine and my poor country's to command:
Whither indeed, before thy here-approach,
Old Siward, with ten thousand warlike men,
Already at a point[61], was setting forth.
Now we'll together; and the chance of goodness
Be like our warranted quarrel![62] Why are you silent?

[55] **trains:** tricks
[56] **modest wisdom…haste:** caution prevents me from believing people too quickly
[57] **abjure:** renounce
[58] **Unknown to woman:** a virgin
[59] **forsworn:** have lied
[60] **coveted:** desired enviously
[61] **at a point:** ready for battle
[62] **the chance…warranted quarrel:** Let the possibility of success be as likely as the justice of our cause.

Macduff
Such welcome and unwelcome things at once
'Tis hard to reconcile.
[Enter a DOCTOR]

Malcolm
Well, more anon. – Comes the King forth, I pray you?

Doctor
Ay, sir; there are a crew of wretched souls
That stay his cure:[63] their malady convinces
The great assay of art; but at his touch –
Such sanctity hath heaven given his hand –
They presently amend.

[63] **there are…his cure:** There are a group of suffering people who wait to be cured. King Edward (the Confessor) was said to be able to heal the sick.

Malcolm
I thank you, doctor.
[Exit DOCTOR]

Macduff
What's the disease he means?

Malcolm
'Tis called the evil:
A most miraculous work in this good king;
Which often, since my here-remain in England,
I have seen him do. How he solicits[64] heaven,

[64] **solicits:** gets helps from

Himself best knows: but strangely-visited people,
All swoln[65] and ulcerous, pitiful to the eye,
The mere despair of surgery[66], he cures,
Hanging a golden stamp about their necks,
Put on with holy prayers: and 'tis spoken,
To the succeeding royalty he leaves
The healing benediction[67]. With this strange virtue,
He hath a heavenly gift of prophecy,
And sundry blessings hang about his throne,
That speak him full of grace.
[Enter ROSS]

[65] **swoln:** swollen
[66] **despair of surgery:** those who cannot be cured by medicine
[67] **benediction:** blessing/power of healing

MACDUFF
See, who comes here?

MALCOLM
My countryman; but yet I know him not.

MACDUFF
My ever-gentle cousin, welcome hither.

MALCOLM
I know him now. Good God, betimes remove
The means that makes us strangers!

ROSS
Sir, amen.

MACDUFF
Stands Scotland where it did?

ROSS
Alas, poor country!
Almost afraid to know itself. It cannot
Be called our mother, but our grave; where nothing,
But who knows nothing, is once seen to smile;
Where sighs and groans and shrieks that rend[68] the air
Are made, not marked;[69] where violent sorrow seems
A modern ecstasy;[70] the dead man's knell
Is there scarce asked for who;[71] and good men's lives
Expire before the flowers in their caps,
Dying or ere they sicken.

[68] **rend:** tear apart
[69] **not marked:** unnoticed
[70] **modern ecstasy:** recent emotional state
[71] **the dead man's...for who:** Rarely does anybody ask who the funeral bell tolls for.

MACDUFF
O, relation
Too nice, and yet too true!

MALCOLM

What's the newest grief?

ROSS

That of an hour's age doth hiss the speaker:
Each minute teems a new one.[72]

MACDUFF

How does my wife?

ROSS

Why, well.

MACDUFF

And all my children?

ROSS

Well too.

MACDUFF

The tyrant has not battered at their peace?

ROSS

No; they were well at peace[73] when I did leave 'em.

MACDUFF

Be not a niggard of your speech:[74] how goes't?

ROSS

When I came hither to transport the tidings,
Which I have heavily borne, there ran a rumour
Of many worthy fellows that were out;[75]
Which was to my belief witnessed the rather,
For that I saw the tyrant's power a-foot:
Now is the time of help; your eye in Scotland[76]
Would create soldiers, make our women fight,
To doff their dire distresses.[77]

MALCOLM

Be't their comfort
We are coming thither. Gracious England hath
Lent us good Siward and ten thousand men;
An older and a better soldier none
That Christendom gives out.

ROSS

Would I could answer
This comfort with the like! But I have words

[72] **That of an hour's...new one:** Anybody who reports news an hour old will be hissed at, as each minute brings new suffering.

[73] **well at peace:** well and peaceful/ resting in peace, i.e. dead

[74] **Be not...speech:** Don't hold back in what you say.

[75] **fellows that were out:** men preparing for war

[76] **your eye in Scotland:** a sighting of you in Scotland

[77] **To doff...distresses:** to throw off their awful misery

That would be howled out in the desert air,
Where hearing should not latch[78] them.

Macduff

What concern they?
The general cause? or is it a fee-grief
Due to some single breast?[79]

Ross

No mind that's honest
But in it shares some woe; though the main part
Pertains to you alone.

Macduff

If it be mine,
Keep it not from me, quickly let me have it.

Ross

Let not your ears despise my tongue for ever,
Which shall possess them with the heaviest sound
That ever yet they heard.

Macduff

Hum! I guess at it.

Ross

Your castle is surprised; your wife and babes
Savagely slaughtered: to relate the manner,
Were, on the quarry of these murdered deer,
To add the death of you.[80]

Malcolm

Merciful heaven!
What, man! Ne'er pull your hat upon your brows;
Give sorrow words.[81] The grief that does not speak
Whispers the o'er-fraught heart and bids it break.[82]

Macduff

My children too?

Ross

Wife, children, servants, all
That could be found.

Macduff

And I must be from thence!
My wife killed too?

[78] **latch:** catch

[79] **is it a fee-grief...single breast?:** Is it the personal grief of one individual?

[80] **to relate...death of you:** To tell you the way in which they were murdered would be to add your body to the pile which looks like a heap of dead deer.

[81] **Ne'er pull...sorrow words:** Don't hide your grief, talk about your sorrow.

[82] **The grief...bids it break:** Unspoken grief overwhelms the heart and breaks it.

Ross

I have said.

Malcolm

Be comforted:
Let's make us medicines of our great revenge,
To cure this deadly grief.

Macduff

He has no children. All my pretty ones?
Did you say all? O hell-kite![83] All?
What, all my pretty chickens and their dam
At one fell swoop?

Malcolm

Dispute it like a man.

Macduff

I shall do so;
But I must also feel it as a man:[84]
I cannot but remember such things were,
That were most precious to me. Did heaven look on,
And would not take their part?[85] Sinful Macduff,
They were all struck for thee! Naught that I am,
Not for their own demerits[86], but for mine,
Fell slaughter on their souls. Heaven rest them now!

Malcolm

Be this the whetstone[87] of your sword: let grief
Convert to anger; blunt not the heart, enrage it.

Macduff

O, I could play the woman with mine eyes
And braggart[88] with my tongue! But, gentle heavens,
Cut short all intermission; front to front
Bring thou this fiend of Scotland and myself;
Within my sword's length set him; if he 'scape,
Heaven forgive him too!

Malcolm

This tune goes manly.
Come, go we to the King; our power is ready;
Our lack is nothing but our leave;[89] Macbeth
Is ripe for shaking, and the powers above
Put on their instruments.[90] Receive what cheer you may:
The night is long that never finds the day.[91]
[Exeunt]

83 **hell-kite!:** 'kite' as in bird of prey

84 **I must also feel it as a man:** There is an echo of Act I, Scene 7 in which Macbeth and Lady Macbeth discussed the idea of manliness.

85 **not take their part:** not defend them

86 **demerits:** faults

87 **whetstone:** sharpener

88 **braggart:** boaster

89 **Our lack...leave:** All we need do is leave.

90 **Put on their instruments:** arm themselves

91 **The night...the day:** It's a long night that doesn't end in dawn.

Key Quotations

MALCOLM *...all things foul would wear the brows of grace, / Yet grace must still look so.*

MALCOLM *The grief that does not speak / Whispers the o'er-fraught heart and bids it break.*

MACDUFF *Sinful Macduff,*
They were all struck for thee! Naught that I am,
Not for their own demerits, but for mine,
Fell slaughter on their souls.

Commentary

- In this scene, Malcolm displays himself as a prudent character in his testing of Macduff's loyalty. He recognises that both good and evil individuals may appear good: 'all things foul would wear the brows of grace, / Yet grace must still look so'. Malcolm reveals himself to be less trusting of those around him than Duncan was. Although a good king, Duncan was too trusting of both the former Thane of Cawdor and of Macbeth himself. In contrast, Malcolm is cautious of Macduff and slow to place his trust in him. It should be noted how transparent Malcolm's test of Macduff is and how Macduff lacks the insight to see through it.

- The scene comments on the idea of kingship. A highly complimentary image of the English King, Edward the Confessor, is provided. Edward is depicted as blessed with divine healing powers:

  'With this strange virtue,
  He hath a heavenly gift of prophecy,
  And sundry blessings hang about his throne,
  That speak him full of grace'

  This contrasts with the portrayal of Macbeth as an agent of hell whose actions, 'Strike heaven on the face'. Macduff clearly aligns Macbeth with hell: 'Not in the legions / Of horrid hell can come a devil more damned / In evils to top Macbeth'. Shakespeare is keen to reinforce the idea of the King as God's natural representative on earth. This is done by contrasting the divinely inspired Edward and the devilish Macbeth.

- Malcolm asks Macduff why he left his family so vulnerable to attack. The question is never answered. Some commentators feel that Macduff puts the good of Scotland above the security of his family and that this is a sign of his unwavering loyalty. Others see it as a character flaw. Macduff himself echoes this sentiment when he blames himself for their deaths: 'Sinful Macduff, / They were all struck for thee! Naught that I am, / Not for their own demerits, but for mine, / Fell slaughter on their souls.'

- The discussion of what it means to be a man is explored in this scene. When Macduff learns that his family have been murdered he is naturally upset. Malcolm encourages him to express his sorrow openly, arguing that unexpressed grief will destroy the heart: 'The grief that does not speak / Whispers the o'er-fraught heart and bids it break.' As Macduff weeps, Malcolm tells him to 'Dispute it like a man'. Macduff replies that he will, but he must also 'feel it as a man'. Macduff then expresses a typical 'manly' thirst for revenge and promises to kill Macbeth.

Malcolm's response is 'This tune goes manly'. Macduff embraces the idea of courageous and violent manliness but is also rounded enough to express his grief openly thus posing the question of what constitutes typical 'manly' behaviour.

Questions

1. *'Malcolm is wisely a much more suspicious character than his father.'* Do you agree with this statement? Explain your viewpoint by referring to this scene and to the character of Duncan.
2. Finding evidence from this scene, describe Scotland under Macbeth's rule.
3. (a) Describe the portrayal of King Edward in this scene. Use quotations in your response.
   (b) What do you think is the significance of this description?
4. What do we learn about Macduff from this scene?
5. What do you think this scene says about the issue of manliness?

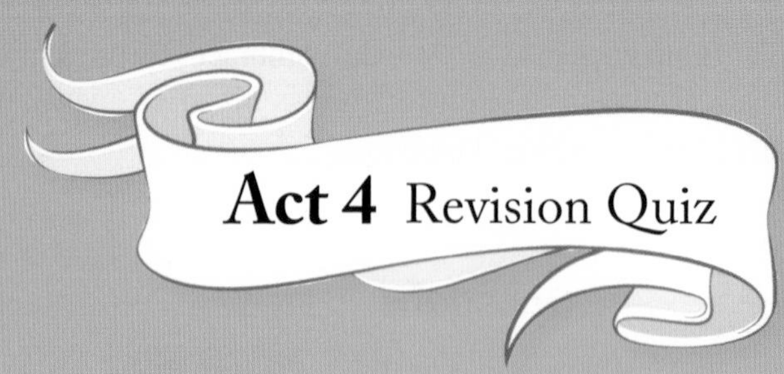

1. In Scene 1, what are the witches doing as Macbeth comes to meet them?

2. What do each of the three apparitions tell Macbeth?

3. After the three apparitions disappear, what vision is shown to Macbeth?

4. What prompts Macbeth to say 'The very firstlings of my heart shall be / The firstlings of my hand'.

5. Which members of Macduff's family do the audience see on stage just before they are murdered?

6. How does Malcolm test Macduff's loyalty?

7. What is the name of the English King?

8. What special power is the English King reported to have?

9. Who tells Macduff the awful news about his family?

10. Who says each of the following?:

(a) *'Double, double toil and trouble;*
Fire burn and cauldron bubble

(b) *'Whither should I fly?*
I have done no harm. But I remember now
I am in this earthly world; where to do harm
Is often laudable, to do good sometime
Accounted dangerous folly'

(c) *'Bring thou this fiend of Scotland and myself;*
Within my sword's length set him; if he 'scape,
Heaven forgive him too!'

Act 5 Scene 1

Scene Summary

- A doctor and a gentlewoman (lady-in-waiting) watch Lady Macbeth as she sleepwalks.
- In a dream, Lady Macbeth washes blood from her hands and relives the night Duncan was murdered.
- Lady Macbeth also mentions Banquo's death and the murder of Macduff's family.

Dunsinane. Macbeth's castle. Ante-room[1].
Enter a Doctor of Physic and a Waiting-Gentlewoman

DOCTOR
I have two nights watched with you, but can perceive no truth in your report. When was it she last walked?

GENTLEWOMAN
Since his Majesty went into the field,[2] I have seen her rise from her bed, throw her night-gown upon her, unlock her closet, take forth paper, fold it, write upon't, read it, afterwards seal it, and again return to bed; yet all this while in a most fast sleep.

DOCTOR
A great perturbation in nature,[3] to receive at once the benefit of sleep, and do the effects of watching! In this slumbery agitation,[4] besides her walking and other actual performances, what, at any time, have you heard her say?

GENTLEWOMAN
That, sir, which I will not report after her.

DOCTOR
You may to me, and 'tis most meet[5] you should.

GENTLEWOMAN
Neither to you nor any one; having no witness to confirm my speech.
[Enter LADY MACBETH, with a taper[6]]
Lo you, here she comes! This is her very guise;[7] and, upon my life, fast asleep. Observe her; stand close.

DOCTOR
How came she by that light?

1 **Ante-room:** a room leading to another room/a waiting room

2 **into the field:** into battle

3 **perturbation in nature:** disturbance in her being

4 **slumbery agitation:** activity while asleep

5 **most meet:** most fitting

6 **taper:** candle

7 **This is her very guise:** This is exactly how she behaves.

Gentlewoman
Why, it stood by her: she has light by her continually; 'tis her command.

Doctor
You see, her eyes are open.

Gentlewoman
Ay, but their sense is shut.[8]

Doctor
What is it she does now? Look, how she rubs her hands.

Gentlewoman
It is an accustomed action with her, to seem thus washing her hands. I have known her continue in this a quarter of an hour.

Lady Macbeth
Yet here's a spot.

Doctor
Hark! she speaks. I will set down what comes from her, to satisfy my remembrance the more strongly.

Lady Macbeth
Out, damned spot! out, I say! – One: two: why, then, 'tis time to do't. – Hell is murky! – Fie,[9] my lord, fie! A soldier, and afeard? What need we fear who knows it, when none can call our power to account? – Yet who would have thought the old man to have had so much blood in him.

Doctor
Do you mark[10] that?

Lady Macbeth
The Thane of Fife had a wife: where is she now? – What, will these hands ne'er be clean? – No more o' that, my lord, no more o' that: you mar all with this starting.[11]

Doctor
Go to, go to; you have known what you should not.

Gentlewoman
She has spoke what she should not, I am sure of that: heaven knows what she has known.

[8] **their sense is shut:** She can't actually see with them (her eyes).

[9] **Fie:** For shame

[10] **mark:** hear

[11] **you mar all with this starting:** You spoil everything with this jumpiness.

Lady Macbeth
Here's the smell of the blood still: all the perfumes of Arabia will not sweeten this little hand. Oh, oh, oh!

Doctor
What a sigh is there! The heart is sorely charged.[12]

Gentlewoman
I would not have such a heart in my bosom for the dignity of the whole body.

Doctor
Well, well, well –

Gentlewoman
Pray God it be, sir.

Doctor
This disease is beyond my practice:[13] yet I have known those which have walked in their sleep who have died holily[14] in their beds.

Lady Macbeth
Wash your hands, put on your nightgown; look not so pale. – I tell you yet again, Banquo's buried; he cannot come out on's grave.

Doctor
Even so?

Lady Macbeth
To bed, to bed! There's knocking at the gate: come, come, come, come, give me your hand. What's done cannot be undone. – To bed, to bed, to bed!
[Exit]

Doctor
Will she go now to bed?

Gentlewoman
Directly.

Doctor
Foul whisperings are abroad. Unnatural deeds
Do breed unnatural troubles; infected minds
To their deaf pillows will discharge their secrets.
More needs she the divine than the physician.[15]

12 **sorely charged:** is burdened (with guilt)

13 **my practice:** my medical knowledge

14 **died holily:** i.e. died without any evil deeds on their conscience

15 **More needs...the physician:** She requires help from a priest or God, more than a doctor.

God, God forgive us all! Look after her;
Remove from her the means of all annoyance,[16]
And still keep eyes upon her. So, good night:
My mind she has mated,[17] and amazed my sight.
I think, but dare not speak.

[16] **Remove...all annoyance:** Take away anything with which she could harm herself.
[17] **mated:** confused

GENTLEWOMAN
Good night, good doctor.
[Exeunt]

Key Quotations

LADY MACBETH *Out, damned spot!*

LADY MACBETH *Here's the smell of the blood still: all the / perfumes of Arabia will not sweeten this little / hand.*

DOCTOR *Unnatural deeds / Do breed unnatural troubles; infected minds / To their deaf pillows will discharge their secrets*

Commentary

- This scene provides an intimate vision of Lady Macbeth sleepwalking. Like the doctor and the gentlewoman, the audience watches with horror as she reveals her guilt for the crimes she has committed with Macbeth.

- In Acts 1 and 2, Lady Macbeth seemed able to deal with the consequences of her actions. It was she who chided Macbeth for his inability to put the murders behind him and coldly announced, 'A little water clears us of this deed.' However, in Act 3 Lady Macbeth signals that the role of Queen has brought her no contentment: ''Tis safer to be that which we destroy / Than by destruction dwell in doubtful joy.' The sleepwalking scene develops this idea and illustrates the heavy burden of guilt that Lady Macbeth carries. She keeps a light by her side continually as a source of comfort; this suggests a traumatised mind. Shakespeare cleverly uses the device of sleepwalking to reveal her inner torment as it provides unrestrained access to her thoughts and feelings. Through her sleepwalking, Lady Macbeth illustrates her great unhappiness and fraying mental state. Her earlier statement: 'These deeds must not be thought / After these ways; so, it will make us mad,' (Act 2, Scene 2) now seems remarkably prophetic.

- The burden of guilt that Lady Macbeth carries is dramatically shown here. She is seen washing her hands, attempting to cleanse herself of the memory of Duncan's murder: 'Out, damned spot!... who would have thought the old man / to have had so much blood in him.' However, her efforts are in vain as the imagined smell of blood remains: 'Here's the smell of the blood still: all the / perfumes of Arabia will not sweeten this little / hand.' Lady Macbeth realises the role she played in encouraging Macbeth to murder Duncan; she now bears the guilt for the evil Macbeth has unleashed on Scotland.

Questions

1. How does Shakespeare reveal Lady Macbeth's guilt in this scene? Refer to the text in your answer.
2. Contrast how Lady Macbeth and Macbeth deal with their guilt within the play.
3. Why do you think the doctor in this scene advises the gentlewoman to *'Remove from her the means of all annoyance'*?
4. Where else in *Macbeth* does the idea of sleeplessness arise?
5. At the start of this scene, the gentlewoman refers to how Lady Macbeth has been seen writing and sealing a letter in her sleep. Write down what you imagine is contained in this letter.

Act 5 Scene 2

Scene Summary

- The thanes meet and approach Macbeth's castle at Dunsinane.
- They discuss the strength of their troops and how Macbeth's control over his own forces is wavering.

The countryside near Dunsinane.
Drum and colours[1]. Enter MENTEITH, CAITHNESS, ANGUS, LENNOX, and Soldiers

Menteith
The English power is near, led on by Malcolm,
His uncle Siward and the good Macduff.
Revenges burn in them; for their dear causes
Would to the bleeding and the grim alarm
Excite the mortified man.[2]

Angus
Near Birnam wood
Shall we well meet them; that way are they coming.

Caithness
Who knows if Donalbain be with his brother?

Lennox
For certain, sir, he is not: I have a file
Of all the gentry: there is Siward's son,
And many unrough youths[3] that even now
Protest their first of manhood.[4]

Menteith
What does the tyrant?

Caithness
Great Dunsinane he strongly fortifies:
Some say he's mad; others that lesser hate him
Do call it valiant fury;[5] but, for certain,
He cannot buckle his distempered cause
Within the belt of rule.[6]

Angus
Now does he feel
His secret murders sticking on his hands;
Now minutely revolts upbraid his faith-breach;[7]

1 **colours:** banners displaying each thane's colours and crest

2 **for their dear causes...mortified man:** Their noble reason for rebellion would inspire even a dead man to answer their bloody call to battle.

3 **unrough youths:** boys that don't shave yet

4 **Protest their first of manhood:** announce for the first time that they are men

5 **valiant fury:** mad courage

6 **He cannot buckle...of rule:** He cannot control his diseased mind/he cannot keep order in his kingdom.

7 **Now minutely...faith-breach:** Every minute a revolt erupts to reproach him for his disloyalty (to Duncan).

Those he commands move only in command,
Nothing in love:[8] now does he feel his title
Hang loose about him, like a giant's robe
Upon a dwarfish thief.[9]

Menteith

Who then shall blame
His pestered senses to recoil and start,
When all that is within him does condemn
Itself for being there?[10]

Caithness

Well, march we on,
To give obedience where 'tis truly owed:
Meet we the medicine of the sickly weal,
And with him pour we in our country's purge
Each drop of us.[11]

Lennox

Or so much as it needs,
To dew the sovereign flower and drown the weeds.[12]
Make we our march towards Birnam.
[Exeunt, marching]

8 **Those he...in love:** His soldiers only obey him because they are commanded to, not because they are loyal.

9 **now does he feel...dwarfish thief:** Now he feels he can't live up to the title of King, like a dwarf who has stolen the robe of a giant only to find it doesn't fit him.

10 **Who then...being there?:** Who can blame Macbeth's worried nerves for being jumpy when Macbeth condemns himself?

11 **Meet we ...drop of us:** Let us meet with the cure (Malcolm) to this diseased sore (Macbeth) and use our blood to cleanse Scotland.

12 **Or so much ... drown the weeds:** Or as much blood as is required to nourish the flower of kingship (Malcolm) and kill the weeds (Macbeth).

Key Quotations

Caithness *He cannot buckle his distempered cause / Within the belt of rule.*

Angus *now does he feel his title / Hang loose about him, like a giant's robe / Upon a dwarfish thief.*

Mentieth *...all that is within him does condemn / Itself for being there.*

Caithness *Meet we the medicine of the sickly weal, / And with him pour we in our country's purge / Each drop of us.*

Commentary

- This short scene displays how the thanes have collectively turned against Macbeth and pledged their support to Malcolm. They are selflessly willing to sacrifice themselves for the good of Scotland: 'Meet we the medicine of the sickly weal, / And with him pour we in our country's purge / Each drop of us.' Their motivations seem far removed from the self-serving actions of Macbeth.

- Macbeth's cruel reign and 'secret murders' have inspired little support and as a result his troops obey him simply because they are commanded to: 'Those he commands move only in command, / Nothing in love.' Macbeth fails to earn the love and respect a rightful king would inspire. Angus pictures him as a thief swamped by the robes of power and he states that Macbeth now realises he is unfit to be King: 'now does he feel his title / Hang loose about him, like a giant's robe / Upon a dwarfish thief.'

- The thanes discuss Macbeth's motivation for holding out against his enemies: 'Some say he's mad; others that lesser hate him / Do call it valiant fury.' They recognise that Macbeth is a conflicted and flawed individual: 'all that is within him does condemn / Itself for being there.'

Questions

1. What evidence is there in this scene that Macbeth's control over Scotland and his own troops is slipping?

2. Would you agree that the thanes express great loyalty to Malcolm in this scene? Explain your viewpoint by referring to the text.

3. (a) Shakespeare uses clothing imagery, a medical image and an image of natural fertility in this scene. Write down each.

(b) Rewrite each of these images in your own words using modern English.

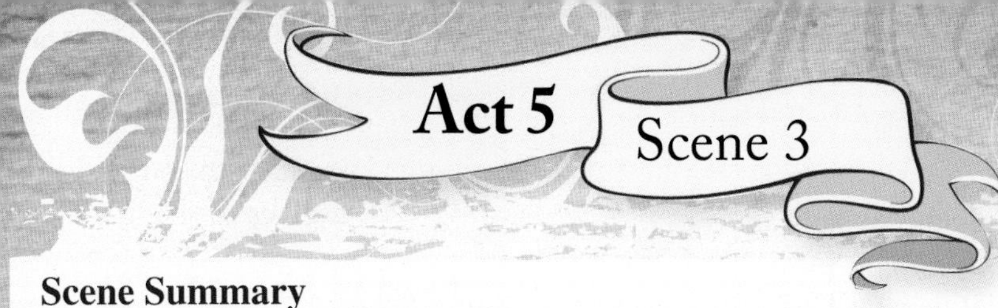

Act 5 Scene 3

Scene Summary

- Macbeth prepares for battle. He learns that the thanes and the English forces are gathering against him.
- Macbeth says he is unafraid because of the witches' prophecies.
- Seyton, Macbeth's lieutenant, helps Macbeth with his armour.
- The doctor informs Macbeth that Lady Macbeth is mentally unwell.

Dunsinane. A room in Macbeth's castle.
Enter MACBETH, Doctor, and Attendants

Macbeth
Bring me no more reports; let them fly all:[1]
Till Birnam wood remove to Dunsinane,
I cannot taint[2] with fear. What's the boy Malcolm?
Was he not born of woman? The spirits that know
All mortal consequences have pronounced me thus:
'Fear not, Macbeth; no man that's born of woman
Shall e'er have power upon thee.' Then fly, false thanes,
And mingle with the English epicures:[3]
The mind I sway by[4] and the heart I bear
Shall never sag with doubt nor shake with fear.
[Enter a Servant]
The devil damn thee black, thou cream-faced loon![5]
Where got'st thou that goose look?

Servant
There is ten thousand –

Macbeth
Geese, villain!

Servant
Soldiers, sir.

Macbeth
Go prick thy face,[6] and over-red thy fear,
Thou lily-livered[7] boy. What soldiers, patch?[8]
Death of thy soul! Those linen cheeks of thine
Are counsellors to fear. What soldiers, whey-face?[9]

Servant
The English force, so please you.

1 **fly all:** all desert me

2 **taint:** weaken

3 **English epicures:** soft/spoilt English

4 **sway by:** rule with

5 **cream-faced loon:** white-faced fool (the servant is pale with fear)

6 **Go prick thy face:** Go pinch your cheeks (to redden them)
7 **lily-livered:** cowardly
8 **patch:** clown
9 **whey-face:** white face

MACBETH
Take thy face hence.
[Exit Servant]
Seyton! – I am sick at heart,
When I behold – Seyton, I say! – This push
Will cheer me ever, or disseat me now.[10]
I have lived long enough: my way of life
Is fall'n into the sear,[11] the yellow leaf;
And that which should accompany old age,
As honour, love, obedience, troops of friends,
I must not look to have; but, in their stead,[12]
Curses, not loud but deep, mouth-honour,[13] breath,
Which the poor heart would fain deny, and dare not.[14] Seyton!
[Enter SEYTON]

SEYTON
What is your gracious pleasure?

MACBETH
What news more?

SEYTON
All is confirmed, my lord, which was reported.

MACBETH
I'll fight, till from my bones my flesh be hacked.
Give me my armour.

SEYTON
'Tis not needed yet.

MACBETH
I'll put it on.
Send out more horses; skirr[15] the country round;
Hang those that talk of fear. Give me mine armour. –
How does your patient,[16] doctor?

DOCTOR
Not so sick, my lord,
As she is troubled with thick coming fancies,[17]
That keep her from her rest.

MACBETH
Cure her of that.
Canst thou not minister to a mind diseased,
Pluck from the memory a rooted sorrow,
Raze[18] out the written troubles of the brain
And with some sweet oblivious antidote[19]

[10] **This push...me now:** This military attack will give me confidence or dethrone me.

[11] **fall'n into the sear:** withered

[12] **in their stead:** in their place

[13] **mouth-honour:** false praise

[14] **breath / Which...dare not:** words which the speaker would like to deny but doesn't dare

[15] **skirr:** scour/search

[16] **your patient:** i.e. Lady Macbeth

[17] **thick coming fancies:** persistent delusions

[18] **Raze:** erase

[19] **oblivious antidote:** medicine that will make her forget

Cleanse the stuffed bosom of that perilous stuff
Which weighs upon the heart?[20]

Doctor

Therein the patient
Must minister to himself.[21]

Macbeth

Throw physic[22] to the dogs; I'll none of it. –
Come, put mine armour on; give me my staff.
Seyton, send out. – Doctor, the thanes fly from me. –
Come, sir, dispatch. If thou couldst, doctor, cast
The water of my land,[23] find her disease,
And purge it to a sound and pristine health,[24]
I would applaud thee to the very echo,
That should applaud again. – Pull't off, I say. –
What rhubarb, senna or what purgative drug,[25]
Would scour these English hence? Hear'st thou of them?

Doctor

Ay, my good lord; your royal preparation
Makes us hear something.

Macbeth

Bring it after me. –
I will not be afraid of death and bane,[26]
Till Birnam Forest come to Dunsinane.
[Exeunt all but the Doctor]

Doctor

Were I from Dunsinane away and clear,
Profit again should hardly draw me here.
[Exit]

[20] **Cleanse...the heart:** Clean the burdened heart of those dangerous thoughts which weigh upon it.

[21] **Therein...to himself:** This is something that only the patient can cure.

[22] **physic:** medicine

[23] **cast/the water of my land:** analyse the urine of (i.e. to diagnose)

[24] **And purge...health:** Cleanse it so that it's healthy.

[25] **rhubarb, senna or ...purgative drug:** laxatives

[26] **bane:** destruction

Key Quotations

Macbeth *I have lived long enough: my way of life*
Is fall'n into the sear, the yellow leaf;
And that which should accompany old age,
As honour, love, obedience, troops of friends,
I must not look to have; but, in their stead,
Curses, not loud but deep, mouth-honour, breath,
Which the poor heart would fain deny, and dare not.

Macbeth *I'll fight, till from my bones my flesh be hacked.*

Commentary

- Macbeth is overconfident and aggressive for much of this scene. He brashly disregards the reports of his enemies' whereabouts and refers to the witches' prophecies as the source of his self-belief:

  'Bring me no more reports; let them fly all:
  Till Birnam wood remove to Dunsinane,
  I cannot taint with fear. What's the boy Malcolm?
  Was he not born of woman?'

  He shows his resolve to fight to the end: 'I'll fight, till from my bones my flesh be hacked.'

- Macbeth places great emphasis on bravery in battle and prides himself on being a courageous soldier. This leads him to cruelly rebuke the fearful looking servant, describing him as a 'cream-faced loon' and 'lily-livered'. Macbeth later decrees, 'Hang those that talk of fear.'

- However, Macbeth is mercurial (changeable) in this scene and soon lapses into a melancholic meditation on life. With a note of resignation he says, 'I have lived long enough: my way of life / Is fall'n into the sear'. Macbeth is now world-weary and recognises the meaningless lip service paid to him ('mouth-honour'), not out of respect, but out of fear: 'breath, / Which the poor heart would fain deny, and dare not'. Macbeth is coming to understand the emptiness of his own ambition. This mounting recognition helps to earns the audience's sympathy.

- Macbeth realises that he is a soldier, not a ruler. This is conveyed by his eagerness to discard his kingly robes and put on armour. He calls out for his battledress with great urgency and ignores Seyton's protest that it is not needed yet: 'Come, put mine armour on.'

Questions

1. (a) Describe Macbeth's attitude to the pending attack of the English and Scottish thanes.
   (b) What has inspired this attitude?
2. Do you think Macbeth is sympathetic or unsympathetic to Lady Macbeth in this scene? Explain your answer by referring to the text.
3. Which word do you feel best describes Macbeth in this scene: *brave, reckless, desperate* or *hopeless*? Refer to the scene in your answer.
4. Explain the significance of Macbeth exchanging his kingly robes for armour.
5. How is Macbeth growing in wisdom in this scene?
6. What does the doctor mean in the final two lines of this scene?

Act 5 Scene 4

Scene Summary

- The thanes arrive at Birnam Wood.
- Malcolm instructs the soldiers to cut down branches from the trees. They are told to carry them as they march in order to conceal their numbers.

Countryside near Birnam Wood.
Drum and colours. Enter MALCOLM, SIWARD and YOUNG SIWARD, MACDUFF, MENTEITH, CAITHNESS, ANGUS, LENNOX, ROSS, and Soldiers, marching

MALCOLM
Cousins, I hope the days are near at hand
That chambers[1] will be safe.

MENTEITH
We doubt it nothing.

SIWARD
What wood is this before us?

MENTEITH
The wood of Birnam.

MALCOLM
Let every soldier hew him down a bough[2]
And bear't before him: thereby shall we shadow
The numbers of our host and make discovery
Err in report of us.[3]

SOLDIERS
It shall be done.

SIWARD
We learn no other but the confident tyrant
Keeps still in Dunsinane, and will endure
Our setting down before 't.[4]

MALCOLM
'Tis his main hope:
For where there is advantage to be given,
Both more and less have given him the revolt,[5]
And none serve with him but constrained things
Whose hearts are absent too.[6]

1 **chambers:** bedrooms

2 **hew...bough:** cut down a branch

3 **thereby shall we...report of us:** By doing so we will disguise how many of us there are and scouts will give incorrect reports of our number.

4 **will endure...before't:** is willing to resist our siege of the castle

5 **more and less...revolt:** Nobles and common men have deserted him.

6 **And none serve...absent too:** and the only people to serve him are forced to do so, but their hearts aren't in it

Macduff

Let our just censures
Attend the true event, and put we on
Industrious soldiership.[7]

Siward

The time approaches
That will with due decision make us know
What we shall say we have and what we owe.[8]
Thoughts speculative their unsure hopes relate,
But certain issue strokes must arbitrate:[9]
Towards which advance the war.
[Exeunt, marching]

7 **Let our just...soldiership:** We'll know the truth of that after the event (i.e. the battle). Let's conduct ourselves like hardworking soldiers.

8 **owe:** possess

9 **Thoughts speculative...arbitrate:** We can speculate that they (Macbeth's army) don't have a chance but the battle will decide the outcome.

Commentary

- The order for every soldier to 'hew him down a bough' effectively shows the audience how Macbeth's faith in the witches' prophecies is misplaced. We realise that Birnam Wood is literally about to move to Dunsinane Hill.
- The thanes seem optimistic about their prospects in the battle, but Shakespeare is keen to stress their caution: 'Let our just censures / Attend the true event.' This serves as a counterpoint to Macbeth's overconfidence and arrogance. It also shows that the thanes are aware that Macbeth is a formidable soldier.
- Although this scene is short, it allows Shakespeare to build the tension between the two opposing forces. The audience now wait expectantly for the ultimate battle between Macbeth and Macduff.

Questions

1. Which of the witches' prophecies does this scene relate to?
2. If you were directing this play, how would you stage the moment when the soldiers cut down branches from Birnam Wood?
3. What do you think is the dramatic purpose of this scene?

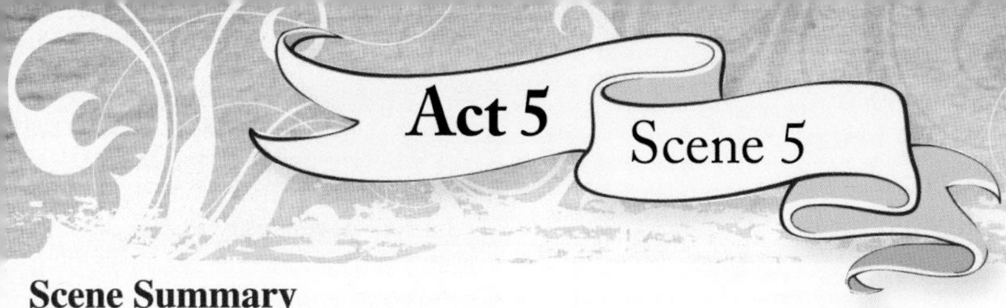

Act 5 Scene 5

Scene Summary

- While Macbeth is giving orders, he hears women crying.
- He asks what the noise is and reflects on how he has forgotten the experience of fear.
- Macbeth learns that Lady Macbeth is dead. Macbeth's reaction is strangely detached.
- A messenger tells Macbeth that Birnam Wood is moving.
- Macbeth now suspects the witches' prophecies are misleading.
- He resolves to die fighting.

Dunsinane. Within Macbeth's castle.
Enter MACBETH, SEYTON and Soldiers, with drum and colours

MACBETH
Hang out our banners on the outward walls;
The cry is still 'They come'. Our castle's strength
Will laugh a siege to scorn.[1] Here let them lie
Till famine and the ague[2] eat them up.
Were they not forced with those that should be ours,[3]
We might have met them dareful,[4] beard to beard,
And beat them backward home.
[A cry of women within]
What is that noise?

SEYTON
It is the cry of women, my good lord.
[Exit]

MACBETH
I have almost forgot the taste of fears.
The time has been, my senses would have cooled
To hear a night-shriek, and my fell of hair[5]
Would at a dismal treatise[6] rouse and stir
As life were in't. I have supped full with horrors;[7]
Direness, familiar to my slaughterous thoughts
Cannot once start me.[8]
[Re-enter SEYTON]
Wherefore was that cry?

SEYTON
The Queen, my lord, is dead.

MACBETH
She should have died hereafter;[9]
There would have been a time for such a word.[10]

1 **Our castle's strength...to scorn:** The strength of our castle will mock their siege.
2 **ague:** fever
3 **Were they...ours:** Were the enemy's ranks not reinforced with our soldiers (i.e. deserters)
4 **dareful:** in a daring/brave manner

5 **my fell of hair:** hair on my skin
6 **dismal treatise:** terrifying story
7 **I have supped full with horrors:** I have drunk my fill of horror.

8 **Cannot once start me:** cannot shock me as it once did

9 **She should have died hereafter:** She should have died later OR she would have died sometime.
10 **There would...such a word:** There would have been a better time for this/ This news is inevitable.

Tomorrow, and tomorrow, and tomorrow,
Creeps in this petty pace from day to day[11]
To the last syllable of recorded time,
And all our yesterdays have lighted fools
The way to dusty death.[12] Out, out, brief candle!
Life's but a walking shadow, a poor player[13]
That struts and frets[14] his hour upon the stage
And then is heard no more. It is a tale
Told by an idiot, full of sound and fury,
Signifying nothing.
[Enter a MESSENGER]
Thou comest to use thy tongue; thy story quickly.

MESSENGER
Gracious my lord,
I should report that which I say I saw,
But know not how to do it.

MACBETH
Well, say, sir.

MESSENGER
As I did stand my watch upon the hill,
I looked toward Birnam, and anon, methought,
The wood began to move.

MACBETH
Liar and slave!

MESSENGER
Let me endure your wrath, if't be not so.
Within this three mile may you see it coming;
I say, a moving grove.

MACBETH
If thou speak'st false,
Upon the next tree shalt thou hang alive,
Till famine cling thee.[15] If thy speech be sooth,[16]
I care not if thou dost for me as much.
I pull in resolution,[17] and begin
To doubt the equivocation of the fiend
That lies like truth: 'Fear not, till Birnam Wood
Do come to Dunsinane'; and now a wood
Comes toward Dunsinane. Arm, arm, and out!
If this which he avouches[18] does appear,
There is nor flying hence nor tarrying[19] here.
I 'gin to be aweary of the sun,[20]
And wish the estate o' the world were now undone.[21]

[11] **Creeps in...day to day:** Time crawls slowly, one day after the next.

[12] **And all our...dusty death:** All of our time has just been a candle lighting the path towards the grave.

[13] **poor player:** bad/unfortunate actor

[14] **struts and frets:** parades and causes commotion

[15] **Till famine cling thee:** until you starve and wither

[16] **sooth:** truth

[17] **I pull in resolution:** I feel less confident now.

[18] **avouches:** swears is true

[19] **tarrying:** waiting

[20] **I 'gin...the sun:** I am growing tired of the sun.

[21] **And wish...undone:** And wish that the whole world would collapse

Ring the alarum-bell! Blow, wind! Come, wrack![22]
At least we'll die with harness[23] on our back.
[Exeunt]

[22] **wrack:** wreck/destroy
[23] **harness:** armour

Key Quotations

MACBETH *I have almost forgot the taste of fears.*

MACBETH *I have supped full with horrors;/ Direness, familiar to my slaughterous thoughts / Cannot once start me.*

MACBETH *Tomorrow, and tomorrow, and tomorrow,*
Creeps in this petty pace from day to day
To the last syllable of recorded time,
And all our yesterdays have lighted fools
The way to dusty death. Out, out, brief candle!
Life's but a walking shadow, a poor player
That struts and frets his hour upon the stage
And then is heard no more. It is a tale
Told by an idiot, full of sound and fury,
Signifying nothing.

MACBETH *I pull in resolution, and begin / To doubt the equivocation of the fiend / That lies like truth*

MACBETH *I 'gin to be aweary of the sun,*
And wish the estate o' the world were now undone.
Ring the alarum-bell! Blow, wind! Come, wrack!
At least we'll die with harness on our back.

Commentary

- At the start of this scene Macbeth is blindly confident of victory: 'Our castle's strength / Will laugh a siege to scorn. Here let them lie / Till famine and the ague eat them up.' This self-assurance stems from his faith in the apparitions' prophecies.

- When Macbeth hears the horrified crying of women, he realises that he has 'almost forgot the taste of fears.' Macbeth's horrendous deeds have hardened him to the point where he can barely remember the fears and doubts he experienced in the earlier part of the play: 'I have supped full with horrors; / Direness, familiar to my slaughterous thoughts / Cannot once start me.' At this point, Macbeth realises that his engagement with evil has almost destroyed his ability to feel normal human emotions.

- Lady Macbeth's death brings Macbeth's growing awareness into focus. His strangely detached reaction to the news of her death, 'She should have died hereafter', reveals his mounting despair. Macbeth is now devoid of hope and accepts the inevitability of death.

- Macbeth is prompted into a melancholic reflection on the meaninglessness of existence. He sees life as a futile succession of days, inevitably leading towards death: 'Tomorrow, and tomorrow, and tomorrow, / Creeps in this petty pace from day to day… And all our yesterdays have lighted fools / The way to dusty death.'

- The image of a candle being snuffed out signals Macbeth's disillusionment with life and reveals a soul tortured to the point where all meaning and purpose have been extinguished:

  'Out, out, brief candle!
  Life's but a walking shadow, a poor player
  That struts and frets his hour upon the stage
  And then is heard no more. It is a tale
  Told by an idiot, full of sound and fury,
  Signifying nothing'.

  The image of the 'poor player' strutting and fretting upon the stage, encapsulates Macbeth's disillusionment with human effort and ambitious striving. He now comes to accept that life is short, death is inevitable and human ambition is meaningless.

- The news that Birnam Wood is moving causes Macbeth to suspect the equivocal nature of the witches' prophecies: 'I pull in resolution, and begin / To doubt the equivocation of the fiend / That lies like truth.' As this realisation grows, his confidence shrinks.

- By the end of the scene Macbeth is resolved to die fighting. Although he now sees death as inevitable, he is determined to meet it as a soldier: 'Blow, wind! Come, wrack! / At least we'll die with harness on our back.' His pride in himself as a soldier and a man remains.

Questions

1. After seeing Banquo's ghost (Act 3, Scene 4), Macbeth proclaimed, *'My strange and self-abuse / Is the initiate fear that wants hard use/ We are yet but young in deed'.* What evidence from Act 5, Scene 5 shows that this is no longer the case?
2. How does Macbeth react to the news that Lady Macbeth has died?
3. Lady Macbeth's death happens offstage. From what you learned in the sleepwalking scene (Act 5, Scene 1), how do you think she died? Explain your answer.
4. Using quotations, describe Macbeth's outlook on life in this scene.
5. Rewrite Macbeth's *'Tomorrow, and tomorrow, and tomorrow'* soliloquy in modern English.
6. What is Macbeth's reaction to the news that Birnam Wood is moving?

Act 5 Scene 6

Scene Summary

- Malcolm gives instructions for the attack on Macbeth's castle.

Dunsinane. Before Macbeth's castle.
Drum and colours. Enter MALCOLM, SIWARD, MACDUFF, and their Army, with boughs

MALCOLM
Now near enough; your leafy screens[1] throw down,
And show like those you are. You, worthy uncle,
Shall, with my cousin, your right-noble son,
Lead our first battle.[2] Worthy Macduff and we
Shall take upon's what else remains to do,
According to our order.[3]

SIWARD
Fare you well.
Do we but find the tyrant's power to-night,
Let us be beaten, if we cannot fight.

MACDUFF
Make all our trumpets speak; give them all breath,
Those clamorous harbingers[4] of blood and death.
[Exeunt]

1 **leafy screens:** the branches from Birnam Wood

2 **first battle:** the main army

3 **order:** military strategy

4 **clamorous harbingers:** noisy announcers

Questions

1. How is Malcolm portrayed in this scene?
2. Do you agree that Macbeth's enemies appear confident in this scene? Explain your answer.
3. Imagine you are Macbeth watching the soldiers throw their 'leafy screens' down. Write your thoughts.

Act 5 Scene 7

Scene Summary

- Macbeth kills Young Siward.
- Malcolm's forces enter Macbeth's castle.
- Macduff continues his hunt for Macbeth.

Another part of the Field.
Alarums. Enter MACBETH

MACBETH
They have tied me to a stake; I cannot fly,
But, bear-like,[1] I must fight the course. What's he
That was not born of woman? Such a one
Am I to fear, or none.
[Enter YOUNG SIWARD]

YOUNG SIWARD
What is thy name?

MACBETH
Thou'lt be afraid to hear it.

YOUNG SIWARD
No; though thou call'st thyself a hotter name
Than any is in hell.

MACBETH
My name's Macbeth.

YOUNG SIWARD
The devil himself could not pronounce a title
More hateful to mine ear.

MACBETH
No, nor more fearful.

YOUNG SIWARD
Thou liest, abhorred[2] tyrant; with my sword
I'll prove the lie thou speak'st.

[They fight and YOUNG SIWARD is slain]

[1] **bear-like:** a reference to bear-baiting. This was the practice of tying a bear to a stake and then setting dogs upon it.

[2] **abhorred:** hated

Macbeth

Thou wast born of woman
But swords I smile at, weapons laugh to scorn,
Brandished[3] by man that's of a woman born.
[Exit]
[Alarums. Enter MACDUFF]

Macduff

That way the noise is. Tyrant, show thy face!
If thou be'st slain and with no stroke of mine,[4]
My wife and children's ghosts will haunt me still.
I cannot strike at wretched kerns,[5] whose arms
Are hired to bear their staves. Either thou, Macbeth,
Or else my sword with an unbattered edge
I sheathe again undeeded.[6] *[Alarums]* There thou shouldst be;
By this great clatter, one of greatest note
Seems bruited.[7] Let me find him, Fortune!
And more I beg not.
[Exit. Alarums]
[Enter MALCOLM and SIWARD]

Siward

This way, my lord – the castle's gently rendered.[8]
The tyrant's people on both sides do fight;
The noble thanes do bravely in the war;
The day almost itself professes yours,[9]
And little is to do.

Malcolm

We have met with foes
That strike beside us.[10]

Siward

Enter, sir, the castle.
[Exeunt. Alarums]

3 **Brandished:** waved (a weapon)

4 **If thou...of mine:** If you have been killed, and not by my sword

5 **kerns:** hired Irish soldiers

6 **Or else...undeeded:** or else my undamaged sword will be replaced in its sheath unused

7 **By this great...bruited:** By all this noise it seems that someone of importance must be here.

8 **rendered:** surrendered

9 **The day almost itself professes yours:** You have very nearly won the day.

10 **foes/That strike beside us:** enemies who fight with us (i.e. deserters from Macbeth's army)

Key Quotations

Macbeth *They have tied me to a stake; I cannot fly, / But, bear-like, I must fight the course.*

Commentary

- Macbeth recognises he is doomed as his enemies hem him in. He depicts himself as a bear set upon by dogs: 'They have tied me to a stake; I cannot fly, / But, bear-like, I must fight the course.' Macbeth sees himself as strong (like a bear), but also trapped. Just as a baited bear is worn down and eventually killed by dogs, Macbeth understands that his own death is imminent. Despite this realisation and his mounting desperation, Macbeth is still determined to fight to the end. Macbeth's helplessness in this moment awakens the audience's sympathy. We pity the strong bear set upon by lesser dogs.

- Although Macbeth knows he was misled by the witches' prophecy about Birnam Wood, he still takes some comfort in their other prediction: 'What's he / That was not born of woman? Such a one / Am I to fear, or none.' This confidence is bolstered after he kills Young Siward, 'Thou wast born of woman / But swords I smile at, weapons laugh to scorn, / Brandished by man that's of a woman born.' Although his ambition to be King has now deserted him, he still prides himself on his strength and skill in battle.

- Macduff is portrayed as a vengeful character as he furiously searches the castle for Macbeth: 'Tyrant, show thy face! / If thou be'st slain and with no stroke of mine, / My wife and children's ghosts will haunt me still.'

- The scene ends with a foreshadowing of the unity Malcolm will bring to Scotland. Macbeth's army has largely deserted him and now fights under Malcolm's banner: 'We have met with foes / That strike beside us.' Shakespeare is keen to reinforce the notion of Malcolm as a goodly king who will heal Scotland's wounds. The pitiful image of Macbeth isolated and alone is also reinforced here.

Questions

1. Even though Macbeth's army is deserting him and his castle is being stormed, he is still determined to fight on. Why do you think this is?
2. Increasingly throughout the play Macbeth is associated with hell and the devil. Find examples of this in this scene.
3. Describe Macduff's attitude in this scene.
4. Rewrite Macbeth's final lines in this scene using modern English: 'But swords I smile at, weapons laugh to scorn, / Brandished by man that's of a woman born.'

Act 5 Scene 8

Scene Summary

- Macduff confronts Macbeth.
- Macbeth tells Macduff that he cannot be harmed by any man born of woman.
- Macduff reveals that he was delivered by caesarean section.
- Macbeth fights him regardless and is killed.

Another part of the Field.
Enter MACBETH

MACBETH
Why should I play the Roman fool,[1] and die
On mine own sword? Whiles I see lives,[2] the gashes
Do better upon them!
[Enter MACDUFF]

MACDUFF
Turn, hell-hound, Turn!

MACBETH
Of all men else I have avoided thee. –
But get thee back; my soul is too much charged[3]
With blood of thine already.

MACDUFF
I have no words:
My voice is in my sword – thou bloodier villain
Than terms can give thee out![4]
[They fight]

MACBETH
Thou losest labour:[5]
As easy may'st thou the intrenchant air
With thy keen sword impress as make me bleed:[6]
Let fall thy blade on vulnerable crests;[7]
I bear a charmed[8] life, which must not yield,
To one of woman born.

MACDUFF
Despair thy charm! –
And let the angel whom thou still hast served
Tell thee, Macduff was from his mother's womb
Untimely ripped.[9]

1 **Roman fool:** Roman warriors often committed suicide after defeat.
2 **lives:** living enemies
3 **charged:** weighed down/burdened
4 **thou bloodier villain...thee out:** You are a bloodier villain than words can express.
5 **Thou losest labour:** You are wasting effort.
6 **As easy may'st...me bleed:** It would be easier to wound the uncuttable air with your sword than make me bleed.
7 **crests:** heads
8 **charmed:** protected by supernatural powers
9 **Macduff...Untimely ripped:** i.e. Macduff was delivered by caesarean section and therefore not 'born' of woman.

Macbeth

Accursed be that tongue that tells me so,
For it hath cowed my better part of man![10]
And be these juggling fiends[11] no more believed,
That palter with us in a double sense;[12]
That keep the word of promise to our ear,
And break it to our hope![13] – I'll not fight with thee.

Macduff

Then yield thee, coward,
And live to be the show and gaze o' the time.[14]
We'll have thee, as our rarer monsters are,
Painted upon a pole,[15] and underwrit,[16]
'Here may you see the tyrant.'

Macbeth

I will not yield,
To kiss the ground before young Malcolm's feet,
And to be baited with the rabble's curse.[17]
Though Birnam Wood be come to Dunsinane,
And thou opposed, being of no woman born,
Yet I will try the last.[18] Before my body
I throw my warlike shield. Lay on, Macduff,
And damned be him that first cries, 'Hold,[19] enough!'
[Exeunt, fighting. Alarums. Re-enter fighting, and MACBETH is killed. Exit MACDUFF, dragging Macbeth's body]

[10] **For it...part of man!:** as it has overawed the best part of me, i.e. it has stripped me of my confidence.
[11] **juggling fiends:** deceiving devils
[12] **That palter...sense:** that trick us with double meanings
[13] **That keep...our hope!:** that whisper promises in our ear but then destroy our hopes

[14] **show and gaze o' the time:** a spectacle of the age

[15] **Painted upon a pole:** Macbeth's image painted on a banner
[16] **underwrit:** written underneath

[17] **baited with the rabble's curse:** mocked and teased by the mob

[18] **try the last:** fight to the end

[19] **Hold:** Stop

Key Quotations

Macbeth *But get thee back; my soul is too much charged / With blood of thine already.*

Macbeth *For it hath cowed my better part of man!*
And be these juggling fiends no more believed,
That palter with us in a double sense;
That keep the word of promise to our ear,
And break it to our hope!

Macbeth *I will not yield, / To kiss the ground before young Malcolm's feet, / And to be baited with the rabble's curse.*

Commentary

- Macbeth's final moments are as bloody and violent as his life was. However, as Macbeth encounters Macduff he seems reluctant to fight him: 'But get thee back; my soul is too much charged / With blood of thine already'. Some commentators argue that Macbeth has the first of the apparition's warning in mind: 'Beware Macduff!' and is therefore eager to avoid a battle with Macduff. However this does not fit neatly with Macbeth's later boast to Macduff that he can only be hurt by 'one of woman born'. Many commentators see Macbeth's reluctance to fight Macduff as an expression of guilt for murdering Macduff's family.

- Macbeth attempts to hold onto his pride in his final moments: 'I will not yield, / To kiss the ground before young Malcolm's feet, / And to be baited with the rabble's curse .' Rather than be mocked and tortured, Macbeth chooses to 'try the last' and fight to the death. Considering Macbeth's hopelessness in Scene 5 and his moral collapse throughout the play, it is perhaps unsurprising that he embraces death at the end. This arouses great sympathy in the audience.

Questions

1. Why does Macbeth refer to the witches as *'juggling fiends'*?
2. What evidence is there in this scene that Macbeth feels guilt for the murder of Macduff's family?
3. Why does Macbeth fight to the death rather than give up?
4. Macbeth has changed throughout the course of the play. However, are there any similarities between Macbeth in this final scene and the Macbeth that is discussed in Act 1, Scene 2?
5. Do you feel pity for Macbeth at the end of this scene? Explain your answer by referring to the play.
6. Some productions have Macbeth killed offstage and Macduff returning to the stage with Macbeth's severed head in Scene 9. What is the advantage of this?

Scene Summary

- Ross tells Siward that Young Siward has been killed.
- Siward is proud to learn that his son died fighting.
- Macduff enters carrying Macbeth's head and hails Malcolm as King.
- Malcolm invites all to attend his coronation at Scone.

Inside Macbeth's castle.
Retreat and flourish. Enter, with drum and colours, MALCOLM, SIWARD, ROSS, the other thanes, and soldiers

MALCOLM
I would the friends we miss were safe arrived.

SIWARD
Some must go off: and yet, by these I see,
So great a day as this is cheaply bought.

MALCOLM
Macduff is missing, and your noble son.

ROSS
Your son, my lord, has paid a soldier's debt.[1]
He only lived but till he was a man;[2]
The which no sooner had his prowess[3] confirmed
In the unshrinking station[4] where he fought,
But like a man he died.

SIWARD
Then he is dead?

ROSS
Ay, and brought off the field. Your cause of sorrow
Must not be measured by his worth, for then
It hath no end.

SIWARD
Had he his hurts before?[5]

ROSS
Ay, on the front.

SIWARD
Why then, God's soldier be he!

1 **soldier's debt:** i.e. his life
2 **He only...was a man:** He lived only long enough to be called a man.
3 **prowess:** bravery/capabilities in battle
4 **unshrinking station:** unretreating position

5 **Had...hurts before?:** Were his wounds on the front of his body? i.e. Did he die facing his enemy rather than running away?

Had I as many sons as I have hairs,
I would not wish them to a fairer death:
And so, his knell is knolled.[6]

MALCOLM

He's worth more sorrow,
And that I'll spend for him.

SIWARD

He's worth no more
They say he parted well, and paid his score;[7]
And so, God be with him! Here comes newer comfort.
[Enter MACDUFF, with MACBETH's head]

MACDUFF

Hail, King! for so thou art. Behold, where stands
The usurper's[8] cursed head. The time is free.
I see thee compassed with thy kingdom's pearl,[9]
That speak my salutation in their minds;[10]
Whose voices I desire aloud with mine:
Hail, King of Scotland!

ALL

Hail, King of Scotland!
[Flourish]

MALCOLM

We shall not spend a large expense of time
Before we reckon with[11] your several loves,
And make us even with you. My thanes and kinsmen,
Henceforth be earls, the first that ever Scotland
In such an honour named. What's more to do,
Which would be planted newly[12] with the time,
As calling home our exiled friends abroad
That fled the snares of watchful tyranny;
Producing forth the cruel ministers
Of this dead butcher and his fiend-like queen,
Who, as 'tis thought, by self and violent hands
Took off her life;[13] this, and what needful else
That calls upon us, by the grace of Grace,[14]
We will perform in measure, time and place.
So, thanks to all at once, and to each one,
Whom we invite to see us crowned at Scone.
[Flourish. Exeunt]

6 **knell is knolled:** His funeral bell has rung.

7 **score:** debt

8 **usurper:** someone who takes power without a legal right

9 **compassed with thy kingdom's pearl:** surrounded by your kingdom's nobility

10 **That speak...minds:** that salute you in their thoughts as I do out loud

11 **reckon with:** reward

12 **planted newly:** given a new beginning

13 **by self and...her life:** i.e. Lady Macbeth killed herself.

14 **by the grace of Grace:** with the favour of God

Key Quotations

MALCOLM ...*this dead butcher and his fiend-like queen*

Commentary

- In the play's final scene, Malcolm is confirmed as the rightful heir to the throne. He is seen as a goodly king who is honoured by Macduff and all of the other thanes. Malcolm promises to reward all those who supported him: 'We shall not spend a large expense of time / Before we reckon with your several loves, / And make us even with you.' Malcolm pledges to justly punish Macbeth's agents: 'Producing forth the cruel ministers / Of this dead butcher' and affirms the notion of his rule being divinely ordained: 'by the grace of Grace'. Shakespeare makes it clear that Malcolm will be a just and fair ruler.

- However, this final scene echoes Act 1, Scene 2. Like Malcolm, Duncan was a good king. Malcolm promises to reward the thanes for their loyalty in battle just as Duncan rewarded his thanes (such as Macbeth) following the battle with Macdonwald. The play ends much like it starts, thus suggesting a cycle of violence which is set to begin again.

- The issue of manliness is raised here once again. Siward is keen to know if his son has 'his hurts before' (wounds on the front). It consoles him that Young Siward died facing his enemy. Ross celebrates Young Siward's courage in battle: 'like a man he died' and this prompts Siward to call his son 'God's soldier'. The importance of bravery in battle as an emblem of masculinity is explored yet again. Throughout *Macbeth* Shakespeare asks what it means to be a man. Siward (much like Macbeth) equates masculinity with courage.

- The once noble warrior, Macbeth, meets an ignoble ending, bereft of dignity. His severed head is a fitting end to his villainy and bloody reign.

- By the end of the play the audience appreciates how Macbeth's pride and ambition overcame his conscience. Without forgiving him his crimes, we sympathise with a potentially great man, who, through intense suffering, comes to understand his own flawed humanity. What resonates at the end of *Macbeth* is a vision of its protagonist's tortured soul and humanity's capacity for evil. The audience learns to fear the consequences and moral cost of unrestrained ambition and unchecked pride.

Questions

1. Why does Siward feel that his son died an honourable death?
2. Malcolm describes Macbeth and Lady Macbeth as 'this dead butcher and his fiend-like queen'. Do you think this is a fair and accurate description? Explain your answer.
3. Do you feel that Malcolm will make a better king than Macbeth? Explain your answer.
4. (a) In what ways does this final scene recall Act 1, Scene 2?
   (b) What is Shakespeare suggesting by this?
5. Why does the audience pity Macbeth at the end of the play?

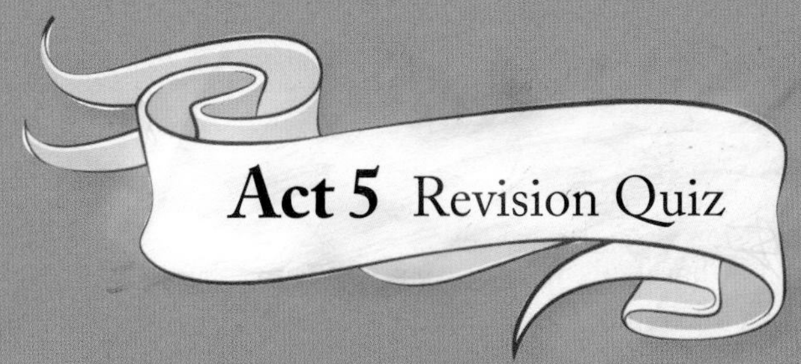

1. Why do the doctor and gentlewoman spy on Lady Macbeth?

2. Find one quotation in Scene 1 that reveals Lady Macbeth as burdened by guilt.

3. What is the name of Macbeth's lieutenant?

4. What prompts Macbeth to say, *'Throw physic to the dogs; I'll none of it.'*

5. What does Malcolm order the soldiers to do in Birnam Wood?

6. Whose son does Macbeth kill in Act 5?

7. Why does Macbeth initially not fear Macduff?

8. What does Macbeth learn that changes his mind?

9. Who says each of the following?:
(a) *'Out, damned spot!'*
(b) *'He cannot buckle his distempered cause / Within the belt of rule'*
(c) *'I have supped full with horrors;*
Direness, familiar to my slaughterous thoughts
Cannot once start me'

10. Fill in the blanks:
(a) *'now does he feel his* title
Hang loose about him, like a giant's *robe*
Upon a dwarfish *thief'*
(b) *'I have almost forgot the taste of* fears *'*
(c) *'Out, out, brief* candle *!*
Life's but a walking shadow, a poor player
That struts and frets *his hour upon the stage*
And then is heard no more. It is a tale
Told by an idiot *, full of sound and* fury *,*
Signifying nothing*'*

Tragedy is a form of drama that deals with human suffering. There are many definitions of what constitutes tragedy. Broadly speaking, tragedy depicts a hero who thrives at the beginning of a story but then, because of a tragic act, experiences a reversal of fortune. The tragic hero experiences great suffering and hardship in the drama but through this gains greater awareness about himself or the world. A tragedy often concludes with the hero's death.

Macbeth can be understood as a typical tragedy as it contains the follows tragic elements:

- The hero (Macbeth) is initially a person of **high social status** and has the **potential for greatness**. At the start of the play, Macbeth is a brave warrior who is honoured by King Duncan with the title Thane (i.e. Lord) of Cawdor.
- Despite his/her potential for greatness, the hero has a **tragic flaw**. In Macbeth's case this is his excessive 'vaulting ambition' and excessive pride.
- The hero commits a **tragic act** that eventually contributes to his/her downfall. In Macbeth's case it is the murder of Duncan.
- The hero experiences a **reversal of fortune**. Macbeth was once celebrated as a noble warrior; by the end of the play he is despised by all of Scotland.
- Through suffering, the **hero gains wisdom**. Towards the end of the play, Macbeth realises the meaninglessness of his immoral life. He understands the pointlessness of his own ambition and his inability to control his fate.
- The tragic hero **inspires pity**. The audience pities Macbeth's flawed humanity which caused his moral blindness.
- The tragedy also **excites fear**. The audience of *Macbeth* feel fear for themselves. If a potentially great man like Macbeth can bring about his own downfall, it is very possible for others to destroy themselves.

Potential for Greatness and High Social Status

At the beginning of a tragedy, the tragic hero prospers and exhibits the potential for greatness. Macbeth begins the play as a celebrated soldier whose bravery and nobility earn him respect and new titles from King Duncan. Macbeth is hailed as 'brave Macbeth', 'Valour's minion' and 'Bellona's bridegroom' in praise of his heroics. Duncan displays his affection for Macbeth by referring to him as his 'valiant cousin' (Act 1, Sc 2).

Macbeth is awarded the title of Thane of Cawdor for his courage. This honour elevates him socially. Duncan explains how highly he esteems him and points to Macbeth's potential to grow in greatness: 'I have begun to plant thee, and will labour / To make thee full of growing' (Act 1, Sc 4).

Macbeth recognises his newly earned respect and tells Lady Macbeth that he is reluctant to disregard this in hasty pursuit of the crown:

> 'He [Duncan] hath honoured me of late; and I have bought
> Golden opinions from all sorts of people,
> Which would be worn now in their newest gloss,
> Not cast aside so soon' (Act 1, Sc 7)

Shakespeare stresses how much Macbeth has to lose. **His eventual state of wretchedness is all the more tragic as he falls from a position of such favour and prosperity** (see Tragic Reversal on page 140).

Tragic Flaw

In all tragedies, the tragic hero has a flaw that contributes to his/her downfall. This allows the audience to learn some moral lesson and also understand how a great figure can experience such a dramatic reversal of fortune. **Macbeth's tragic flaw is his excessive ambition.** This grows out of his pride in himself as a man.

It is his overwhelming desire to be King of Scotland that encourages him to kill Duncan. Even though Macbeth is reluctant to commit the crime, the lure of power is irresistible to him.

Both the witches and Lady Macbeth play on this aspect of Macbeth's personality to encourage him to do evil. The witches promise him greatness while Lady Macbeth directly appeals to his desire to be king: 'Wouldst thou have that / Which thou esteem'st the ornament of life' (Act 1, Sc 7). Macbeth recognises this flaw within his character but does little to control it:

> 'I have no spur
> To prick the sides of my intent, but only
> Vaulting ambition, which o'erleaps itself
> And falls on the other' (Act 1, Sc 7)

Lady Macbeth encourages Macbeth to seize the crown by presenting the murder of Duncan as a courageous act. This appeals to Macbeth's pride in himself as a man: 'When you durst do it, then you were a man! / And, to be more than what you were, you would / Be so much more the man' (Act 1, Sc 7). Here the idea of being a man is bound up with the prospect of power. Lady Macbeth criticises his reluctance to murder Duncan as cowardice: 'Art thou afeard / To be the same in thine own act and valour / As thou art in desire?' (Act 1, Sc 7). Macbeth is encouraged to realise his ambition to be king as it is equated with masculinity and bravery.

He becomes morally blinded by his overwhelming ambition to be king. This sets him on a path towards self-destruction. Shakespeare highlights that this is indeed a character flaw within Macbeth through comparison with Banquo. Banquo is also given a favourable prophecy by the witches but does nothing to bring it about. This is because Banquo lacks the excessive sense of ambition that Macbeth has. As a result, he is suspicious of the witches' motives:

> 'And oftentimes, to win us to our harm,
> The instruments of darkness tell us truths,
> Win us with honest trifles, to betray's
> In deepest consequence' (Act 1, Sc 3)

In contrast with Banquo, **Macbeth undergoes a moral descent. His overwhelming guilt, spiritual collapse and eventual death all stem from his tragic flaw.**

Tragic Act

Macbeth's tragic flaw leads him to murder Duncan. This tragic act sets him on a path of self-destruction and begins a bloody chain of events: the murder of Banquo, the slaughter of Macduff's family. It ends in Macbeth's fight to the death with Macduff.

Macbeth himself suspects that his murder of Duncan will be his downfall:

> 'we but teach
> Bloody instructions, which, being taught, return
> To plague the inventor. This even-handed justice
> Commends the ingredients of our poisoned chalice
> To our own lips' (Act 1, Sc 7)

After he commits the crime, Macbeth instinctively recognises how the consequences of his crime will only grow. As he tries to wash Duncan's blood from his hands, he imagines the pool of blood spreading and changing the colour of the ocean:

'Will all great Neptune's ocean wash this blood
Clean from my hand? No, this my hand will rather
The multitudinous seas incarnadine,
Making the green one red' (Act 2, Sc 2)

Macbeth rightly suspects that this tragic act will have far-reaching consequences.

Tragic Reversal

Macbeth's tragic act brings about a dramatic reversal of fortune. Due to his own flawed humanity and moral blindness, he falls from a state of prosperity. His tyrannical rule and murderous crimes make him despised by all of Scotland. He is described as a 'tyrant', 'fiend', 'butcher' and is associated with the devil: 'Not in the legions / Of horrid hell can come a devil more damned / In evils to top Macbeth' (Act 4, Sc 3). Through his own actions he has lost the respect he had earned in the first Act (see Potential for Greatness on page 138).

Typically of tragedy, **Macbeth's reversal of fortune leads him to experience great suffering and unhappiness**. The audience sees throughout the play how he suffers great emotional anguish. He feels considerable guilt for his murders. This is most keenly illustrated through the vision of Banquo's ghost. Macbeth suffers spiritually as he is numbed by his actions: 'I have supped full with horrors; / Direness, familiar to my slaughterous thoughts / Cannot once start me' (Act 5, Sc 5). He becomes world-weary and wholly disinterested in life: 'I have lived long enough: my way of life / Is fall'n into the sear, the yellow leaf' (Act 5, Sc 3). This state of wretchedness is typical of tragic heroes.

By the end of the play Macbeth becomes an isolated figure at war with the thanes of Scotland and the forces from England. The grotesque spectacle of Macbeth's severed head displayed by Macduff at the play's end dramatically highlights the tragic hero's fall from grace and his radical reversal of fortune.

Tragic Recognition

In tragedy, **the hero comes to realise the errors he has made or gains profound insight into life through a process of tragic recognition**. Aristotle, an ancient Greek philosopher, defines this tragic recognition as a 'change from ignorance to awareness'. The hero's revelation compounds the sense of tragedy as he sees the mistakes he has made but is powerless to change his circumstances.

Macbeth sees that he has set himself on an inescapable path of bloodshed and unhappiness. After the murder of Banquo he says, 'I am in blood / Stepped in so far that, should I wade no more, / Returning were as tedious as go o'er' (Act 3, Sc 4). The image of wading through a river of blood illustrates the great suffering he has brought upon himself.

Macbeth's revelation allows him to see the futility of an immoral life. Happiness and contentment can only be achieved by living ethically. By the end of the play, he recognises that all that he values has been undone by his immoral actions. The crown should bring respect, love and friendship, but the dishonourable way in which Macbeth achieved power means that he is reviled, unloved and alone:

'And that which should accompany old age,
As honour, love, obedience, troops of friends,
I must not look to have; but, in their stead,
Curses, not loud but deep, mouth-honour, breath,
Which the poor heart would fain deny, and dare not' (Act 5, Sc 3)

Macbeth grows in wisdom throughout the play. He comes to understand his own nature as that of a warrior not a ruler. This is keenly reflected in his eagerness to exchange his kingly robes for armour in Act 5, Scene 3.

After Macbeth hears a report that Birnam Wood has actually moved, his confidence slips and he starts to doubt the witches:

'I pull in resolution, and begin
To doubt the equivocation of the fiend
That lies like truth' (Act 5, Sc 5)

As the play progresses Macbeth sees that the witches' promises were equivocal and buoyed him with false confidence. This recognition however comes too late for him to change his future.

In Act 5, Scene 5 **Macbeth recognises the pointlessness of his own ambition.**

'Out, out, brief candle!
Life's but a walking shadow, a poor player
That struts and frets his hour upon the stage
And then is heard no more. It is a tale
Told by an idiot, full of sound and fury,
Signifying nothing.'

He imagines life as a puffed-up actor who 'struts and frets' vainly but 'then is heard no more'. He labels the excitable passions of humanity as merely the 'sound and fury' of a tale, 'Signifying nothing'.

In this soliloquy Macbeth also recognises that death is unavoidable. Just as a candle inevitably burns out, life must come to an end. His pride and ambition saw him try to resist Fate by attempting to murder Fleance in Act 3, Scene 3. As the play draws to its close, Macbeth understands that Fate cannot be beaten and death cannot be escaped.

His wisdom about his situation is all the more tragic as he is powerless to change the course he has embarked upon. This arouses great sympathy in the audience.

Inspires Pity and Fear

It is vital in a tragedy that the audience feels pity for the tragic hero. Pity helps to create the feeling of loss at the end of the play.

Despite Macbeth's repeated acts of villainy and his increasingly murderous reign, **he evokes pity in the audience**. The initial presentation of Macbeth as a courageous and noble soldier means that the audience is well disposed towards him from the beginning. Through the reports given by the bleeding sergeant and Ross, Shakespeare stresses Macbeth's courage (Act 1, Sc 2). Like Duncan, the audience at this stage trusts Macbeth and is encouraged to admire his bravery. The audience recognises his potential as a noble individual and his downfall is therefore all the more tragic.

Macbeth succumbs to his own tragic flaw and this inspires pity. The audience pities a man who has destroyed himself through his own moral blindness. Without forgiving him for the murder of Duncan, the audience understands Macbeth as a man overwhelmed by his excessive ambition and spurred on by the witches and Lady Macbeth.

Macbeth suffers greatly throughout the play. **His anxiety, deep sense of guilt, paranoia and eventual world-weariness combine to create a pitiful figure wracked by regret** (see Tragic Reversal and Tragic Recognition on page 140).

Because of the pity that Macbeth inspires, his eventual death creates a sense of tragic loss. His function in the play is to illustrate how a good man can easily turn astray. Although his villainous actions are condemned, the audience can't help but feel that Macbeth's potential for good was never realised – the tragedy is therefore felt all the more.

At the end of *Macbeth*, the audience also experiences fear for themselves. If a figure with potential for greatness such as Macbeth can be destroyed by his own flawed humanity, then anybody can be potentially undone. This disquieting idea excites fear in the audience and serves as a moral warning.

The Development of Macbeth as a Tragic Hero

Potential for Greatness	• At the beginning of the play Macbeth is a noble and loyal figure, commended by King Duncan for his bravery. • He is made Thane of Cawdor in recognition of this bravery.
Tragic Flaw	• Macbeth's tragic flaw is his excessive ambition. • This is bound up with his pride in himself as a man. • His tragic flaw leads him to his downfall as he pursues his desire for power at all costs.
Tragic Act	• Macbeth's tragic act is the murder of Duncan. • This creates a chain of bloody events concluding in Macbeth's death.
Tragic Reversal	• From a state of prosperity and favour, Macbeth becomes despised by all of Scotland and is eventually killed. • He suffers hugely throughout the play. • He is denied dignity even in death as his head is paraded by Macduff.
Tragic Recognition	• Macbeth comes to see the true nature of the witches' prophecies. • He sees that the bloody path he has set upon is inescapable. • He recognises the futility and meaninglessness of his own ambition and pride.
Inspires Pity and Fear	• The audience pities Macbeth for his flawed humanity. • *Macbeth* excites fear in the audience as people realise their own potential for self-destruction.

Macbeth

Macbeth is one of Shakespeare's most intriguing tragic figures. He **paradoxically inspires both revulsion and sympathy in the audience** as we watch the horror of his crimes played out against the backdrop of his increasingly guilty conscience. It is this contradiction within the character of Macbeth that casts him in the roles of both tragic hero and central villain.

Ambitious

All tragic heroes are undone by a flaw in their character. In Macbeth's case, **ambition leads him on a path towards self-destruction**. This is first evident in his meeting with the witches. When Macbeth learns that he will be Thane of Cawdor and king he is lost for words; Banquo notes how he is 'rapt withal'.

Even at this early stage of the play, **Shakespeare connects Macbeth's ambition with his violent crimes**. As the witches make their prophecies, Macbeth's mind immediately turns to murder as the only way to satisfy his ambitious nature: 'why do I yield to that suggestion / Whose horrid image doth unfix my hair / And make my seated heart knock at my ribs' (Act 1, Sc 3). Similarly, his destructive sense of ambition is apparent when he hears Duncan name Malcolm as his successor:

> 'The Prince of Cumberland! That is a step
> On which I must fall down, or else o'er-leap,
> For in my way it lies. Stars, hide your fires!
> Let not light see my black and deep desires' (Act 1, Sc 4)

It is the prospect of power that encourages Macbeth's dark and murderous thoughts. He himself recognises the danger of his excessive ambition. He reflects on the immorality of killing Duncan and realises that his sole motivation is his ambitious nature:

> 'I have no spur
> To prick the sides of my intent, but only
> Vaulting ambition, which o'erleaps itself
> And falls on the other' (Act 1, Sc 7)

The image here is of an overly eager jockey who ambitiously jumps too far and falls on the other side. He clearly recognises how excessive ambition can potentially bring disaster.

Lady Macbeth also acknowledges Macbeth's ambition. She encourages him to kill Duncan by appealing to this side of his character: 'Wouldst thou have that / Which thou esteem'st the ornament of life' (Act 1, Sc 7).

Macbeth's tragic act stems from his overwhelming desire to be king. It is this excessive sense of ambition that leaves him vulnerable to the suggestive influence of the witches and Lady Macbeth.

Proud

However, Macbeth is also undone by his excessive pride. He considers himself to be a courageous, manly figure and this **pride contributes towards his moral blindness**.

Lady Macbeth appeals to Macbeth's pride in himself as a brave man to encourage him to murder Duncan. She accuses him of dishonourably breaking a promise to her: 'What beast was't, then, / That made you break this enterprise to me?' and calls him a coward for his reluctance in proceeding with the murder: 'Art thou afeard / To be the same in thine own act and valour / As thou art in desire?' (Act 1, Sc 7). The idea of manliness is central here as Lady Macbeth argues that Macbeth would be a real man if he kills Duncan: 'When you durst do it, then you were a man! / And, to be more than what you were, you would / Be so much more the man.'

The witches' apparitions bolster Macbeth's pride by appealing to his view of himself as an undefeatable soldier. They tell him to be 'lion-mettled, proud' as he 'shall never vanquished be until / Great Birnam wood to high Dunsinane hill / Shall come against him' (Act 4, Sc 1). The predictions encourage Macbeth to think of himself as invincible. **By playing on his innate pride, the witches, like Lady Macbeth, spur Macbeth on towards greater evil.**

As his castle is besieged and his army deserts him, Macbeth confidently defies his enemies. His pride prevents him from submitting, and in a grotesque image, he announces. 'I'll fight till from my bones my flesh be hacked' (Act 5, Sc 3). He dismisses the enemy's siege of his castle: 'Our castle's strength / Will laugh a siege to scorn. Here let them lie / Till famine and the ague eat them up' (Act 5, Sc 5). At this point he cannot accept that he will lose the battle.

Macbeth is lead by his pride throughout the play. Even at the end when he knows he is doomed, his prideful nature inspires him to embrace death rather than be mocked and forced to submit: 'I will not yield, / To kiss the ground before young Malcolm's feet, / And to be baited with the rabble's curse' (Act 5, Sc 8).

Courageous

Macbeth is presented as **a brave and noble warrior at the beginning of the play**. A bleeding sergeant reports to Duncan how Macbeth exhibited incredible courage and loyalty on the battlefield against the rebels. He is referred to as 'brave Macbeth', 'Valour's minion' and 'Bellona's bridegroom' in praise of his heroics. Duncan commends him and warmly calls him his 'valiant cousin' (Act 1, Sc 2).

Macbeth is described as single-handedly pushing through the enemy's ranks and personally killing the rebel leader: 'Like Valour's minion carved out his passage / Till he faced the slave' (Act 1, Sc 2). However, some commentators note that **his ferocious behaviour on the battlefield seems excessively violent**. We learn that he 'unseamed' the rebel leader, Macdonwald, 'from the nave to the chops' (Act 1, Sc 2) and fixed his head upon the battlements. Whether it is pure bravery or battle-lust, the audience is encouraged to admire Macbeth for his courage and loyalty to his king.

However, his courage is limited to violent action. He lacks moral courage because of his excessive ambition and pride. In a long soliloquy (Act 1, Sc 7) Macbeth recognises that murdering Duncan would be an immoral action but he lacks the moral courage to resist his ambition.

Readily Influenced

Although Macbeth clearly makes the decision to kill Duncan himself, the influence of the witches and Lady Macbeth cannot be discounted. Without taking away responsibility for the crime from Macbeth, it can still be argued that **he is influenced by the equivocal suggestions of the witches and his wife's manipulative strategies**.

From the start of the play the witches strive to influence his actions. They prophesise that he will be made Thane of Cawdor and then king. Despite the fact that their statements are true, they purposefully neglect to tell him about the great personal toll and moral sacrifice he will have to make in order to get the throne. Banquo instinctively distrusts the witches and questions their motives; he realises that they seek to influence Macbeth through equivocation:

> 'to win us to our harm,
> The instruments of darkness tell us truths,
> Win us with honest trifles, to betray's
> In deepest consequence' (Act 1, Sc 3)

However, Macbeth is convinced by the witches. He allows himself to be readily influenced as they play on his innate ambition to encourage him towards evil.

This is repeated later in the play when the witches' apparitions give Macbeth false hope. Hecate realises that overconfidence can be the downfall of a man: 'And you all know, security / Is mortals' chiefest enemy' (Act 3, Sc 5). The apparitions tell Macbeth that 'none of woman born / Shall harm Macbeth' (Act 4, Sc 1) and that he has nothing to fear until Birnam Wood comes to Dunsinane Hill. He seeks the witches out at this point in the play and actively courts evil. His **overconfidence is in part due to these equivocal predictions**.

Similarly, Lady Macbeth influences Macbeth. Because she worries that her husband is 'too full o' the milk of human kindness', she plans to persuade him to murder Duncan: 'Hie thee hither, / That I may pour my spirits in thine ear, / And chastise with the valour of my tongue' (Act 1, Sc 5). **She exerts her influence on him by using persuasive rhetoric:**

'Was the hope drunk
Wherein you dressed yourself? Hath it slept since?
And wakes it now, to look so green and pale
At what it did so freely?' (Act 1, Sc 7)

The audience watch as **Macbeth is cajoled, taunted and flattered** into agreeing to proceed with the murder.

Although he does make the decision to kill Duncan himself, and his later crimes are his alone, the influence of the witches and Lady Macbeth help him along a destructive and violent path.

Burdened by Guilt

One the most compelling features of Macbeth's personality is the guilt he feels for his murderous actions. The vision of a man torn between his 'black and deep desires' and the 'milk o' human kindness' creates a **psychological spectacle evoking both sympathy and moral revulsion.**

From the moment he first entertains the idea of killing Duncan, Macbeth is troubled by his conscience: 'My thought, whose murder yet is but fantastical, / Shakes so my single state of man' (Act 1, Sc 3). It is this aspect of his personality that makes Macbeth a **reluctant murderer**. In a long soliloquy, he outlines a number of reasons for not killing Duncan. He sees that he has a moral obligation to Duncan, noting that as both his guest and relative, Duncan is in 'double trust'. He realises that he 'should against his murderer shut the door, / Not bear the knife' (Act 1, Sc 7). After he wrestles with his strong sense of ambition, he seems resolved not to commit the murder. He says to Lady Macbeth: 'We will proceed no further in this business' and although he later changes his mind, Macbeth reveals here the conscionable side of his character.

However, **he lacks the moral courage to resist the temptation of power and the attack on his manhood**. He gives into the pressure from Lady Macbeth and his own personal desires. After murdering Duncan, he is deeply remorseful for what he has done. As he washes Duncan's blood from his hands he listens to the knocking at the gate and laments, 'Wake Duncan with thy knocking! I would thou couldst!' (Act 2, Sc 2).

The spectacle of Banquo's ghost dramatically personifies Macbeth's guilt. We understand that Macbeth is haunted by his crimes. His response to the burden of guilt is to harden himself. He believes that he can make himself numb to his crimes by committing further acts of violence: 'My strange and self-abuse / Is the initiate fear that wants hard use: / We are yet but young in deed' (Act 3, Sc 4). It is at this point that his moral decline accelerates as he grows increasingly tyrannical, murderous and callous. He reigns cruelly over Scotland inspiring terror rather than respect. This is dramatically represented through his vicious slaughter of Macduff's wife and children. It appears that as the play progresses, **Macbeth suppresses his conscience and attempts to use violence to smother his guilt**.

Ultimately this strategy fails as he reveals his burdened conscience in his confrontation with

Macduff. Macbeth seems reluctant to fight and says, 'get thee back; my soul is too much charged / With blood of thine already' (Act 5, Sc 8). In this final moment of his life, Macbeth expresses remorse for murdering Macduff's family.

The audience is fascinated by the vision of a man tortured by guilt and burdened by regret. This suffering partly explains the sympathy that is extended to him by the audience.

Anxious and World-Weary

Macbeth suffers hugely as a result of his crimes. He becomes increasingly isolated and emotionally overwrought as the play progresses. This taxing emotional state leads to his eventual world-weariness and deep sense of despair.

The crown fails to give Macbeth any contentment or inner peace. After killing Duncan, he imagines voices saying, 'Macbeth shall sleep no more.' This foreshadows the paranoia and 'saucy doubts and fears' of which he later complains. He becomes increasingly distrustful of Banquo and complains to Lady Macbeth that his mind is 'full of scorpions'. He is agitated and suffers nightmares having to 'sleep / In the affliction of these terrible dreams / That shake us nightly' (Act 3, Sc 2). Murdering Banquo brings no relief from his sense of insecurity.

After killing Banquo and Macduff's family, Macbeth becomes increasingly disillusioned with life. He pictures himself as a withered leaf, stripped of its vitality: 'I have lived long / enough: my way of life / Is fall'n into the sear' (Act 5, Sc 3). **He comes to see life as futile, and existence as meaningless**. He imagines life as a candle that will inevitably burn out and also compares it to a poor actor who is soon forgotten:

> 'Out, out, brief candle!
> Life's but a walking shadow, a poor player
> That struts and frets his hour upon the stage
> And then is heard no more. It is a tale
> Told by an idiot, full of sound and fury,
> Signifying nothing' (Act 5, Sc 5)

The absolute despair of these lines signals Macbeth's world-weariness. **His ambition, bravery and troubled conscience have given way to a profound sense of hopelessness.**

A Tragic Hero

Macbeth is both the chief villain and the tragic hero of the play. He experiences a reversal of fortune: beginning from a privileged position in Duncan's favour, he becomes a despised tyrannical ruler. He is also identifiable as a tragic hero by the flaws in his character: his excessive pride and ambition. This leads him on a path towards self-destruction. As his life spirals towards its tragic conclusion, he gains insight into the emptiness of his ambition. He becomes filled with remorse but is unable to change the course of his life. This inspires pity in the audience. (For a more detailed discussion of Macbeth as a tragic hero, see the Tragedy section of this book on page 138.)

Macbeth:

- Ambitious
- Proud
- Courageous
- Readily influenced
- Burdened by guilt
- Anxious and world-weary
- A tragic hero

Lady Macbeth

Ambitious

Like her husband, Lady Macbeth is **characterised by ruthless ambition**. When Macbeth writes to her about the witches' prophecies, her thoughts immediately spring to murder as the most expedient way of attaining power. Unlike Macbeth, this dark idea is not tempered by any moral considerations. For Lady Macbeth, **the prospect of power is all consuming**: 'Which shall to all our nights and days to come / Give solely sovereign sway and masterdom' (Act 1, Sc 5).

Her unrestrained ambition is signalled by her eagerness to kill Duncan; she seems to almost relish the idea: 'The raven himself is hoarse / That croaks the fatal entrance of Duncan / Under my battlements' (Act 1, Sc 5). It is interesting that she says '**my** battlements' thus signalling her personal ambitions. She **embraces the idea of murder** in her appeal to evil spirits:

'Come, you spirits
That tend on mortal thoughts, unsex me here,
And fill me from the crown to the toe top-full
Of direst cruelty!' (Act 1, Sc 5)

Here she hopes to suppress her conscience to facilitate her desire to be queen.

When Macbeth returns to Dunsinane, Lady Macbeth displays her **obsession with power**. Her first words to her husband seek to flatter and appeal to his sense of ambition: 'Great Glamis! Worthy Cawdor! / Greater than both, by the all-hail hereafter!' (Act 1, Sc 5).

Manipulative

Lady Macbeth is **instrumental in encouraging Macbeth to proceed with the murder** of Duncan. Upon reading Macbeth's letter, she fears that her husband lacks the necessary murderous resolve: 'yet do I fear thy nature; / It is too full o' the milk of human kindness / To catch the nearest way' (Act 1, Sc 5). She therefore states her intention to aggressively manipulate Macbeth: 'Hie thee hither, / That I may pour my spirits in thine ear, / And chastise with the valour of my tongue' (Act 1, Sc 5).

In Act 1, Scene 7, Lady Macbeth uses her **powers of persuasion** to overcome Macbeth's reservations. She **appeals to his ambition** by focusing his attention on the crown: 'Wouldst thou have that / Which thou esteem'st the ornament of life'. When he displays his reservations about the murder she **uses emotional blackmail** 'From this time / Such I account thy love' and then proceeds to taunt him: 'Wouldst thou…live a coward in thine own esteem, / Letting "I dare not" wait upon "I would," / Like the poor cat i' the adage?'

She attacks Macbeth's masculinity in an attempt to play upon his pride in himself as a man: 'When you durst do it, then you were a man!'. Finally she shocks Macbeth with the chilling image of murdering her own child to illustrate her commitment to him:

'I have given suck, and know
How tender 'tis to love the babe that milks me:
I would, while it was smiling in my face,
Have plucked my nipple from his boneless gums,
And dashed the brains out, had I so sworn as you
Have done to this'.

This appeals to his sense of honour, making him feel that he has broken a promise to his wife. As a manipulative character, Lady Macbeth cleverly focuses on Macbeth's ambition, manly pride and sense of honour.

Her influence over Macbeth wanes as she becomes an increasingly marginalised character. This is most evident when Macbeth fails to consult with her about the murders of Banquo and Macduff's family. He says, 'Be innocent of the knowledge, dearest chuck, / Till thou applaud the deed' (Act 3, Sc 2). Lady Macbeth's manipulative personality influences Macbeth at the start of the play. However, her sway lessens as the play continues.

Calculating

Lady Macbeth possesses a mind that is **coldly calculating**. It is she rather than Macbeth who devises the plan to kill Duncan. Macbeth notes her **steely determination and unfeeling nature**: 'Bring forth men-children only; / For thy undaunted mettle should compose / Nothing but males' (Act 1, Sc 7).

She recognises the power of deception and uses it in a calculating way to avoid suspicion. She instructs Macbeth to 'look like the innocent flower, / But be the serpent under't' (Act 1, Sc 5). Before the banquet she makes a similar plea: 'sleek o'er your rugged looks; / Be bright and jovial among your guests tonight' (Act 3, Sc 2).

After Macbeth kills Duncan's chamberlains, Macduff begins to question Macbeth's motives. Lady Macbeth's fainting spell distracts the thanes from her husband. She may faint because she is overcome by emotion or is shocked by Macbeth's killing of the chamberlains, but most commentators see this as another example of her calculating nature.

Composed

After Duncan is murdered (Act 2, Sc 2) both Lady Macbeth and Macbeth appear nervous and shaken by the crime. However, while Macbeth remains distraught throughout the scene, Lady Macbeth regains a **chilling calm**. Macbeth is so distressed that he mistakenly forgets to leave the daggers in Duncan's room. With **implacable composure** his wife returns to the room to 'gild the faces of the grooms' with Duncan's blood. While Macbeth hears imaginary voices and expresses immediate remorse, Lady Macbeth remains **practically focused** on the task of getting away with murder. She coldly tells Macbeth 'A little water clears us of this deed'.

During the banquet scene (Act 3, Sc 4), Lady Macbeth exhibits similar composure. Overwrought by his crimes, Macbeth becomes hysterical at the sight of Banquo's ghost. Lady Macbeth remains calm and attempts to explain away Macbeth's behaviour as resulting from illness: 'my lord is often thus, / And hath been from his youth: pray you, keep seat; / The fit is momentary' (Act 3, Sc 4).

However, as the play begins to reach a conclusion **she loses her self-control as she becomes consumed by her own guilt**.

Burdened by Guilt

Although Lady Macbeth is complicit in the murder of Duncan, she is still a conscionable character. As she contemplates regicide, she calls on evil spirits to 'Stop up the access and passage to remorse' (Act 1, Sc 5). However, the spirits do not answer her prayers. Unable to suppress her conscience, she is left burdened with guilt over Duncan's death.

Unlike Macbeth, **Lady Macbeth never publicly expresses her doubts** about the murder of Duncan. **As she is a guarded individual, the audience only witnesses her personal guilt in her most private moments**.

Shakespeare suggests a more human side to her character when she privately confesses that she could not bring herself to murder Duncan as he looked like her father: 'Had he not resembled / My father as he slept, I had done't' (Act 2, Sc 2). This aspect of her personality is emphasised in the second half of the play as she reveals her guilt and remorse.

The first signal of regret appears in Act 3. In a short soliloquy, **Lady Macbeth explains that power has brought her no contentment and confesses that she envies the peace Duncan has achieved in death**:

> 'Nought's had, all's spent,
> Where our desire is got without content:
> 'Tis safer to be that which we destroy
> Than by destruction dwell in doubtful joy' (Act 3, Sc 2)

It is interesting to note that once Macbeth arrives on stage, she makes no mention of these personal doubts and instead chides him for appearing sorrowful.

Lady Macbeth's guilt reaches its fullest expression in the sleepwalking scene (Act 5, Sc 1). As she is a very guarded character it seems appropriate for Shakespeare to expose her most personal fears through the device of sleepwalking. It gives the audience an uncensored look at her subconscious. **The arresting vision of Lady Macbeth attempting to wash her hands of blood dramatically conveys the depth of her guilt**. She is unable to rid herself of the memory of her crimes: 'Here's the smell of the blood still: all the / perfumes of Arabia will not sweeten this little / hand.' She also makes reference to the murders of Banquo and Macduff's family; evidently she feels responsible for helping to unleash the evil in Macbeth. The sleepwalking scene reveals Lady Macbeth's unhappiness and fraying mental state. Ominously the doctor tells the gentlewoman to 'Remove from her the means of all annoyance, / And still keep eyes upon her', thus foreshadowing her eventual suicide.

Her suicide happens offstage, indicating how marginalised she has become as a character. The means of her death compounds the idea of her as a woman overwhelmingly burdened by guilt.

Lady Macbeth:

- Ambitious
- Manipulative
- Calculating
- Composed
- Ultimately burdened by guilt

Banquo

Banquo is an important figure within *Macbeth*. **He functions as a foil (contrast) to Macbeth**. His distrust of the witches, his innate goodness and the fact that he commits no evil deeds set him apart from Macbeth. Banquo is also ambitious: he harbours private ambitions for his children's succession to the crown. However, unlike Macbeth, he is unwilling to compromise his morality to pursue these ambitions.

A Foil (Contrast) to Macbeth

One of the main functions of Banquo within the play is to highlight Macbeth's shortcomings. This is done by contrasting how Macbeth and Banquo deal with temptation. This is most evident when both characters meet the witches. Macbeth appears desperate to hear the witches' prophecies: 'Stay, you imperfect speakers, tell me more' whereas Banquo boldly shows a refusal to fear or beg the weird sisters: 'Speak then to me, who neither beg nor fear / Your favours nor your hate' (Act 1, Sc 3).

While Macbeth is 'rapt withal' by the witches' prophecies, Banquo's instinct is to question their motives:

> '...to win us to our harm,
> The instruments of darkness tell us truths,
> Win us with honest trifles, to betray's
> In deepest consequence' (Act 1, Sc 3)

Banquo's innate goodness causes him to interrogate evil. Unlike Macbeth, he does not try to actively bring about the witches' equivocal promises.

Although Banquo is affected by dark thoughts **he is portrayed as resistant to the lure of evil**. Shortly before Duncan is murdered, Banquo is unable to sleep as he is troubled by thoughts of the witches. He appeals to heaven to help resist the temptations prompted by the evil witches' prophecies:

'A heavy summons lies like lead upon me,
And yet I would not sleep. Merciful powers,
Restrain in me the cursed thoughts that nature
Gives way to in repose!' (Act 2, Sc 1)

Where Macbeth embraces evil, Banquo resists it.

Ambitious

Banquo is nonetheless an ambitious character. The witches prophesised that his descendents shall be kings; he articulates his private ambitions for himself as the father of a long line of kings:

'But that myself should be the root and father
Of many kings. If there come truth from them –
As upon thee, Macbeth, their speeches shine –
Why, by the verities on thee made good,
May they not be my oracles as well,
And set me up in hope?' (Act 3, Sc 1)

However, Banquo is unwilling to allow his ambitions to compromise him morally. **He remains morally forthright** when Macbeth warily tries to gauge his loyalty. Macbeth tells Banquo that he will be favoured if he remains loyal to him: 'If you shall cleave to my consent, when 'tis, / It shall make honour for you'. Banquo replies that he can only act in good conscience and with honour. He says that this concerns him more than titles:

'So I lose none
In seeking to augment it, but still keep
My bosom franchised and allegiance clear' (Act 2, Sc 1)

His honourable and uncompromising loyalty to the King contrasts with Macbeth's increasingly corrupt thoughts. Although ambitious, Banquo values his honour above all.

Suspicious of Macbeth

Some commentators question why Banquo fails to act against Macbeth. However, he never has any concrete evidence that Macbeth killed Duncan. He only suspects Macbeth. In Act 3, Scene 1 Banquo says:

'Thou hast it now: King, Cawdor, Glamis, all,
As the weird women promised, and, I fear,
Thou play'dst most foully for't'

His suspicions and implied condemnation align him with the forces of good within the play.

Virtuous

Like Macbeth, Banquo is initially presented as a **loyal subject of Scotland** who risked his life on the battlefield. Duncan looks upon him favourably and commends his nobility:

'Noble Banquo,
That hast no less deserved, nor must be known
No less to have done so – let me enfold thee
And hold thee to my heart' (Act 1, Sc 4)

Banquo is later identified as a virtuous figure in his reaction to the murder of Duncan. At first he expresses his shock but he quickly calls for an investigation to root out treason: 'In the great hand of God I stand; and thence / Against the undivulged pretence I fight / Of treasonous malice' (Act 2, Sc 3). As a virtuous individual he aligns himself with God and the need to uncover the truth.

According to Macbeth, **Banquo possesses many virtues and kingly qualities**. It is this aspect of his personality that encourages Macbeth to fear him:

'Our fears in Banquo
Stick deep, and in his royalty of nature
Reigns that which would be feared: 'tis much he dares;
And, to that dauntless temper of his mind,
He hath a wisdom that doth guide his valour
To act in safety. There is none but he
Whose being I do fear' (Act 3, Sc 1)

When *Macbeth* was written it was thought that King James I was a direct descendent of Banquo. The witches show Macbeth a procession of kings followed by Banquo. This illustrates the notion that Banquo is an ancestor of the British monarchs. Shakespeare was therefore keen to please James I by stressing **Banquo's innate nobility and 'royalty of nature'.**

Banquo:

- A foil (contrast) to Macbeth
- Ambitious but not corruptible
- Suspicious of Macbeth
- Virtuous

Macduff

Macduff represents moral fortitude, patriotism and the forces of good within the play. However, because Macduff is undeveloped as a character, his triumph over evil fails to inspire the audience. He is also a flawed character: he makes many unwise choices within the play.

Patriotic and Loyal

From the first moment he enters the stage, **Macduff reveals the intensity of his loyalty to king and country**. He is the most visibly distressed by the news of Duncan's murder. So traumatised is he by the sight of Duncan's body that he struggles to articulate what he has discovered: 'O horror! Horror! Horror! Tongue nor heart / Cannot conceive nor name thee!' (Act 2, Sc 3).

His **reverence for Duncan** is displayed when he uses religious terminology to describe Duncan:

'Most sacrilegious murder hath broke ope
The Lord's anointed temple, and stole thence
The life o' the building!' (Act 2, Sc 3)

Macduff echoes the Elizabethan concept of a king being God's representative on earth.

His patriotism is evident throughout the play. It is he who goes to England to enlist the help of King Edward and Malcolm. Macduff's loyalty to Scotland is tested by Malcolm who falsely presents himself as unfit to be king. This test of Macduff's loyalty is obvious and transparent. However Macduff lacks the wisdom to see this; his immediate reaction is a passionate outburst lamenting Scotland's future:

'O nation miserable,
With an untitled tyrant bloody-sceptred,
When shalt thou see thy wholesome days again,
Since that the truest issue of thy throne
By his own interdiction stands accursed,
And does blaspheme his breed?' (Act 4, Sc 3)

As a loyal patriot, his emotions are bound up with the fate of his country.

Uncompromising

Throughout *Macbeth*, Macduff is portrayed as **a highly moral character who refuses to compromise his principles**. In a bold snub of Macbeth, he declines to go to the coronation at Scone. His suspicions may stem from the fact that Macbeth killed the chamberlains (Macduff did question Macbeth in this regard). Macduff is also the only thane to reject Macbeth's invitation to the coronation banquet. Although the other thanes may be suspicious of Macbeth, only Macduff has the unwavering principles to deny Macbeth's bidding.

Lacks Wisdom

However, again questions can be asked of Macduff's wisdom. As he believes Macbeth is treacherous enough to murder Duncan's murderers, it would be more prudent to keep this to himself until proof could be found. Instead he snubs Macbeth; this prompts Macbeth to move against him.

So uncompromising are Macduff's ideals that he even **puts Scotland ahead of his family's welfare**. He leaves his family vulnerable by going to England to meet with Malcolm. Lady Macduff herself questions his motives for doing this:

'... to leave his wife, to leave his babes,
His mansion and his titles in a place
From whence himself does fly? He loves us not;
He wants the natural touch' (Act 4, Sc 2)

And when he learns of the murder of his family he immediately blames himself:

'Sinful Macduff,
They were all struck for thee! Naught that I am,
Not for their own demerits, but for mine,
Fell slaughter on their souls' (Act 4, Sc 3)

An Uninspiring Figure

There is a logic to the fact that it is Macduff who finally kills Macbeth and displays his decapitated head. He pursues Macbeth through Dunsinane Castle and confronts him with single-minded intensity: 'I have no words: / My voice is in my sword – thou bloodier villain / Than terms can give thee out!' (Act 5, Sc 8). This completes his function within the play, allows him to take revenge for his family's murder and fulfils the witches' prophecies.

However, despite the fact that Macduff signals the triumph of good over evil, what endures is a vision of Macbeth, the play's tragic figure. **Macduff's actions fail to inspire the audience** partly because he remains undeveloped as a character and partly because the audience has been intently focused on Macbeth throughout the play.

Macduff:

- Patriotic and loyal
- Uncompromising
- Lacks wisdom
- Ultimately an uninspiring figure

Malcolm

Malcolm plays a relatively minor role within *Macbeth*, but he is important as a symbol of goodness and kingship. He can be admired for his prudence and ability to lead an army, but his opposition to Macbeth is uninspiring in the final act. This is because Shakespeare does not want to distract the audience's attention away from the tragic figure of Macbeth.

Duncan names Malcolm as his successor. Although this seems natural by right of birth, it also suggests that Malcolm has the necessary qualities needed to lead the country.

One of these admirable qualities is apparent immediately after Duncan's body is found. Macbeth and the other thanes make a public spectacle of their grief. Malcolm shows himself to be **a shrewd judge of character** when he suspects one of the thanes to be responsible for the crime: 'To show an unfelt sorrow is an office / Which the false man does easy' (Act 2, Sc 3). Malcolm is clearly aware that he is surrounded by treachery.

Malcolm is also **a prudent character**: while in the court of King Edward he is slow to trust Macduff. As he says, 'modest wisdom plucks me / From over-credulous haste' (Act 4, Sc 3). This quality was sorely lacking in Duncan, who trusted both the former Thane of Cawdor and Macbeth – both of whom betrayed him.

Malcolm also reveals himself to be **a capable leader** in his role as head of the allied forces. He confidently proclaims his army as agents of God and affirms the moral justification for ousting Macbeth: 'Macbeth / Is ripe for shaking, and the powers above / Put on their instruments' (Act 4, Sc 3). He displays his **tactical wisdom** when he orders his men to mask their numbers by carrying branches from Birnam Wood thus giving an appearance of fewer soldiers.

Despite the fact that he occupies a relatively minor role within the play, Malcolm asserts his importance as **a symbol of kingship and social order** at the play's close. He delivers the final lines dismissing the 'dead butcher and his fiend-like queen' and inviting all to witness his coronation.

Despite his admirable qualities and his ability to lead, Malcolm remains **uninspiring for the audience**. Macbeth arouses both horror and pity; Malcolm and the forces of good are somewhat lost in the midst of this. Although Macbeth is a deplorable and tyrannical king, his plight occupies the imagination of the audience. Malcolm's story neatly concludes the play but is not intended to move the audience. Instead the audience is kept focused on the tragic figure of Macbeth.

Malcolm:	• Possessed of kingly virtues • Ultimately uninspiring for the audience

Duncan

A Virtuous King

In Shakespeare's time the king was the political leader of the country and was thought to be God's representative on earth. Duncan exhibits the qualities of a strong and virtuous king. He is described in religious terms that align him with God and is presented as a trusting character. These factors mark him as an innocent victim and therefore emphasise the evil of Macbeth's crime.

Duncan is portrayed as a confident and kind leader. In the second scene of the play he acts decisively to punish the former Thane of Cawdor for his treachery. In the same scene, he also displays compassion in his concern for the bleeding sergeant who reports on the battle.

Duncan is seen as generous in his willingness to reward those who have displayed loyalty. He is quick to confer the title of Thane of Cawdor on Macbeth and appears genuinely grateful for Macbeth's part in the battle: 'Only I have left to say, / More is thy due than more than all can pay'. He promises to favour Macbeth in the future: 'I have begun to plant thee, and will labour / To make thee full of growing' (Act 1, Sc 4). His gratitude to Banquo is similarly expressed. **Duncan displays virtues that ensure his popularity as a king: decisiveness, generosity and graciousness**.

In soliloquy, Macbeth questions whether he should proceed with the murder and reflects on Duncan as a leader. **Macbeth himself acknowledges Duncan as a virtuous and popular king**. He notes that Duncan has used his power with restraint and acted with honesty in his important role:

> '... Duncan
> Hath borne his faculties so meek, hath been
> So clear in his great office, that his virtues
> Will plead like angels, trumpet-tongued, against
> The deep damnation of his taking-off' (Act 1, Sc 7)

Macbeth sees that there will be a public outcry following Duncan's death, that will serve as a testimony to his virtuousness:

'And pity, like a naked new-born babe,
Striding the blast, or heaven's cherubim, horsed
Upon the sightless couriers of the air,
Shall blow the horrid deed in every eye,
That tears shall drown the wind' (Act 1, Sc 7)

Trusting

Duncan is also a very trusting character and this is perhaps his downfall. He recognises this characteristic in himself. He relates how he placed too much trust in the former Thane of Cawdor who then betrayed him:

'There's no art
To find the mind's construction in the face:
He was a gentleman on whom I built
An absolute trust' (Act 1, Sc 4)

This foreshadows Macbeth's breach of trust. A wiser king may have taken stricter measures to guarantee his own safety and shown better judgement of character.

Saintly

Duncan is presented as a saintly figure, particularly after his death. Macduff uses religious terminology upon discovering Duncan's body, comparing him to a sacred temple: 'Most sacrilegious murder hath broke ope / The Lord's anointed temple, and stole thence / The life o' the building' (Act 2, Sc 3). Macduff reinforces this idea later in the play by describing Duncan as 'a most sainted king' (Act 4, Sc 3). Ross clearly links Duncan to heaven when he speaks to the old man about the strange darkness that clouds the sky after Duncan's death: 'Thou seest, the heavens, as troubled with man's act, / Threaten his bloody stage: by the clock, 'tis day, / And yet dark night strangles the travelling lamp' (Act 2, Sc 4).

Innocent victim

Duncan's virtuous nature, trusting personality and saintly qualities evoke the audience's sympathy. These traits add to the idea of him as an innocent victim, making Macbeth's crimes seem all the more despicable. However, Duncan is not fully developed as a character in the play as Shakespeare's intention is to keep the audience focused on the tragic figure of Macbeth.

Duncan:

- A virtuous king
- Trusting
- Saintly
- Innocent victim

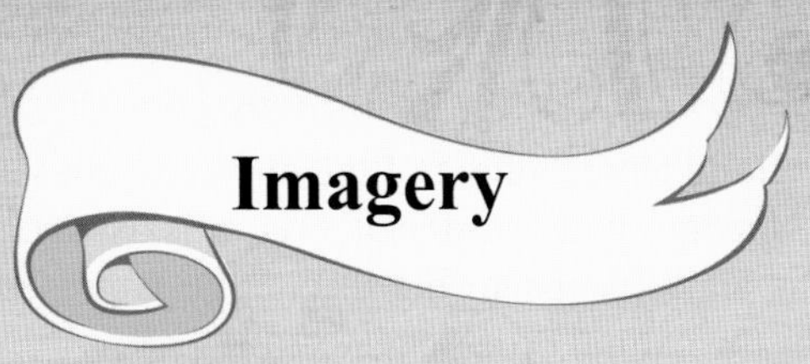

Imagery

The rich imagery of *Macbeth* brings the themes of the play into sharp focus. Shakespeare uses poetic language to metaphorically explore key ideas. The play's imagery also helps to create atmosphere and enriches the audience's understanding of the characters. In particular, four recurring images are interwoven into the text:

- darkness and light
- fertility and disease
- blood
- clothing and masks.

Darkness and Light

By setting many of the important scenes of *Macbeth* at night, Shakespeare reflects the moral darkness of the play. The murder of Duncan, the killing of Banquo, the banquet scene and the sleepwalking scene all take place at night. Light and darkness serve as metaphors for good and evil through the imagery of the play.

As emblems of evil, the witches are referred to by Macbeth as 'black, and midnight hags' (Act 4, Sc 1); Banquo calls them 'instruments of darkness' (Act 1, Sc 3). It is therefore fitting that the night of Duncan's murder is characterised by an unusually starless sky: 'There's husbandry in heaven; / Their candles are all out' (Act 2, Sc 1). After his death, a strange darkness grips the land. Ross and an old man discuss how the sun fails to rise: 'by the clock, 'tis day, / And yet dark night strangles the travelling lamp' (Act 2, Sc 4).

When Macbeth seeks the courage to kill Duncan, he imagines all light being blotted out to provide cover for his evil desires: 'Stars, hide your fires! / Let not light see my black and deep desires' (Act 1, Sc 4). Similarly, as he prepares for the murder of Banquo, he calls on the night to blindfold the light of day: 'Come, seeling night, / Scarf up the tender eye of pitiful day' (Act 3, Sc 2).

When Lady Macbeth invokes evil spirits, she imagines darkness smothering her actions, screening the deed from her conscience:

'Come, thick night,
And pall thee in the dunnest smoke of hell,
That my keen knife see not the wound it makes,
Nor heaven peep through the blanket of the dark,
To cry 'Hold, hold!'' (Act 1, Sc 5)

Towards the end of the play, as she starts to suffer from a guilty conscience, Lady Macbeth keeps a light by her bed continuously.

In Act 5, Scene 5, Macbeth imagines life as a candle that will inevitably burn out. This pessimistic image illustrates how the dark forces of evil have coloured his view of the world. For Macbeth, darkness has consumed light leaving him with a desperately bleak outlook: 'Out, out, brief candle! / Life's but a walking shadow…signifying nothing' (Act 5, Sc 5).

In contrast, images of light help to highlight the essential goodness of Duncan and Malcolm. It is no coincidence that scenes focusing on these characters generally take place during the day.

Duncan equates nobility and goodness with light: 'But signs of nobleness, like stars, shall shine / On all deservers' (Act 1, Sc 4). Malcolm equates Macbeth's reign with darkness and his marching army with the coming dawn: 'Receive what cheer you may: / The night is long that never finds the day' (Act 4, Sc 3).

Fertility and Disease

An Elizabethan audience would have thought of the monarchy system as part of the natural order. This idea is reflected in *Macbeth* where Duncan's reign is associated with fertility and bounty. Because Macbeth isn't the rightful heir to the throne, he is presented as a blight on Scotland, threatening the harmony of the natural order.

From the beginning of the play, images of growth are bound up with ideas about power and the social order. A connection is made between the idea of fertility and power when Banquo asks the witches to predict his future titles: 'If you can look into the seeds of time, / And say which grain will grow and which will not, / Speak then to me' (Act 1, Sc 3).

Duncan is associated with images of harvest and growth. This helps to portray him as a good king and head of the natural social order. Duncan compares Macbeth to a plant that he will nurture and strengthen: 'I have begun to plant thee, and will labour / To make thee full of growing' (Act 1, Sc 4). The image communicates Duncan's generosity and nourishing leadership. When Duncan compliments Banquo after the battle, Banquo continues the fertility metaphor: 'There if I grow, / The harvest is your own.' Shakespeare is keen to stress the mutually beneficial power structure of monarchy. Images of fertility and growth poetically underscore the harmony within Scotland under a goodly king.

In contrast to this is the recurring imagery of sickness and disease. Many of the characters associate Macbeth's tyrannical reign with disease and infertility. When Ross cries out for his 'poor country', he laments that 'good men's lives / Expire before the flowers in their caps, / Dying or ere they sicken' (Act 4, Sc 3). This idea is reflected when Caithness describes Macbeth's rule as a 'distempered cause' (Act 5, Sc 2). Distemper was a disease of the abdomen that caused swelling.

Caithness also depicts Macbeth as a diseased sore on the skin of Scotland and Malcolm's army as the cure: 'Meet we the medicine of the sickly weal' (Act 5, Sc 2). In *Macbeth*, the forces of good are presented as a cure for the nation's ills through the image of Edward the Confessor. King Edward is blessed with divine healing power; not only can he cure the sick but his forces will also bring health to Scotland.

Macbeth himself sees Scotland as blighted by disease. He asks the doctor to diagnose the sickness that plagues the country: 'If thou couldst, doctor, cast / The water of my land, find her disease, / And purge it to a sound and pristine health' (Act 5, Sc 3). His actions not only induce disease in Scotland but also in Lady Macbeth whose mental illness eventually leads to her suicide.

The diseased nature of Scotland stems from its tyrannical king. Macbeth himself highlights his own illness and compares himself to a withered leaf: 'I am sick at heart… I have lived long enough: my way of life / Is fall'n into the sear, the yellow leaf' (Act 5, Sc 3).

Scotland's only cure is the coronation of the rightful king. This natural harmony can only occur once Scotland is purged of Macbeth. As Lennox remarks, the battle against Macbeth will 'dew the sovereign flower and drown the weeds' (Act 5, Sc 2). In the final moments of the play Malcolm describes himself in the same terms as 'newly planted'. Now the natural order has returned, the characters of *Macbeth* feel that Scotland can grow once again.

Blood

Macbeth is a most bloody play. Shakespeare's bloody imagery, including the vision of blood-spattered characters, allows him to create an atmosphere of horror and violence. Blood also represents guilt within the play. As *Macbeth* draws to a close, the blood-drenched imagery expresses the idea of Scotland suffering under the oppression of Macbeth's rule.

The violence of the world of *Macbeth* is established with the appearance of the bleeding sergeant (Act 1, Sc 2). We soon learn about Macbeth's gruesome participation in the battle: how his sword 'smoked with bloody execution' as he 'carved out his passage' through enemy soldiers. When

Macbeth finally faced Macdonwald, he 'unseamed him from the nave to the chops, / And fixed his head upon [the] battlements.' The characters' celebration of such violence clearly establishes Scotland in this period as a violent and dangerous place.

When Macbeth sees the vision of the dagger (Act 2, Sc 1), the sudden appearance of blood on the blade and handle ominously prefigures the impending murder: 'I see thee still, / And on thy blade and dudgeon gouts of blood, / Which was not so before.' This adds to the overall sense of horror within the play.

Images of blood also illustrate guilt within *Macbeth*. The disquieting vision of Macbeth's blood-soaked hands dramatically highlights the gruesome nature of his crime, but his efforts to cleanse them represent his desperation to rid himself of his own guilt:

'Will all great Neptune's ocean wash this blood
Clean from my hand? No, this my hand will rather
The multitudinous seas incarnadine,
Making the green one red' (Act 2, Sc 1)

Here Macbeth recognises that the violence of his actions will spread rather than be washed away. This foreshadows his grim proclamation later in the play that 'blood will have blood' (Act 3, Sc 4).

Similarly, the appearance of Banquo's bloody ghost (Act 3, Sc 4) with 'twenty trenched gashes on his head' dramatically illustrates Macbeth's guilt. As the ghost shakes his 'gory locks' the audience understand that Macbeth is literally haunted by what he has done.

In a most telling image, Macbeth pictures himself wading through a river of blood. He is so consumed by the horror of his crimes that his actions now seem to have little significance: 'I am in blood / Stepped in so far that, should I wade no more, / Returning were as tedious as go o'er' (Act 3, Sc 4).

Although Lady Macbeth never publicly admits her feelings of guilt, the bloody imagery she employs in the sleepwalking scene (Act 5, Sc 1) illustrates the depth of her remorse. She imagines a persistent blood stain: 'Out, damned spot!' and the ever-present smell of blood on her hands: 'Here's the smell of the blood still: all the / perfumes of Arabia will not sweeten this little / hand.' As with Macbeth, bloody imagery serves to highlight Lady Macbeth's feelings of guilt.

Towards the end of the play, images of blood also communicate Scotland's disorder. Macduff cries, 'Bleed, bleed, poor country!' (Act 4, Sc 3) and Malcolm describes how under Macbeth's rule Scotland 'bleeds; and each new day a gash / Is added to her wounds' (Act 4, Sc 3). Caithness proclaims that loyal patriots are willing to sacrifice their own blood to help Scotland: 'pour we in our country's purge / Each drop of us' (Act 5, Sc 2).

Fittingly the play ends as bloodily as it begins, with Macduff carrying Macbeth's decapitated head. Just as the play began with a bloody battle, it ends with one. Shakespeare is suggesting that the bloody cycle of violence is due to begin again.

Masks and Clothing

Images of masks illustrate the idea of deception at the heart of *Macbeth*. The audience realises how Macbeth and Lady Macbeth seek to maintain power through the appearance of virtue, hiding the fact that their power stems from an appalling act of treachery.

From the beginning of the play, Duncan highlights the connection between deception and disloyalty. Explaining how his trust in Macdonwald was misplaced, Duncan says, 'There's no art / To find the mind's construction in the face' (Act 1, Sc 4). As leader of the rebellion, Macdonwald hid his treasonous plans beneath a mask of allegiance.

Lady Macbeth also stresses the importance of deception and its relationship to power. She realises that Macbeth's outward appearance must be fitting to a goodly king, even if his inner thoughts are evil: 'look like the innocent flower, / But be the serpent under't' (Act 1, Sc 5).

Macbeth comes to realise how necessary it is to present himself falsely to the world and mask his dark thoughts: 'False face must hide what the false heart doth know' (Act 1, Sc 7). He consciously looks to disguise his villainy to retain the loyalty of the thanes: 'And make our faces vizards to our hearts, / Disguising what they are' (Act 3, Sc 2).

Images of clothing stress the inappropriateness of Macbeth's role as king. Characters connect Macbeth's unsuitability for the title of king by imagining him dressed in ill-fitting or borrowed clothes. Indeed, he himself uses this kind of imagery to express his surprise upon receiving the title of Thane of Cawdor: 'The Thane of Cawdor lives: why do you dress me / In borrowed robes?' (Act 1, Sc 3). Banquo echoes this sentiment by comparing Macbeth's elevated status to newly worn clothes: 'New honours come upon him, / Like our strange garments, cleave not to their mould / But with the aid of use' (Act 1, Sc 3).

The clothing metaphor is continued when Macbeth argues that he should remain loyal to Duncan who has rewarded him for bravery:

> 'He hath honoured me of late; and I have bought
> Golden opinions from all sorts of people,
> Which would be worn now in their newest gloss,
> Not cast aside so soon' (Act 1, Sc 7)

Macduff uses the image of new clothes to question the suitability of Macbeth as king. He fears that Macbeth's reign will compare poorly with Duncan's: 'Lest our old robes sit easier than our new!' (Act 2, Sc 4).

This idea is mirrored when Caithness describes Macbeth's inability to maintain order as an ill-fitting belt: 'He cannot buckle his distempered cause / Within the belt of rule' (Act 5, Sc 2).

Angus extends the metaphor and pictures Macbeth as pathetically swamped by the trappings of power. He images how Macbeth must feel 'his title / Hang loose about him, like a giant's robe / Upon a dwarfish thief' (Act 5, Sc 2). The grotesque comedy used here serves to mock Macbeth and stress the inappropriateness of him as King of Scotland.

Shakespeare uses clothing imagery to suggest that Macbeth comes to see himself as unsuited to the role of king. Before the final battle he is presented as frantically casting off his kingly robes in favour of his armour (see Act 5, Sc 3).

Imagery	Function
Darkness and Light	• Darkness adds to the sinister atmosphere of the play and represents the evil forces within *Macbeth*. • Light represents goodness.
Fertility and Disease	• Images of growth serves as a metaphor for the natural order. • Images of disease highlight the destructive nature of Macbeth's rule and represent evil.
Blood	• Adds to the horror of the play • Represents guilt • Serves as a metaphor for the disorder within Scotland • Represents the notion of loyal self-sacrifice
Masks and Clothing	• Explores the relationship between deception and power • Stresses Macbeth's inability to rule • Highlights the theme of appearance and reality • Draws attention to Macbeth's own realisation that he is unfit to rule

Kingship

In *Macbeth*, Shakespeare presents a vision of idealised kingship through the figures of Duncan, Malcolm and Edward. These three goodly kings provide a stark contrast to Macbeth. Shakespeare uses this contrast to highlight the desirable qualities of a king and to make the connection between kingship and social harmony.

In Shakespeare's time, the king was considered God's representative on earth. Duncan, Malcolm and Edward are all established as blessed figures within the play, whereas Macbeth is associated with hell and evil. After he is murdered, Duncan is presented using imagery that connects him with godliness. Macduff compares Duncan's body to a temple: 'Most sacrilegious murder hath broke ope / The Lord's anointed temple' (Act 2, Sc 3) and later in the play says to Malcolm: 'Thy royal father / Was a most sainted king' (Act 4, Sc 3). The idea of **Duncan as an agent of God** is reinforced when his death provokes strange unnatural events, as if his murder has offended God himself. Ross tells the old man that Duncan's death has upset heaven, and as a result the sun refuses to rise: 'Thou seest, the heavens, as troubled with man's act, / Threaten his bloody stage: by the clock, 'tis day, / And yet dark night strangles the travelling lamp' (Act 2, Sc 4).

Similarly, **Shakespeare emphasises King Edward's saintliness**, presenting him as blessed with divine healing powers. Malcolm tells Macduff how the sick queue to be healed by Edward's heavenly power and how 'He hath a heavenly gift of prophecy, / And sundry blessings hang about his throne, / That speak him full of grace' (Act 4, Sc 3).

Duncan and Edward are seen as saintlike whereas **Macbeth is presented as a devil**. Macduff stresses this idea in his meeting with Malcolm: 'Not in the legions / Of horrid hell can come a devil more damned / In evils to top Macbeth' (Act 4, Sc 3). He is referred to in terms that reinforce this notion: 'Devilish Macbeth' (Act 4, Sc 3), 'fiend of Scotland' (Act 4, Sc 3) and his meetings with the witches dramatically align him with dark supernatural forces. It is therefore fitting that as he prepares to marshal his troops against Macbeth, Malcolm commends his army as agents of heaven: 'the powers above / Put on their instruments' (Act 4, Sc 3). **Shakespeare presents the king as divinely ordained; opponents of this 'natural' order should be considered as evil.**

Shakespeare also recognises that a good king will inspire love in his subjects. Duncan is evidently loved and respected by the whole of Scotland. Macbeth himself testifies to this and offers it as a reason not to kill Duncan. He sees how Duncan's death would lead to a public outcry causing the whole nation to weep:

> 'And pity, like a naked new-born babe,
> Striding the blast, or heaven's cherubim, horsed
> Upon the sightless couriers of the air,
> Shall blow the horrid deed in every eye,
> That tears shall drown the wind' (Act 1, Sc 7)

Malcolm too inspires love and respect in his followers. He leads a loyal army against Macbeth. At the end of the play, Malcolm is enthusiastically hailed as King of Scotland.

In direct contrast, **Macbeth is reviled and distrusted by his subjects**. Where Malcolm can inspire an army to attack Macbeth's castle, Macbeth's army desert him, leaving him isolated and alone. Macbeth sees that he lacks the love that should naturally accompany a king, and instead receives curses and false praise:

'And that which should accompany old age,
As honour, love, obedience, troops of friends,
I must not look to have; but, in their stead,
Curses, not loud but deep, mouth-honour, breath' (Act 5, Sc 3)

Shakespeare sees a successful king as a steward of his country who promotes social harmony. Duncan is effective in dealing with dissent and moves decisively to quash the rebellion led by Macdonwald. He pronounces the death of the treacherous former Thane of Cawdor; stability and order are soon restored in Scotland. As a generous king, Duncan rewards loyalty: Macbeth is quickly made the new Thane of Cawdor. Duncan looks to nurture his subjects so that they may excel in the future, as he says to Macbeth: 'I have begun to plant thee, and will labour / To make thee full of growing' (Act 1, Sc 4).

Echoing his father's style of leadership, Malcolm too rewards his subjects' loyalty. At the end of the play he announces his desire to quickly recognise the thanes that have helped to depose Macbeth: 'We shall not spend a large expense of time / Before we reckon with your several loves, / And make us even with you' (Act 5, Sc 9). Malcolm pronounces that the thanes should be known as earls from this point on as further appreciation of their loyalty. By the end of the play the vision of unity suggests that Malcolm will restore the social harmony that was lost during Macbeth's reign.

In contrast, **Macbeth is seen as a king who promotes chaos over order**. Ross comments on the disorder and air of fear over which Macbeth reigns. He says to Lady Macduff:

'But cruel are the times, when we are traitors
And do not know ourselves, when we hold rumour
From what we fear, yet know not what we fear,
But float upon a wild and violent sea
Each way and move' (Act 4, Sc 2)

And in his meeting with Macduff and Malcolm, Ross outlines Scotland's woes:

'Alas, poor country!
Almost afraid to know itself. It cannot
Be called our mother, but our grave; …
Where sighs and groans and shrieks that rend the air
Are made, not marked; where violent sorrow seems
A modern ecstasy; the dead man's knell
Is there scarce asked for who; and good men's lives
Expire before the flowers in their caps,
Dying or ere they sicken' (Act 4, Sc 3)

Macbeth himself describes Scotland as a diseased state but fails to recognise himself as the source of the country's problems:

'If thou couldst, doctor, cast
The water of my land, find her disease,
And purge it to a sound and pristine health,
I would applaud thee to the very echo,
That should applaud again' (Act 5, Sc 3)

Shakespeare highlights the king's role as a promoter of social harmony by illustrating the deficits in Macbeth's character. Where Duncan and Malcolm offer a vision of what a king ought to be, Macbeth is presented as unfit to wear the 'golden round'.

Kingship

Godliness	• Duncan, Edward and Malcolm are presented as saintly or as agents of heaven. • Macbeth is aligned with evil and presented as a devil.
Beloved	• Duncan is loved by his subjects. • Malcolm inspires loyalty and respect. • Macbeth's followers desert him and curse him in secret.
Promotes social harmony	• Duncan quashes rebellion and honours his followers. • Malcolm restores order to Scotland and also rewards those loyal to him. • Macbeth's reign promotes social chaos.

Evil

The spectre of supernatural evil is central to the play, *Macbeth*. Shakespeare dramatically presents evil in the form of the witches. **The play also explores humanity's capacity for evil**. Through the figures of Macbeth and Lady Macbeth, Shakespeare illustrates how people can be drawn to and eventually consumed by evil deeds.

The witches personify pure evil in *Macbeth*. They are aligned with hell throughout the play: Banquo refers to them as 'instruments of darkness' and 'the devil' (Act 1, Sc 3). They cast ghoulish spells using a mixture of grotesque ingredients: 'Fillet of fenny snake…Eye of newt…tongue of dog' (Act 4, Sc 1). Their unholy worship of the goddess Hecate compounds the vision of them as agents of evil.

In keeping with Christian theology, **supernatural evil exerts an influence on individuals through temptation**; it is unable to actively participate in evil actions. For this reason, the witches seek to tempt Macbeth, but cannot actually force him to commit any evil deeds. They do this through equivocation, i.e. by telling Macbeth half-truths. Banquo recognises the witches as equivocating agents of evil early on in the play, but his objections do little to undermine Macbeth's interest in their prophecies:

'And oftentimes, to win us to our harm,
The instruments of darkness tell us truths,
Win us with honest trifles, to betray's
In deepest consequence' (Act 1, Sc 3)

Although too late, Macbeth eventually comes to the same conclusion at the end of the play:

'And be these juggling fiends no more believed,
That palter with us in a double sense;
That keep the word of promise to our ear,
And break it to our hope!' (Act 5, Sc 8)

Shakespeare highlights the idea that evil can only be realised through the actions of humanity. Although evil is a supernatural force, it only has the power to influence. More dangerous is the evil found in the hearts of people. The evil actions of Macbeth and Lady Macbeth reveal humanity's capacity for evil. In Act 1, Scene 7 Macbeth outlines a number of reasons not to kill Duncan:

- Macbeth is his subject and his kinsman ('He's here in double trust: / First, as I am his kinsman and his subject, / Strong both against the deed').
- Macbeth is his host ('as his host, / Who should against his murderer shut the door, / Not bear the knife myself').
- Duncan is a good king ('Duncan / … hath been / So clear in his great office, that his virtues / Will plead like angels, trumpet-tongued, against / The deep damnation of his taking-off').
- All of Scotland shall mourn Duncan's loss ('And pity, …/ Shall blow the horrid deed in every eye, / That tears shall drown the wind').

Despite these moral objections Macbeth still carries out the murder, knowing that it is wrong. **What is most disquieting about his behaviour is that he consciously commits evil.** The rest of Macbeth's crimes (the murders of Banquo and Macduff's family) all evolve from this evil decision.

Shakespeare distinguishes between supernatural evil and humanity's capacity for evil. The witches are evil for evil's sake. They gain nothing from their actions bar the sinister satisfaction of watching Macbeth's life destroyed. This separates them from the human characters in the play who perpetrate evil. Macbeth and Lady Macbeth are motivated by the power they hope to personally gain from their evil deeds.

This distinction is furthered in that **the human characters suffer severe psychological consequences for their evil actions.** Lady Macbeth privately expresses her doubts about killing Duncan: "Tis safer to be that which we destroy / Than by destruction dwell in doubtful joy' (Act 3, Sc 2). This is explored more fully in the sleepwalking scene where we see her trying to wash imaginary blood from her hand: 'Here's the smell of the blood still: all the / perfumes of Arabia will not sweeten this little / hand' (Act 5, Sc 1). Her eventual suicide tragically illustrates the depth of her remorse.

Macbeth too is burdened with the guilt of his evil actions. Immediately after killing Duncan, he wishes that the knocking at the gate could revive the king: 'Wake Duncan with thy knocking! I would thou couldst!' (Act 2, Sc 2). Macbeth's guilt is dramatically presented by the spectacle of Banquo's ghost. Macbeth is forced to physically confront the results of his evil actions and is appalled at what he sees: 'Thy bones are marrowless, thy blood is cold; / Thou hast no speculation in those eyes / Which thou dost glare with!' (Act 3, Sc 4). Macbeth's guilt eventually gives way to world-weariness. By the end of the play, life has lost all meaning for him. In a memorable soliloquy he compares life to a candle that will inevitably burn out and to a poor actor whose words are ultimately meaningless:

> 'Out, out, brief candle!
> Life's but a walking shadow, a poor player
> That struts and frets his hour upon the stage
> And then is heard no more. It is a tale
> Told by an idiot, full of sound and fury,
> Signifying nothing' (Act 5, Sc 5)

Shakespeare's rich psychological development of *Macbeth*'s central characters reveals the inevitable outcome of evil. Lady Macbeth's prophetic statement: 'These deeds must not be thought / After these ways; so, it will make us mad' (Act 2, Sc 2) seems fitting here.

***Macbeth* concludes with the triumph of good over evil.** The celebration of Malcolm's impending coronation and the vision of Macbeth's severed head all point to the predominance of good. Through his characters, Shakespeare reveals how humanity has the capacity for both good and evil. Although evil is tempting, the burden of guilt and evil's inability to defeat the forces of good affirm the moralising ending of *Macbeth.*

Evil

Supernatural evil	• The witches personify evil in the play. • They conduct evil for evil's sake, not for personal gain. • The witches cannot commit evil directly. • They can only tempt individuals to commit evil deeds.
Humanity's capacity for evil	• Macbeth and Lady Macbeth perform many evil deeds. • Macbeth is conscious that his killing of Duncan is immoral.
Consequences of evil	• Lady Macbeth expresses her guilt privately and eventually commits suicide as a result. • Macbeth is consumed by his guilt. • Macbeth eventually becomes world-weary and suffers a spiritual death as a result of his evil crimes.
Triumph of good over evil	• In the end, the forces of good defeat Macbeth, and Malcolm prepares for his coronation. • The spectacle of Macbeth's decapitated head serves as a warning against the dangers of evil.

Appearance vs Reality

Shakespeare's exploration of appearance and reality is an intriguing aspect of *Macbeth.* The witches' paradoxical chant in the opening scene, 'Fair is foul, and foul is fair' establishes an air of confusion, where nothing is what it seems. In this play Shakespeare considers how equivocation and deception can mask reality with truly evil results. The theme is furthered by the characters' hallucinations which allow Shakespeare to communicate the protagonists' fraying mental states.

Equivocation is the use of ambiguous language to mislead or trick. Equivocators don't lie, instead they tell half-truths to mask reality. Equivocation was a serious issue when *Macbeth* was written. After a failed assassination attempt on King James I (the Gunpowder Plot) one of the accused plotters, Father Garnet, equivocated at his trial in order to hide information that was given to him during confession. He was found guilty and executed but his equivocal testimony provoked huge discussion. Shakespeare intended to flatter King James I in *Macbeth* and as a result aligned equivocation with evil in the play.

The witches use equivocal language to mislead Macbeth. In Act 1, Scene 3 they tell Macbeth that he 'shalt be king hereafter!'. Although this statement is true, the witches fail to warn him of the dire consequences that will result from pursuing this ambition. Macbeth recognises that the witches are 'imperfect speakers' but grows to trust them as they correctly predict that he will become Thane of Cawdor. However, Banquo is suspicious of the witches' motives and warns Macbeth that their predictions may mask a darker reality:

> 'And oftentimes, to win us to our harm,
> The instruments of darkness tell us truths,
> Win us with honest trifles, to betray's
> In deepest consequence' (Act 1, Sc 3)

Macbeth fails to heed Banquo's advice; **the witches' equivocal language appeals to Macbeth's sense of ambition, and as a result he chooses a murderous path.**

Later in the play (Act 4, Sc 1) **the witches equivocate again, presenting Macbeth with three apparitions which also influence his behaviour**. He is shown an armed head that warns him: 'Beware Macduff'. He then sees a bloody child that says, 'none of woman born / Shall harm Macbeth.' Finally he is presented with a crowned child that predicts, 'Macbeth shall never vanquished be until / Great Birnam wood to high Dunsinane hill / Shall come against him.' These equivocal predictions encourage Macbeth to attack Macduff's family and also give him false courage. He doesn't realise that Macduff was not technically 'of woman born' as he was delivered by caesarean section. Similarly, the idea that Birnam Wood could move seems implausible until Malcolm orders his soldiers to cut down branches from the wood to disguise their numbers. The decisions Macbeth makes are based upon the witches' equivocation. Hecate realises that Macbeth's confidence will be his final undoing, 'And you all know, security / Is mortals' chiefest enemy' (Act 3, Sc 5). The equivocal apparitions encourage this overconfidence and play on Macbeth's prideful nature.

The theme of appearance vs reality is also explored through the many acts of deception in the play. Ironically, Duncan is the first to recognise deception as a threat. He describes how he placed much trust in the former Thane of Cawdor and was then deceived by this apparently loyal subject: 'There's no art / To find the mind's construction in the face' (Act 1, Sc 2).

In an echo of this, **Lady Macbeth uses deception as a strategy within the play.** She sees how important deception is in attaining power. She worries that Macbeth may appear troubled by the murder and warns him to 'look like the innocent flower, / But be the serpent under't' (Act 1, Sc 5). She continues to use deception to divert suspicion away from Macbeth. She frames the chamberlains for Duncan's murder by smearing their bodies with blood: 'I'll gild the faces of the grooms withal; / For it must seem their guilt' (Act 2, Sc 2). After the body is discovered, Macduff questions why Macbeth killed the chamberlains; Lady Macbeth diverts attention from her husband by fainting. Many commentators believe this to be a feigned swoon and further testimony to her deceptive nature. In the banquet scene, Lady Macbeth tries to deceive the thanes by explaining away Macbeth's bizarre outburst as a fit he suffers from regularly.

Macbeth also values deception as a tactic. He understands that he must hide his crimes from the public gaze and adopt an innocent appearance. Macbeth pithily sums up this idea shortly before he kills Duncan: 'False face must hide what the false heart doth know' (Act 1, Sc 7). True to his intention, he appears shocked when Macduff discovers Duncan's body: 'Had I but died an hour before this chance, / I had lived a blessed time' (Act 2, Sc 3).

Shakespeare uses the motif of hallucinations to deepen the discussion of appearance vs reality. Shortly before he murders Duncan, Macbeth sees the vision of a dagger floating in the air (Act 2, Sc 1): 'Is this a dagger which I see before me, / The handle toward my hand?' Macbeth suspects the vision is a product of the stress he is under, that it is a 'dagger of the mind, a false creation, / Proceeding from the heat-oppressed brain'. **Shakespeare uses this visual spectacle to reveal how Macbeth's hold on reality is slipping**. The same idea is continued after the murder. Macbeth, in a state of confusion, thinks he hears voices: ' '...sleep no more! / Macbeth does murder sleep' ' (Act 2, Sc 2).

Some critics argue that Banquo's ghost is an hallucination of Macbeth's. Lady Macbeth sees it as a mirror of the earlier dagger hallucination, both evolving out of Macbeth's cowardice: 'This is the very painting of your fear: / This is the air-drawn dagger which, you said, / Led you to Duncan' (Act 3, Sc 4). Banquo's ghost dramatically presents Macbeth's guilt to the audience.

Lady Macbeth's guilt is also revealed in a similar fashion in the sleepwalking scene. In a dream state she imagines her hands soaked in blood and tries desperately to clean them: 'Here's the smell of the blood still: all the / perfumes of Arabia will not sweeten this little / hand' (Act 5, Sc 1). Her nightmare illustrates the depth of her guilt which she has kept so well hidden during her waking hours. **For both Macbeth and Lady Macbeth the confusion between appearance and reality allows Shakespeare to reveal their deep-seated guilt.**

Appearance vs Reality

Equivocation	• Shakespeare aligns equivocation with evil in an attempt to please King James I. • The witches use equivocal language to encourage Macbeth to kill Duncan. • The equivocal apparitions bolster Macbeth's confidence and tempt him towards greater evil.
Deception	• Ironically, Duncan sees how deceptive individuals can falsely win his trust. • Lady Macbeth uses deception as a strategy within the play. • Macbeth also uses deception as a key tactic.
Hallucinations and dreams	• Macbeth's hallucinations reveal his fraying mental state. • Shakespeare uses the motif of hallucinations to reveal Macbeth's guilt. • Lady Macbeth's guilt is revealed through sleepwalking.

Gender Roles

***Macbeth* is a fascinating exploration of masculinity and femininity.** The play interrogates the traditional ideas about gender and examines what it means to be a man or a woman. Throughout the play, many characters subvert the traditional ideas about gender.

***Macbeth* explores what it means to be a man.** The play discusses the connection between masculinity and physical bravery. Shakespeare also examines the idea of emotional composure as a manly trait.

Traditionally, men are idealised as aggressive and brave on the battlefield. The sergeant's report of Macbeth in battle clearly reflects this ideal (Act 1, Sc 2.). The description of 'brave Macbeth' as a violent and courageous warrior is very much applauded by Duncan and the other characters. Macbeth is described as 'Bellona's bridegroom' and 'Valour's minion' and is pictured as a bloodthirsty soldier:

'Disdaining Fortune, with his brandished steel,
Which smoked with bloody execution,
Like Valour's minion carved out his passage
Till he faced the slave;
Which ne'er shook hands, nor bade farewell to him,
Till he unseamed him from the nave to the chops,
And fixed his head upon our battlements.'

Duncan's reaction to this gory account is to commend Macbeth's actions: 'O valiant cousin! worthy gentleman!' This is a clear celebration of the traditional ideal of manhood.

Similarly, Duncan points to the bleeding sergeant's wounds as evidence of his honour on the battlefield: 'So well thy words become thee as thy wounds; / They smack of honour both' (Act 1, Sc 2). This connection between manhood and physical courage continues throughout the play. Lennox suggests that the battlefield is a place where young men may prove their masculinity; he declares that the English army is made up of 'many unrough youths that even now / Protest their first of manhood' (Act 5, Sc 2).

Young Siward's death towards the end of the play also illustrates how **bravery in battle is seen as a manly trait**. When Siward hears of his son's death, he is relieved to learn that Young Siward's wounds were on the front of his body, confirming that he did not run from his enemy. Siward sees this as appropriately manly behaviour:

'Why then, God's soldier be he!
Had I as many sons as I have hairs,
I would not wish them to a fairer death' (Act 5, Sc 9)

Ross views Young Siward's death in a similar fashion, noting that 'like a man he died'.

Macbeth himself plays on this idea. After Duncan's body is discovered he adopts the role of the decisive alpha male. He instructs the other thanes to adopt a manly attitude (possibly arm themselves) to deal with the murder of Duncan: 'Let's briefly put on manly readiness, / And meet i' the hall together' (Act 2, Sc 3). However, some commentators have pointed out that Macbeth is merely playing a role here. Internally he is a much more sensitive individual, badly shaken by his crime in the previous scene.

Lady Macbeth plays on the idea of manliness in her efforts to persuade Macbeth to kill Duncan. When Macbeth expresses his reservations about the crime she asks, 'Art thou afeard / To be the same in thine own act and valour / As thou art in desire?' (Act 1, Sc 7). She suggests her husband is not a real man if he expresses fear: 'When you durst do it, then you were a man! / And, to be more than what you were, you would / Be so much more the man.'

Throughout the play, Shakespeare's characters echo the idea that bravery is a manly trait. When Macduff weeps at the news of his family's death he is told by Malcolm to 'Dispute it like a man' (Act 4, Sc 3). Interestingly Macduff's response is: 'I shall do so; / But I must also feel it as a man'. His emotional behaviour is appropriate here but it does represent a deviation from the typical emotional composure associated with manliness. Shakespeare recognises that human beings are more complex than simple idealised representations of gender allow. However, Macduff does not deny the aggressive side of his character. In typical 'manly' fashion he vows to kill Macbeth himself:

'O, I could play the woman with mine eyes
And braggart with my tongue! But, gentle heavens,
Cut short all intermission; front to front
Bring thou this fiend of Scotland and myself;
Within my sword's length set him' (Act 4, Sc 3)

Emotional composure is also seen as a traditional manly trait. In the Banquet Scene, Lady Macbeth points to Macbeth's hysteria at the sight of Banquo's ghost as unmanly. She asks him, 'Are you a man?' and accuses him of being 'unmanned in folly'. She then charges him with cowardice:

'O, these flaws and starts,
Impostors to true fear, would well become
A woman's story at a winter's fire,
Authorised by her grandam' (Act 3, Sc 4)

Macbeth protests that he is as brave as any man, and that nobody could face a ghost such as this without fear:

'What man dare, I dare:
Approach thou like the rugged Russian bear,
The armed rhinoceros, or the Hyrcan tiger;
Take any shape but that, and my firm nerves
Shall never tremble: or be alive again,
And dare me to the desert with thy sword;
If trembling I inhabit then, protest me
The baby of a girl.' (Act 3, Sc 4)

Ross comes close to tears in his discussion with Lady Macduff about the fate of Scotland. So embarrassed is he by his lack of manly composure that he hurries off: 'should I stay longer, / It would be my disgrace and your discomfort: / I take my leave at once' (Act 4, Sc 2).

As the tragedy continues **Macbeth comes to see the meaninglessness in his pride as a manly warrior**. He characterises life as a puffed-up actor whose brave 'struts and frets' are utterly futile. Just as a candle inevitably burns out, his manly pride seems pointless when confronted with the inevitability of death:

'Out, out, brief candle!
Life's but a walking shadow, a poor player
That struts and frets his hour upon the stage
And then is heard no more. It is a tale
Told by an idiot, full of sound and fury,
Signifying nothing' (Act 5, Sc 5)

Ultimately, **Shakespeare shows how traditional masculinity is a powerful idea in society**. It confers power and motivates the characters. However, as he grows in wisdom, **Macbeth comes to see the hollowness of such manly pride and the play therefore undermines the traditional conception of masculinity.**

***Macbeth* also explores what it means to be a woman.** Why does Shakespeare present the witches as bearded women? Why must Lady Macbeth adopt a more traditionally masculine bearing in the play?

Throughout the play, femininity is traditionally associated with weakness and fragility. Macduff illustrates this idea: following the discovery of Duncan's body he refuses to tell Lady Macbeth the details of the King's murder:

'O gentle lady,
'Tis not for you to hear what I can speak:
The repetition, in a woman's ear,
Would murder as it fell' (Act 2, Sc 3)

He feels, that as a woman, Lady Macbeth is too delicate to hear about such goriness. Little does he know that this murder was planned by Lady Macbeth and that it was she who smeared the blood on the groomsmen. **Shakespeare deftly identifies the traditional view of womanhood and simultaneously undermines it.**

It is interesting however, that **Lady Macbeth plays on the idea of the fragile woman** when she faints in Act 2, Scene 3. Many commentators see this is a feigned swoon as Lady Macbeth looks to distract the attention away from her husband. Again, Shakespeare both illustrates the feminine norm and undermines it at the same time.

Lady Macbeth puts paid to the idea that woman are weak and fragile. Instead, she exhibits a steely nature traditionally associated with masculinity. She dominates her husband at the start of the play, plans the murder of Duncan, uses the bloody daggers to 'gild the faces of the grooms' and acts with resolve and composure following the crime. On the night of Duncan's death she appears stronger than her husband and appears to easily overcome her moral scruples. As she says to Macbeth: 'My hands are of your colour; but I shame / To wear a heart so white' (Act 2, Sc 2).

Some commentators argue that Lady Macbeth can only act in such a way *because* she has renounced her femininity. She calls on evil spirits to 'unsex' her and begs them, 'Come to my woman's breasts, / And take my milk for gall' (Act 1, Sc 5). This is dramatically presented in the infanticide image where Lady Macbeth tells her husband that she would rather kill her own child than break a promise to him:

> 'I have given suck, and know
> How tender 'tis to love the babe that milks me:
> I would, while it was smiling in my face,
> Have plucked my nipple from his boneless gums,
> And dashed the brains out, had I so sworn' (Act 1, Sc 7)

Macbeth recognises these 'masculine' traits in his wife: 'Bring forth men-children only; / For thy undaunted mettle should compose / Nothing but males' (Act 1, Sc 7). Again, the connection between masculinity, violence and emotional detachment is asserted within the play.

When Lady Macbeth calls on evil spirits to 'unsex' her, she is turning her back on her feminine nature. **Shakespeare may be suggesting that femininity (and indeed masculinity) are simply roles that are played in society**. Although these are powerful signifiers, they are not grounded in biology, in any pre-determined way. Shakespeare sees that our perceptions of ourselves as men and women have great social significance, but that these are merely roles that we fill out in a social context. Like 'poor players' we act our part but ultimately these traditional roles have little to do with who we really are.

Gender Roles

Traditional masculinity is linked to physical bravery	• Manliness is equated with bravery on the battlefield in the eyes of society
Traditional masculinity is associated with emotional composure	• Emotional composure is seen as a traditional manly trait
Macbeth's recognition of the emptiness of manly pride	• Macbeth comes to understand the emptiness of his manly pride
Traditional femininity is associated with weakness	• As a woman, Lady Macbeth is thought of as fragile
The character of Lady Macbeth asks questions of the stereotype of the fragile woman	• Through her actions and resolve, Lady Macbeth undermines the traditional view of womanhood
Shakespeare explores how society thinks of men and women. He ultimately undermines the idea that gender is a fixed role and points to the emptiness of traditional gender roles	• Traditional gender roles are interrogated through the actions of the play's central characters: Macbeth and Lady Macbeth

Interesting Fact
During Shakespeare's time it was illegal for women to act. The female characters in his plays were therefore played by men.

Interesting Fact
The average person has an active vocabulary of 10,000 words. Shakespeare's plays contain over 30,000 different words.

The exact details of William Shakespeare's life are unclear. However some facts are known from court and clerical records.

Shakespeare's exact date of birth is unknown but records reveal that he was baptised on 26 April 1564. Due to a scholar's mistake, his birthday is commemorated on 23 April. This date has appealed to commentators as it is also the same date on which he died (23 April 1616).

Shakespeare was born at Stratford-upon-Avon to John Shakespeare and Mary Arden. He was the third child of eight, although three of his siblings died before reaching adulthood.

None of his school records survive, but Shakespeare probably attended the local grammar school: the King's New School. It is thought that he left school at the age of 15.

In 1582, he married Anne Hathaway. He was 18; she was 26. Six months later, Anne gave birth to a daughter, whom they named Susanna. She was followed two years later by the twins: Hamnet and Judith. Sadly, Hamnet, Shakespeare's only son, died at the age of 11; the cause is unknown.

Biographers refer to the years 1585-1592 as 'The Lost Years' as there are no records of Shakespeare's life for this period. Shakespeare is mentioned in the London theatre records in 1592. Various legends suggest Shakespeare's reasons for leaving Stratford-upon-Avon. The most persistent is that Shakespeare fled to avoid prosecution for deer poaching at the Charlecote estate. This is unlikely as Charlecote did not have a deer park for another 100 years. Other biographers believe that he worked as a schoolteacher pointing to the record of a William Shakeshaft in Lancashire. However, Shakeshaft was a relatively popular name at the time.

What is known for certain is that Shakespeare worked as an actor, and wrote plays and poetry. He joined a theatre group called The Lord Chamberlain's Men. In 1603, King James I became the company's royal patron and it changed its name to The King's Men. Shakespeare also owned a share in the Globe Theatre in London which made him a wealthy man.

Shakespeare wrote about 37 plays, including the tragedies: *Romeo and Juliet, Julius Caesar, Hamlet, Othello, King Lear, Macbeth* and *Coriolanus.* His celebrated comedies include *The Tempest, A Midsummer's Night Dream, Much Ado About Nothing* and *The Merchant of Venice.* His dramas are performed regularly throughout the world today.

Shakespeare died in 1616. He left the bulk of his wealth to his daughter Susanna. Famously, Shakespeare left his wife his 'second best bed'. Some commentators see this as an insult to his wife, others argue that this is a reference to the matrimonial bed and therefore a symbolic gesture.

Shakespeare was buried at the Holy Trinity Church.

His epitaph warns against his body being moved:

'Good friend, for Jesus' sake forbear,
To dig the dust enclosed here.
Blessed be the man that spares these stones,
And cursed be he that moves my bones.'
[modern spelling]

Interesting Fact
There are 6 surviving copies of Shakespeare's signature. His name is spelt differently in each, using abbreviated forms. Interestingly his surname is never spelt as 'Shakespeare'. The signatures appear as:

- Willm Shakp
- William Shakspēr
- Wm Shakspē
- William Shakspere
- Willm Shakspere
- William Shakspeare

Ordinary Level – Exam Tips

Answer the question: This may seem obvious but it is vital that you remain focused on what exactly the question is asking.

Structure your answer: Take a few minutes to plan the shape of your answer. Sequence your ideas in a logical order.

Make points. Don't narrate the plot: Although there are times when you will need to explain what has occurred in a scene, it is important that you don't simply retell the story.

Use paragraphs in your answer: Although you are not required to write a long essay, you should use paragraphs where it is appropriate.

Quote and refer: The examiner is keen to see that you have an in-depth knowledge of the play. Illustrate this by using quotations and by making appropriate references.

Watch your timing: Most students spend approximately an hour on the Single Text question.

Ordinary Level – Exam Topics

Key scenes: Focus on scenes that are tense or exciting, act as turning points, illuminate the characters' personalities and/or seem of thematic importance. This is the most common question topic at Ordinary Level.

Characters: Think about how characters are portrayed, the relationship between central characters, the dramatic importance of key characters.

Staging/directing the play.

Your **personal response** to the play

Themes

Ordinary Level Past Exam Questions

2014

Answer **all** of the questions.

1. (a) Describe one episode or incident that shows Macbeth to be a violent man. (10)
   (b) In your opinion, which one of the following words best describes Lady Macbeth?
   Evil Ambitious Loving
   Explain your answer with reference to the text. (10)

2. This text is entitled *Macbeth*. Suggest another title that, in your opinion, would indicate to readers what the play is about. Explain your choice with reference to the text. (10)

3. Answer **ONE** of the following: [Each part carries 30 marks]
   (i) 'In *Macbeth* the female characters are not interesting.'
   To what extent do you agree or disagree with the above statement? Explain your answer, supporting your points with reference to at least one female character from the play.
   OR
   (ii) What aspects of the play *Macbeth* do you think make it appealing to a modern audience? Explain your answer, supporting your points with reference to the text.
   OR
   (iii) Imagine you are one of the witches in the play, *Macbeth*. Write two diary entries: one before you meet Macbeth for the first time and another one after Macbeth's death at the end of the play. Your response should demonstrate your knowledge of the text.

2013

Sample Answer on page 176

Answer **all** of the questions.

1. (a) Describe the actions, taken by Lady Macbeth, when she attempts to conceal the fact that Macbeth has murdered King Duncan. (10)
   (b) In your opinion, is Lady Macbeth a good influence on Macbeth?
   Support your answer with reference to the play. (10)

2. Give one reason why you did or did not enjoy studying the play, *Macbeth*.
   Support your answer with reference to the play. (10)

3. Answer **ONE** of the following: [Each part carries 30 marks]
   (i) 'Lady Macbeth is the real villain of the play.'
   Do you agree with the above statement?
   Give reasons for your answer, based on your knowledge of the text.
   OR
   (ii) Write a piece in which you agree or disagree with the following statement:
   Shakespeare's use of horror and the supernatural added to my enjoyment of the play, *Macbeth*. Support your answer with reference to the play.
   OR
   (iii) Imagine you are a Scottish noble. Write a letter to a friend who lives abroad. In your letter, outline what life is like now that Macbeth is King and express your hopes for Scotland's future. You should base your letter on your knowledge of the play.

2009

Answer **all** of the questions.

1. (a) Describe what happens when Macbeth and Banquo first meet the witches in the early part of the play. (10)

   (b) Did you feel sympathy for Lady Macbeth at any time during the play? Give reasons for your answer, based on your knowledge of the text. (10)

   (c) From the following statements, choose one which, in your opinion, best describes what the play is about. Give reasons for your choice.
   - *It is a play about power*
   - *It is a play about evil*
   - *It is a play about love* (10)

2. Answer **ONE** of the following: [Each part carries 30 marks]

   (i) What is your opinion of the actions and behaviour of Macduff throughout the play, *Macbeth*? Support the points you make by reference to the text.

   OR

   (ii) *Macbeth* continues to be one of the most performed and popular of Shakespeare's plays. Do you think it deserves to remain so popular today? Give reasons for your answer by referring to your own experience of studying and/or watching the play in performance.

   OR

   (iii) Imagine you were asked to direct a new film based on Shakespeare's play, *Macbeth*. Which two actors would you cast in the main roles of Macbeth and Lady Macbeth? Explain your choices with reference to the play.

2007

Answer **all** of the questions.

1. (a) In Act 2, Scene 3, Macduff discovers Duncan's body. Describe Macbeth's reaction to this event. (10)

   (b) Why, in your opinion, does Macbeth decide to murder Banquo? (10)

2. Do you feel pity for Lady Macbeth in the sleepwalking scene in Act 5? Explain your answer. (10)

3. Answer **ONE** of the following: [Each part carries 30 marks]

   (i) 'Although Macbeth is guilty of many evil deeds, he is a brave man.' Would you agree with this opinion of Macbeth? Give reasons for your answer based on your knowledge of the play.

   OR

   (ii) You have been invited to play the part of a character in your school's production of the play *Macbeth*. Describe the qualities of your chosen character which you would wish to make clear to your audience. Support your answer with reference to the text.

   OR

   (iii) Macbeth has been arrested for the murder of Duncan. You are to make a speech either defending or prosecuting him at his trial. Write the speech you would make.

2004

Answer **all** of the questions.

1. (a) Describe what happens during the banquet that Macbeth and Lady Macbeth give after he has become king. (10)

   (b) How does Lady Macbeth behave during the banquet scene? Support your answer by reference to the scene. (10)

   (c) What happens to the relationship between Macbeth and Lady Macbeth from this point until the end of the play? Support your answer by reference to the play. (10)

2. Answer **ONE** of the following: [Each part carries 30 marks]

   (i) 'Lady Macbeth is not an evil woman.'
   What do you think of this view? Support your answer by reference to the play.

   OR

   (ii) Some people think that the play *Macbeth* should not be performed because it is too violent. Do you agree with this view? Explain why or why not, supporting your answer by reference to the play.

   OR

   (iii) Choose one important moment from *Macbeth* and describe how you would show it on the stage or on film. Explain your reasons for showing it in this way, pointing out the effect you would like it to have on the audience.

2003

Answer **all** of the questions.

1. (a) Describe what happens on the night that Macbeth murders Duncan, King of Scotland. (10)

   (b) Do you think that becoming King made Macbeth happy? Give reasons for your answer. (10)

2. As the play progresses, what in your view are the things that finally destroy Macbeth? (10)

3. Answer **ONE** of the following: [Each part carries 30 marks]

   (i) Imagine that, after the death of Macbeth, members of the public could apply for the job of King or Queen of Scotland. Write the letter of application that you would send in for either job.

   OR

   (ii) 'The witches play a very important part in Shakespeare's play, *Macbeth*.'
   To what extent do you agree with the above statement? Support your answer by reference to the play.

   OR

   (iii) '*Macbeth* is a play that is full of action and excitement for the audience.'
   Do you agree with the above view of the play? Support your answer by reference to the play.

Sample Ordinary Level Questions

Sample A

1. (a) In Act 1, Scene 7 Macbeth tells Lady Macbeth that he does not want to kill Duncan. How does Lady Macbeth change his mind? (10)

   (b) Did you feel sympathy for Macbeth in the play? Describe one scene where you felt sympathy for him and explain why you felt so. (10)

   (c) What do you think was Macbeth's downfall? Support your answer by making reference to the play. (10)

2. Answer **ONE** of the following: [Each part carries 30 marks]

   (i) Imagine you are directing *Macbeth*. Write instructions for four actors giving them advice for their performances. In each case you must name the character that the actor is playing.

   OR

   (ii) Which character would you most like to play in a school production of *Macbeth*. Give reasons for your answer based on your knowledge of the play.

   OR

   (iii) Write an article for a school magazine in which you consider whether *Macbeth* is relevant to young people today.

Sample B

1. (a) How do the witches' prophecies affect Macbeth? (10)

   (b) Aside from the witches, who else do you think is to blame for the tragedy in *Macbeth*? Refer to the play in your answer. (10)

   (c) Do you think Duncan was a good King of Scotland? Refer to the play in your answer. (10)

2. Answer **ONE** of the following: [Each part carries 30 marks]

   (a) At the end of the play Malcolm describes Macbeth and Lady Macbeth as *'this dead butcher and his fiend-like queen'*. Do you think this is a fitting description? Give reasons for your answer based on your knowledge of the play.

   OR

   (b) Based on your reading of the play, write a piece beginning with one of the following statements:
   - *Macbeth* is a fascinating play for a modern audience…
   - *Macbeth* is irrelevant to a modern audience…

   OR

   (c) Describe the character and conduct of Macduff in the play. Support your answer with reference to the play.

Ordinary Level Sample Answers 2013

Answer **all** of the questions.

1. (a) **Describe the actions, taken by Lady Macbeth, when she attempts to conceal the fact that Macbeth has murdered King Duncan.** ***(10)***

Lady Macbeth takes a number of actions to conceal Macbeth's terrible crime. Firstly, she drugs Duncan's guards so that they may be framed for the murder. When Macbeth returns to her following the murder of Duncan, he is still carrying the daggers. Lady Macbeth takes the murder weapons back to Duncan's chamber and smears the guards with blood to further place them under suspicion.

Lady Macbeth encourages Macbeth to wash the blood from his hands, 'A little water clears us of this deed' and then to put on a nightgown to make it seem as if he was in bed when the murder occurred.

Following the discovery of Duncan's body, Macbeth is questioned by Macduff as to why he killed the chamberlains. To draw attention from Macbeth, she pretends to faint and distracts Macduff and the others.

Without Lady Macbeth, it seems likely that Macbeth would have been immediately blamed for Duncan's death.

(b) **In your opinion, is Lady Macbeth a good influence on Macbeth? Support your answer with reference to the play.** **(10)**

Lady Macbeth is a terrible influence on Macbeth. This is made clear in the first act of the play when she encourages Macbeth to commit regicide.

After meeting the witches, Macbeth is tempted to kill Duncan so that he can seize the crown for himself. However, he has a crisis of conscience and decides not to go ahead with his murderous plan. He tells Lady Macbeth, 'We will proceed no further in this business'.

Lady Macbeth is infuriated by Macbeth's change of heart and immediately criticises him.

She questions his manhood: 'When you durst do it, then you were a man!' and calls him a coward. This offends Macbeth's pride and his sense of himself as a man. She also appeals to his sense of ambition: 'Wouldst thou have that / Which thou esteem'st the ornament of life' in the hope that Macbeth's dream of being King will encourage him. In order to shock him, Lady Macbeth says she would never break a promise to him, even if that promise was to kill her own child:

'I would, while it was smiling in my face,
Have plucked my nipple from his boneless gums,
And dashed the brains out, had I so sworn as you
Have done to this.'

Lady Macbeth's criticisms and shocking language encourage Macbeth to go ahead with the murder. It is under her influence that he makes his final decision to kill the King.

Furthermore, it is Lady Macbeth who outlines the plan to frame Duncan's guards. She explains how she will spike their drinks allowing Macbeth to kill Duncan while they sleep. To get away with the crime, Lady Macbeth plans to smear the guards with the King's blood 'who shall bear the guilt / Of our great quell'.

Although Macbeth is responsible for killing the King, Lady Macbeth has an important influence on his decision to commit this gruesome murder.

2. Give one reason why you did or did not enjoy studying the play, *Macbeth*. Support your answer with reference to the play. (10)

I truly enjoyed studying Macbeth. The most interesting aspect of the play was how I could feel sympathy for Macbeth, even though he is such a murderous villain. Shakespeare shows how we can pity even the worst of humanity. This was made most clear to me in the Banquet Scene in Act III.

In this scene, Macbeth and Lady Macbeth are hosting a banquet to celebrate Macbeth's coronation. Most of the thanes are there. Macbeth requests everybody to sit and then notices that there is no chair for him. He then sees Banquo's ghost sitting in his chair. The ghost is covered in blood and stares at Macbeth. Macbeth shouts hysterically at the ghost, 'Thou canst not say I did it: never shake / Thy gory locks at me'. The thanes are shocked by Macbeth's behaviour as they cannot see the ghost. Lady Macbeth tries to control the situation and tell the thanes that Macbeth is ill but the ghost returns again and Macbeth continues to rave. The thanes are hurried out of the hall.

The spectacle of bloody Banquo clearly shows Macbeth's violent nature. However, I felt great sympathy for Macbeth at this point as he is clearly losing his grip on reality. Nobody else can see the ghost so it is a clear sign of Macbeth's mental agitation. I feel that the ghost is a symbol of Macbeth's remorse. He is burdened by the guilt of murdering his friend Banquo and is now literally haunted by what he has done.

Rather than encouraging him to make amends for his crimes, the ghost inspires Macbeth to perform more horrible acts. This is because Macbeth feels that he has committed so many foul deeds that more will make little difference: 'I am in blood / Stepped in so far that, should I wade no more, / Returning were as tedious as go o'er'. The idea that a person can feel they are beyond redemption is very saddening. Even though Macbeth has clearly chosen an evil path, I felt sympathy for him as he believed there was now no other way to live.

The Banquet Scene highlights the idea that Macbeth is a cruel and vicious man. However, he is also clearly tortured by regret. The sympathy I felt for him here and throughout the play made Macbeth most rewarding and thought provoking.

3. (i) 'Lady Macbeth is the real villain of the play.' Do you agree with the above statement? Give reasons for your answer, based on your knowledge of the text. (30)

Lady Macbeth, along with her husband, is undoubtedly a central villain of the play. Her ambition drives her to do terrible things and the influence she has over Macbeth encourages him onto evil. Her part in planning and covering up the murder of Duncan shows her to be a villainous character. However, this should not take away from the fact that Macbeth is still responsible for so many murders and crimes. Like Lady Macbeth, he too is a central villain in the play. My feelings towards Lady Macbeth softened towards the end of the play; I came to pity her as she struggles to bear the guilt of her villainy.

Lady Macbeth's ambitious nature is the source of her villainy. Early in the play, when Macbeth writes to her about the witches' prophecies, she immediately expresses her ruthless ambition and her thoughts turn to murder. She worries that Macbeth is 'too full o' the milk of human kindness' and decides that she will use her powers of persuasion to influence him: 'Hie thee hither, / That I may pour my spirits in thine ear, / And chastise with the valour of my tongue'. Lady Macbeth, in soliloquy, calls on evil spirits to give her the necessary cruelty to murder the King: 'Make thick my blood; / Stop up the access and passage to remorse'. I feel that this moment shows how she embraces villainy and looks to fulfil her ambitions to be Queen.

Clearly Lady Macbeth is a villainous influence as she encourages Macbeth to kill Duncan.

When he has second thoughts about killing the King, Lady Macbeth questions his masculinity and criticises him. Disturbingly, she says that she would kill her own child if she had promised to do so. In my view, this influence over Macbeth makes her partly responsible for Duncan's murder. Furthermore, it is Lady Macbeth who plans the murder and it is she who brings the bloody daggers back to Duncan's chamber to frame the chamberlains. She has no small part in the gruesome murder and even acknowledges this to Macbeth: 'My hands are of your colour; but I shame / To wear a heart so white.'

Lady Macbeth's ruthlessness is clear throughout much of the play. Shortly after Macbeth kills the chamberlains, she pretends to faint to divert attention away from her husband. During the Banquet Scene, she calmly tries to explain away Macbeth's hysteria, blaming it on a momentary fit. As an icy villain, she helps Macbeth to conceal his terrible crime.

Ultimately, however, it is Macbeth who kills Duncan. Although influenced by Lady Macbeth, the decision to kill the King is his own. Furthermore, Macbeth orders the murders of Banquo and Macduff's family without discussing it with Lady Macbeth and his vicious rule of Scotland has nothing to do with his wife.

Lady Macbeth, along with her husband, is certainly a key villain in Macbeth. However, my feelings towards her softened towards the end of the play. Although she does not show it publicly, Lady Macbeth is unhappy and anxious in her position as Queen. In a short soliloquy she expresses her fears about her position: ''Tis safer to be that which we destroy / Than by destruction dwell in doubtful joy.' Here she seems to envy the peace Duncan has found in death. Although I cannot forget the terrible things she did, I felt pity for her as a lonely and unhappy woman.

Lady Macbeth pays a high price for her villainy. This is most evident in the Sleepwalking Scene in Act V. Lady Macbeth displays how guilty she feels for her terrible crimes. The line, 'Out, damned spot!' displays the blood on Lady Macbeth's conscience. Burdened by guilt she seems on the edge of madness. We can assume that she takes her own life as a result of this.

Lady Macbeth's part in Duncan's murder, her efforts to conceal Macbeth's guilt and her influence over her husband make her a key villain in the play. This should not take away from the fact that Macbeth is also responsible for terrible crimes. Although she is villainous, I did feel pity for her as she comes to see the horror of her actions. I think it is this combination of traits that makes Lady Macbeth such a fascinating villain in the play.

Higher Level – Exam Tips

Answer the question: This may seem obvious but it is vital that you remain focused on what exactly the question is asking.

Structure your answer: Take a few minutes to plan the shape of your essay. Sequence your ideas in a logical order.

Include an introduction: Address the question directly and outline your general response.

Make points. Don't narrate the plot: Although there are times when you will need to explain what has occurred in a scene, it is important that you don't merely retell the story.

Use a topic sentence: It should be clear to the examiner what the overall point of each paragraph is. This is usually done in the opening sentence of each paragraph.

Make one point per paragraph: Each paragraph should deal with one main idea that is discussed by referring to the play.

Quote and refer: The examiner is keen to see that you have an in-depth knowledge of the play. Illustrate this by using quotations and making appropriate references.

Include a conclusion: This should 'wrap up' your essay by drawing all your main points together.

Watch your timing: Most students spend approximately one hour on the Single Text question.

Higher Level – Exam Topics

Characters: Think about how characters are portrayed, the relationship between central characters, the dramatic importance of key characters.

Themes

Key scenes: Focus on scenes that are tense or exciting, act as turning points, illuminate the characters' personalities and/or seem of thematic importance.

Soliloquies: These are intimate moments when a character reflects on their situation out loud to the audience.

Imagery, **symbolism** and **language**

Your **personal response** to the play

Higher Level – Past Exam Questions

2014

(i) 'Macbeth's relationships with other characters can be seen primarily as power struggles which prove crucial to the outcome of the play.'
Discuss the above statement in relation to at least two of Macbeth's relationships with other characters. Support your answer with suitable reference to the play, *Macbeth*.

OR

(ii) 'Throughout the play, *Macbeth*, Shakespeare makes effective use of a variety of dramatic techniques that evoke a wide range of responses from the audience.' Discuss this view with reference to at least two dramatic techniques used by Shakespeare in the play. Support your answer with suitable reference to the text.

2013 Sample Answer on page 182

(i) 'The variety of significant insights that we gain into Macbeth's mind proves critical in shaping our understanding of his complex character.' Discuss this view, supporting your answer with suitable reference to the play, *Macbeth*.

OR

(ii) 'Shakespeare makes effective use of disturbing imagery in the play, *Macbeth*.'
Discuss this statement, supporting your answer with suitable reference to the text.

2009

(i) 'Macbeth's murder of Duncan has horrible consequences both for Macbeth himself and for Scotland.' Write a response to this statement. You should refer to the play in your answer.

OR

(ii) '*Macbeth* has all the ingredients of compelling drama.'
Write a response to this statement, commenting on one or more of the ingredients, which, in your opinion, make *Macbeth* a compelling drama.

2007 Sample Answer on page 184

(i) 'The relationship between Macbeth and Lady Macbeth undergoes significant change during the course of the play.' Discuss this statement supporting your answer with the aid of suitable reference to the text.

OR

(ii) 'Essentially the play *Macbeth* is about power, its use and abuse.' Discuss this view of the play, supporting your answer with the aid of suitable reference to the text

2004

(i) 'Shakespeare's *Macbeth* invites us to look into the world of a man driven on by ruthless ambition and tortured by regret.'
Write a response to this view of the play, *Macbeth*, supporting the points you make by reference to the text.

OR

(ii) 'The play, *Macbeth*, has many scenes of compelling drama.' Choose one scene that you found compelling and say why you found it to be so. Support your answer by reference to the play.

2003

(i) 'We feel very little pity for the central characters of Macbeth and Lady Macbeth in Shakespeare's play.'
To what extent would you agree with the above view? Support your answer by reference to the play.

OR

(ii) 'In *Macbeth*, Shakespeare presents us with a powerful vision of evil.' Write your response to the above statement. Textual support may include reference to a particular performance of the play you have seen.

Higher Level – Sample Questions

1. 'Although villainous, the character of Macbeth evokes the audience's sympathy.'
To what extent would you agree with the above view? Support your answer by reference to the play, *Macbeth*.

2. 'The women of Shakespeare's *Macbeth* are either frightening in their cruelty or pathetic in their helplessness.'
Discuss this statement, making reference to the play.

3. 'The play, *Macbeth*, highlights the corrupting influence of power.'
Write a response to this statement. Support your answer by reference to the play.

4. 'The struggle between good and evil is one of the central themes of the play, *Macbeth*.'
Discuss this statement supporting your answer with appropriate reference to the text.

5. 'Although good wins out over evil, the audience feels no sense of triumph at the end of play.' Discuss this statement with reference to the play, *Macbeth*.

6. 'Lady Macbeth is a complex character who inspires both revulsion and sympathy in the audience.'
Discuss this statement, making suitable reference to Shakespeare's play *Macbeth*.

7. 'Kingship is a central theme of the play *Macbeth*.'
Write a response to this statement. You should refer to the play in your answer.

8. What is the function of the character of Banquo in the play, *Macbeth*?
Support your answer by reference to the play.

9. 'In Shakespeare's *Macbeth*, the villainous characters are more fascinating than the virtuous ones.'
Discuss this statement with reference to the text.

10. 'In its themes and ideas, *Macbeth* is a most relevant play for a modern audience'.
Discuss this statement supporting your answer with the aid of suitable reference to the play.

Higher Level – Sample Answers

2013

(i) 'The variety of significant insights that we gain into Macbeth's mind proves critical in shaping our understanding of his complex character.' Discuss this view, supporting your answer with suitable reference to the play, *Macbeth*.

Macbeth is truly a complex and fascinating villain. He commits a number of horrendous crimes in the play, but Macbeth is not simply a 'butcher' as Malcolm labels him. Despite his abhorrent villainy, Macbeth evokes sympathy in the audience. Shakespeare encourages us to feel sorry for a once noble man as we watch him succumb to evil and the allure of power. Through his soliloquy and asides, the audience gains insight into Macbeth's mind. These private expressions of his innermost fears and desires shape our appreciation for a character who we both condemn, but ultimately come to pity.

As the tragic hero of the play, Macbeth is a flawed character. His inflated pride and ambition lead him to his downfall. Macbeth's excessive ambition is immediately apparent in his asides in the early scenes in the play. When he first meets the witches, Macbeth is told a series of equivocal half-truths, prophesising that he will be King. The audience immediately gains insight into Macbeth's mind as he reveals his ambition in his asides. When it is confirmed to him that he has become Thane of Cawdor as well as Thane of Glamis, Macbeth's mind immediately turns to the crown: 'Two truths are told / As happy prologues to the swelling act / Of the imperial theme.'

Later in Act I, while standing before Duncan, Macbeth's ambition is revealed to the audience through his aside. Macbeth sees Duncan's heir, Prince Malcolm, as an obstacle to overcome on his journey to absolute power: 'That is a step / On which I must fall down, or else o'er-leap, / For in my way it lies.' He knows that his ambition can only be realised through evil acts but hopes to suppress his conscience:

> *'Let not light see my black and deep desires:*
> *The eye wink at the hand; yet let that be,*
> *Which the eye fears, when it is done, to see.'*

This aside is intriguing in its complexity. On the one hand, Macbeth is embracing evil and darkly plans his way to the throne. However, he is still a man with a conscience, a man who understands the immorality of what he is about to do. Macbeth's moral compass allows him to appreciate the good; the fact that he actively chooses to ignore it makes his actions all the more damning.

This idea is developed further in Macbeth's first soliloquy. As he waits for Lady Macbeth, he reflects deeply on the moral significance of killing Duncan. He offers a number of reasons for not going ahead with the murder. He fears punishment on earth and in the afterlife and he worries that 'Bloody instructions...return / To plague the inventor'. Macbeth recognises his moral obligations to Duncan who is his King and guest, and that he 'should against his murderer shut the door / Not bear the knife'. Furthermore, Macbeth fears that as a virtuous king, Duncan's death would spark a public outcry, 'his virtues / Will plead like angels...against / The deep damnation of his taking-off'.

Most revealing in this soliloquy is Macbeth's ability to see his own flawed nature as overly ambitious. He interrogates his motivation and concludes:

'I have no spur
To prick the sides of my intent, but only
Vaulting ambition, which o'erleaps itself
And falls on the other.'

So uncomfortable is Macbeth with the idea of murdering Duncan that he cannot use the word 'murder'. Instead, he employs a number of euphemisms: 'It', 'surcease', 'the deed', 'his taking-off', 'the horrid deed'.

Even moments before he kills Duncan, Macbeth is presented as a man plagued by doubt but still driven on by the irresistible allure of power. Macbeth's dagger soliloquy dramatically illustrates this inner turmoil. He sees a dagger before him, the blade and handle covered in blood. The dagger points him towards Duncan's room. He pauses as he imagines half the world plunged in darkness and envisages 'withered murder' creeping like a ghost. Again, Macbeth reflects on the brutal evil that he is about to commit but nonetheless proceeds. Shakespeare wants us to see Macbeth not as a flat villain, but rather as a flawed and complex character, reluctant to commit evil but nonetheless unable to resist his 'vaulting ambition'.

As the play proceeds, Macbeth's obsessions and fears change. Our insight into his mind-set is again understood as he speaks in soliloquy. Following the murder of Duncan, Macbeth grows fearful of his friend Banquo. This suspicion grows out of the witches' prophecy that Banquo's heirs will be kings. He bitterly remarks that the witches have 'placed a fruitless crown' upon his head and a 'barren sceptre' in his grip. Macbeth arrogantly looks to change fate by murdering Banquo and his son Fleance.

This soliloquy reveals Macbeth as more at home with the idea of murder. Having realised his ambition to be King, he now desperately looks to hold on to the reigns of power. By this point of the play Macbeth's soul is becoming increasingly mired in blood. His conscience is starting to give way to paranoia and suspicion.

By the final act of the play, Macbeth has become a more frightening, yet more pitiful figure. In a short soliloquy, he reflects on the emptiness of his ambition, how it has left him friendless, unloved and alone. Despairingly he notes, 'I have lived long enough: my way of life / Is fall'n into the sear, the yellow leaf'. Macbeth recognises that although he has gained the crown it is a hollow victory if he is reviled:

'that which should accompany old age,
As honour, love, obedience, troops of friends,
I must not look to have; but, in their stead,
Curses, not loud but deep, mouth-honour breath,
Which the poor heart would fain deny, and dare not.'

Macbeth clearly recognises that he inspires fear – he has after all ruled with a bloody hand – but that this is not enough. This soliloquy offers moving insight into a man who recognises the emptiness of his own pride and ambition. It is perhaps not enough to inspire our forgiveness, but it does evoke our pity for his flawed nature.

Macbeth's spiritual death and utter disillusionment is fully understood by the audience in his final soliloquy. He poetically reflects on the futility of existence. The image of a fading candle and pointless actor reveals Macbeth's world-weary defeatism:

'Out, out, brief candle!
Life's but a walking shadow, a poor player
That struts and frets his hour upon the stage
And then is heard no more. It is a tale

Told by an idiot, full of sound and fury,
Signifying nothing.'

In this soliloquy, Macbeth realises the emptiness of human pride and ambition. The image of a puffed up actor, strutting on stage is presented as no more than vanity. Macbeth has realised the meaninglessness of his own manly pride. Tragically he is unable to change the course of his life. Macbeth earns the audience's sympathy as he comes to the devastating self-knowledge that his pursuit of power was a pointless prideful exercise.

It is through his most private expressions that we gain insight into Macbeth's complex mind. It is horrifically enthralling to see a once moral man become twisted by his desire for power until he gives into the most awful type of despair. The brilliant complexity of Shakespeare's character is that he earns both our condemnation and our pity.

2007

(i) 'The relationship between Macbeth and Lady Macbeth undergoes significant change during the course of the play.' Discuss this statement supporting your answer with the aid of suitable reference to the text.

At the heart of Macbeth is the fascinating relationship between the two central protagonists: Macbeth and Lady Macbeth. The plan to kill Duncan grows out of the toxic alchemy of their relationship. However, it is a relationship whose dynamic changes considerably throughout the play. Lady Macbeth begins the play as a powerful influence over Macbeth but as the drama continues she becomes increasingly marginalised. Macbeth becomes less reliant on his wife. By the final act, Macbeth and Lady Macbeth seem wholly separate, finding themselves alone to cope with the psychological consequences of their murderous deeds.

The plan to kill Duncan is very much a conspiracy between Macbeth and Lady Macbeth. Following his meeting with the witches, Macbeth immediately writes to his wife, confiding in her his ambition to be King. He calls Lady Macbeth 'my dearest partner of greatness' and the murder of Duncan is the result of this partnership.

However, it is a partnership in which Lady Macbeth is a dominant force. Fearing that her husband is 'too full o' the milk of human kindness', she immediately sees it as her role to encourage Macbeth to commit regicide:

> *'...Hie thee hither,*
> *That I may pour my spirits in thine ear*
> *And chastise with the valour of my tongue*
> *All that impedes thee from the golden round'*

It is interesting that Lady Macbeth sees her powers of persuasion, the 'valour' of her 'tongue', as necessary for Macbeth's success. I feel that Lady Macbeth, through a twisted sort of fidelity, is acting in her husband's interests. However, I suspect that she is also motivated by her own desires to be Queen.

As Macbeth later waits to meet Lady Macbeth, he agonises over the justification for killing Duncan. Having considered numerous reasons not to go ahead with the plan, he flatly tells his wife, 'We will proceed no further in this business.' Lady Macbeth is clearly prepared for this and uses all of her powers of persuasion to convince Macbeth otherwise. She firstly appeals to his sense of ambition: 'Wouldst thou have that / Which thou esteem'st the ornament of life'. And then sets about cajoling him by attacking his masculinity ('When you durst do it, then you were a man!') and taunting him ('Wouldst thou...live a coward in thine own esteem, / Letting 'I dare not' wait upon 'I would,' / Like the poor cat i' the adage?').

Most effectively she employs the shocking image of infanticide to illustrate her commitment to her husband and to question his constancy. She tells her husband, had she promised to, she would not hesitate to murder her own child:

> *'I would.../ Have plucked my nipple from his boneless gums*
> *And dashed the brains out, had I so sworn as you*
> *Have done to this'.*

Although Macbeth is responsible for all of his actions, Lady Macbeth proves to be a spur, urging him to realise his darkest ambitions.

As the architect of the plan to murder Duncan, Lady Macbeth is clearly the more dominant at this stage of the relationship. She tells Macbeth that she will drug Duncan's guards so that he can enter the chamber and kill the King. When Macbeth returns to her holding the bloody murder weapons, he relies on his wife's steely nature to take charge. She promptly returns the daggers to the chamber and smears blood on the guards to frame them for the crime.

Following the discovery of Duncan's body, Macbeth again needs his wife to protect him. As Macduff questions Macbeth as to why he killed the guards, Lady Macbeth diverts suspicion away from her husband by feigning a fainting fit.

In the first two acts of the play, it is clear that Lady Macbeth is a dominant force over her husband. However, as the play proceeds we see how the couple interact less and both find themselves wrestling privately with the implications of their crimes.

In the acts that come after the discovery of Duncan's body, Macbeth finds no need to consult or conspire with his wife. He orders the murder of Banquo and the slaughter of Macduff's family without discussing it with her.

The atomisation of their relationship is most evident when they articulate their fears in soliloquy. Lady Macbeth is clearly troubled by her new position of power. She is unable to share this with her husband and instead in a short soliloquy dwells on this privately:

> *'Nought's had, all's spent*
> *Where our desire is got without content:*
> *'Tis safer to be that which we destroy*
> *Than by destruction dwell in doubtful joy.'*

Here she seems to envy Duncan's death, preferring it to the anxiety of her own position. What is most telling is that she hides these doubts from her husband. When he enters the scene, she acts coldly towards him and criticises him for his own dark thoughts. Ironically, she could have directed that criticism at herself.

Macbeth too withdraws from the confidence of Lady Macbeth and faces his fears privately, only expressing them in soliloquy. He recognises that as King he should expect love and respect. Instead, he is reviled:

> *'And that which should accompany old age,*
> *As honour, love, obedience, troops of friends,*
> *I must not look to have; but in their stead,*
> *Curses, not loud but deep, mouth-honour breath,*
> *Which the poor heart would fain deny, and dare not.'*

Macbeth cuts a lonely, world-weary figure here. Where before he had a 'partner of greatness', now he has only his own dark thoughts. Unsupported, unloved and alone, he becomes increasingly disillusioned with life. The collapse of his relationship with Lady Macbeth is central to this despairing isolation.

Lady Macbeth's soliloquys are short and few in the play. Instead, Shakespeare reveals her isolation and innermost fears in the Sleepwalking Scene in Act V. Watched by a doctor and handmaid, Lady Macbeth's spoken nightmare shows the extent of her guilt. She tries to wash imagined blood from her hands, 'Out, damned spot!' and relives the bloody image of Duncan's body. Furthermore, she expresses her anxieties over the death of Macduff's wife. Unable to express her worries and trauma to Macbeth, Lady Macbeth can only work through these feelings in her nightmares. The image of Lady Macbeth vainly trying to cleanse her soul underscores her isolation and the great psychological toll she has paid for her crimes. Without the support of her husband, she must bear the guilt of her actions alone. This culminates in her eventual suicide – a violent and lonely end to her life.

Macbeth's reaction to the news of his wife's death reveals the extent to which their relationship has disintegrated. Rather than lamenting her loss, he callously notes that her death was inevitable: 'She should have died hereafter'. He is then prompted into a reflection on the meaninglessness of existence. Like a 'brief candle' that is soon snuffed out, life for the world-weary Macbeth is 'Signifying nothing'. The bleak conclusion that Macbeth reaches is hardly surprising considering the extent of his crimes. But perhaps the torturous burden of his regret is amplified by the fact that he faces his guilt utterly alone.

At the end of the play Malcolm dubs Macbeth and Lady Macbeth a 'dead butcher and his fiend-like queen'. However, to see them as a united force of evil is to misrepresent the fractured nature of their relationship. Although they began the play as conspirators, they withdraw into their own private worlds of remorse and anxiety, leaving the audience with a vision of how pitifully lonely villainy can be.

Notes

Notes

Notes

Notes

Notes

Notes